Alexander Alberro//Jennifer Allen/
Albrecht Barthel//Mary Bergstein//
Louise Bourgeois//Daniel Buren//S
Chang//Judy Chicago//Lynne Coo
Dawson//Jeffrey Deitch//Manthia Diawara//Brian
Dillon//Briony Fer//Elena Filipovic//Jori Finkel//Jack
Goldstein//Ulrike Groos//Carles Guerra//Elizabeth
Harney//Herzog & de Meuron//Carsten Höller//Amelia
Jones//Caitlin Jones//Caroline A. Jones//Sanford
Kwinter//Henri Lefebvre//Alexander Liberman//Paul
McCarthy//Friedrich Meschede//Laura Meyer//Herbert
Molderings//Valérie Mréjen//Joanna Mytkowska//
Bruce Nauman//Sune Nordgren//Hans Ulrich Obrist//
Francis V. O'Connor//Brian O'Doherty//Gabriel Orozco//
Rozsika Parker//Andrzej Przywara//Lane Relyea//
Frances Richard//Carolee Schneemann//Robert
Smithson//Ann Temkin//Sarah Thornton//Coosje van
Bruggen//Jan Verwoert//Ian Wallace//Bernadette
Walter//Steven Watson//Lawrence Weiner//Lawrence
Weschler//Jon Wood//Linda Yablonsky//Phillip Zarrilli

The Studio

Whitechapel Gallery
London
The MIT Press
Cambridge, Massachusetts

Edited by Jens Hoffmann

Documents of Contemporary Art

In recent decades artists have progressively expanded the boundaries of art as they have sought to engage with an increasingly pluralistic environment. Teaching, curating and understanding of art and visual culture are likewise no longer grounded in traditional aesthetics but centred on significant ideas, topics and themes ranging from the everyday to the uncanny, the psychoanalytical to the political.

The Documents of Contemporary Art series emerges from this context. Each volume focuses on a specific subject or body of writing that has been of key influence in contemporary art internationally. Edited and introduced by a scholar, artist, critic or curator, each of these source books provides access to a plurality of voices and perspectives defining a significant theme or tendency.

For over a century the Whitechapel Gallery has offered a public platform for art and ideas. In the same spirit, each guest editor represents a distinct yet diverse approach – rather than one institutional position or school of thought – and has conceived each volume to address not only a professional audience but all interested readers.

Series Editor: Iwona Blazwick; Commissioning Editor: Ian Farr; Project Editor: Sarah Auld; Editorial Advisory Board: Achim Borchardt-Hume, Roger Conover, Neil Cummings, Mark Francis, David Jenkins, Kirsty Ogg, Gilane Tawadros

THERE WAS

NOTHING

IN THE STUDIO

BECAUSE I DIDN'T HAVE MUCH MONEY FOR MATERIALS.

SO I WAS FORCED TO

EXAMINE MYSELF,

AND WHAT I WAS DOING THERE

Bruce Nauman, Interview with Willoughby Sharp, *Arts Magazine*, March 1970

Really there's nothing here.

It's like a place where you live.

The only useful thing about the studio is that after some time you can imagine something.

A forest, for example.

I walk in it.

Today it is nothing for me, but perhaps in two weeks it will become something

Christian Boltanski, 'Studio Visit', *Tate Magazine*, no. 2, Summer 2005

Jens Hoffmann
Introduction//The Artist's Studio in an Expanded Field

Among the many subjects art has questioned and analysed over the last four decades, the artist's studio has thus far received little attention as a topic for critical examination. While a small number of publications and exhibitions have addressed the topic of the studio, it is due for a more profound critique, just as the museum, the art school and the commercial gallery have been increasingly scrutinized in the recent past.[1] This publication hopes to bring this subject – through a wide selection of historical and recent texts, essays and interviews – to a wider public and contribute to a better understanding of the role and function of the studio in contemporary artistic practice.

Traditionally the studio has been considered the working space of artists, a place where artworks – conventionally mostly paintings or sculptures – are created. When we think of an artist's studio, many of us perhaps imagine a rather romantic situation with a lonely painter standing in front of a canvas in a small and barely furnished room in an attic or loft, surrounded by splatters of paint, somewhere in Montmartre or Soho. Or the grand workshops of the Dutch or Flemish old masters such as Johannes Vermeer, Jan van Eyck or Peter Paul Rubens, full of assistants and wealthy, aristocratic clients. Or maybe a chaotic and noisy place filled with eccentric characters – a mixture of an advertisement agency, film studio and nightclub, like Andy Warhol's Factory. No matter what our first thoughts are, they most likely do not resemble the reality of the working places of artists today. Yet these clichés have endured not only in art history but also in literature and film. People love to cling to romantic conceptions of the creative genius, and artists perhaps cannot be blamed for their complicity in the mythologizing.

It is fair to say that the studio is in many ways the birthplace of art, but it would be wrong to believe that its only function is to be a site for the creation of artworks. Nor is the studio today the only place where art can be made. With the shifts and changes in artistic production over the last century, the death of the studio has been proclaimed at numerous times, especially during the heyday of conceptual art in the late 1960s and 1970s, when the concept of 'art as idea' penetrated more traditional artistic production, suggesting a move away from the 'hand' of the artist, the physical creative act, and perhaps any consideration of skill at all. The moment when the grip of traditional media such as painting and sculpture weakened, the studio in its classic sense began to disappear as well. While many artists indeed do not have typical studios any more, most do maintain some kind of working space. Instead of talking about the end of the studio, then, perhaps we can speak of the expanded concept of the studio, even if it is only a laptop computer on the artist's kitchen table. Some artists' studios have expanded to 'house' a number of functions previously associated with the outside world. They are social and professional spaces where artists meet with curators, other artists, collaborators, dealers and collectors. During these studio visits, the outsiders see new artworks, talk about upcoming exhibitions and conduct business. Following an increased professionalization of the art world, it is not unusual for the artist's assistants to busy themselves not only with the more traditional labour of producing work following the artist's instruction, but also with operational matters such as travel and business scheduling, organizing production that is being outsourced to specialists, and administrating loan requests and shipping. Very successful artists may have staffs numbering in the dozens.

Artists throughout history have conceived of the role and function of the studio in various ways. Many have used it as a starting point and subject for their own work. Some early and well-known paintings in this category include Rembrandt van Rijn's *Artist in His Studio* (*c.* 1629) and Gustave Courbet's *The Artist's Studio* (1855). In the former, the viewer is allowed a glimpse into the studio in the moment the artist steps back from his finished canvas to contemplate the results of his labour. He has moved into the background and is barely visible, giving the artwork centre stage, but interestingly we cannot see what he has made – only a glow emanating from its surface. Courbet's scene could not be more different. In the centre we see the artist himself, painting a landscape surrounded by the main influences of his life; the canvas is filled with characters, real-life acquaintances and fictional figures.[2] Whether these works demonstrate a new-found form of self-reflexivity or simply a glorification of the figure of the artist, they certainly mark a shift in the artists' understanding of the creative act, as well as the role and function of the studio.

My own curiosity about this particular subject came about because of another, rather recent tendency in the art world: the representation and display of complete artists' studios by museums and galleries. The most famous one is probably the atelier of Constantin Brancusi, opposite the Centre Pompidou in Paris. But the Francis Bacon studio at Dublin City Gallery The Hugh Lane (brought there from its original location in South Kensington, London) and the working spaces of Eduardo Paolozzi exhibited at the National Galleries of Scotland in Edinburgh were the two primary encounters that prompted me to think more about what actually happens when the studio of the artist is presented as a work of art in an institutional context. This question led me to organize an exhibition at the Hugh Lane, co-curated with Christina Kennedy, in which we presented the work of more than twenty artists alongside the Bacon studio. The works in the exhibition addressed the studio as a subject, used it as material for the creation of new artworks, treated it as an archive for ideas, and conceptualized it in other ways to speak about its role and function.

This publication brings together more than fifty texts on this subject, organized into four sections. The first, *Being the Artist*, reveals the different ways in which ideas of the studio, and the artist in the studio, are understood by both artists and viewers. Drastically contrasting viewpoints are revealed via transcripts and descriptions of studio visits, demonstrating the range of relationships that different artists have with the studios. We hear directly from Louise Bourgeois, Jack Goldstein, Carsten Höller, Gabriel Orozco and Robert Smithson, and read analyses of the practices of Vito Acconci, Martin Kippenberger, Takashi Murakami and Wolfgang Tillmans. In Paul McCarthy's entry for Hans Ulrich Obrist's 2004 project and book *Do It*, the artist offers sets of instructions for the production of art that imply the irrelevance of a studio: 'Pile dirt on your desk …' And Ulrike Groos analyses McCarthy's video work *Painter*, in which the artist performs a grotesque caricature of the masculine painter-genius in his studio.

Several art-historical texts contextualize these ideas. Svetlana Alpers argues that the theatrical character attributed to Rembrandt's works derives from the way in which the artist 'contrived to see or at least to represent life as if it were a studio event'.[3] Sarah Burns examines the bohemian atmosphere of late nineteenth-century Greenwich Village in New York, telling the story of the artist colony's transition from Victorian to modern, and distinctly American, values. Zipping forward through history to a time when these values were already well established, Alexander Liberman's entry on Alberto Giacometti in his iconic book of photographs *The Artist in His Studio* of 1960, reveals the widespread tendency towards conflating artistic production with biography. He describes the artist at work – 'As he works he springs forward, steps back, scratches his hair' – with as much relish as he does the physical studio setting – 'An ordinary painted chair, the paint all cracked on its rounded, bent back, serves as a bed table.' He voyeuristically and romantically portrays the authentic artist at work as a wildly passionate and brilliant man. In '"The Artist in His Studio": Photography, Art and the Masculine Mystique', Mary Bergstein compellingly takes on such mystical representations of artists, and analyses the writing and photographic work of Liberman in particular. In *Studio and Cube: On the Relationship between Where Art is Made and Where Art is Displayed*, Brian O'Doherty connects the artwork and its making to a larger art-world system by tracking the relationships among places of production, completed artworks and the works' public display, from Schwitters' *Merzbau* to Warhol's Factory. Coming to the present, Linda Yablonsky, in 'The Studio System', attempts to make sense of the position of the contemporary artist in a studio now staffed with numerous assistants.

The second section, *Working with the Situation*, brings together texts that present the art studio as a source of inspiration – a starting point for inquiry and experimentation. In 'The Function of the Studio' (1971) and 'The Function of the Studio Revisited' (2007) Daniel Buren argues that the studio, which he grants can be variously defined, is the primary place of work for artists, and that within the logic of the studio, the complete, finished work is necessarily destined to be exhibited elsewhere. Reversing this relationship, Edgar Arceneaux moves the ever-changing quality of the studio into the exhibition space in his project *Drawings of Removal* (2004).

Also in this section, Seydou Keita's portraits, staged in the photographer's studio, are discussed in terms of the skilful way they articulate transitions between old and new African identities; Lawrence Weiner and Bruce Nauman, often considered part of the 'post-studio' generation, discuss their inextricable links to the studio; and in her essay 'Studio', Briony Fer considers the specific character of the sculptor Eva Hesse's studio works. Several texts deal with the artist's body as an active element of the studio. In 'Eye Body: 36 Transformative Actions', Carolee Schneemann describes the moment in 1963 when her studio environment and her own body – as extensions of painting – fused together as an artwork. In 'Yayoi Kusama's Self-Portrait Photographs', Amelia Jones continues this exploration into the relationship of the artist's body to the creative environment, and the role of photography in the viewer's ultimate ability to understand performative gesture. In 'Sounddance', Coosje van Bruggen examines the performance-based works of Bruce Nauman, executed in the studio with a video camera as the sole witness. Such conceptions of the artist's 'studio work' have given rise to a diversity of practices, from the embodied self-photography of Francesca Woodman or Cindy Sherman, to the deserted *Empty Room* (1995–96) of Fischli and Weiss or the *Atelier* (2001) of Gregor Schneider's *Haus u r*, a physical reconstruction based on memories and associations from the artist's house, in evolution since 1985.

In 'Marcel Duchamp's Studio as a Laboratory of Perception' Herbert Molderings examines Duchamp's workspace as it transformed from a painter's studio to a laboratory for artistic experiments. In 'A Rule of the Game' Hans Ulrich Obrist reflects on the impetus for the exhibition 'Laboratorium', co-curated in 1999 with Barbara Vanderlinden, in which they posited that studios and science labs are ever more interrelated. Continuing these themes of science and art, in 'The Function of the Studio (When the Studio is a Laptop)' Caitlin Jones considers the intersection of technology and art in practices that deal with digital forms and online environments.

The third section, *Retracing the Steps*, looks at the extensive genre of works in which the studio is an archive and source of inspiration. In 'Social Space', Henri Lefebvre argues that space is a complex social construction whose processes of production must be studied closely. In 'The Studio in the Gallery?', Jon Wood explores how these can be presented for the public. In particular he looks at the studios of Francis Bacon and Constantin Brancusi, also considering the studio recreation as artwork, in projects by Mike Nelson and Richard Venlet. In 'Gerhard Richter: Atlas', Lynne Cooke analyses Richter's use of his own massive accumulation of photographs and clippings on diverse subjects, stressing its status not as an archive but as an active element in his practice. Alexander Alberro discusses Robert Smithson's library as an archive of his intellect and Elena Filipovic considers Martha Rosler's participatory artwork in which she made her library available in a public space. Ian Wallace describes his practice which has centred on his relationship to the studio as it has progressed over time. In 'Dieter Roth's Mats', Bernadette Walter considers the grey cardboard mats installed on tables throughout Roth's living and work spaces. He used them as writing surfaces, and they inevitably also accrued other indices of daily life. In 'Edward Krasinski's Studio', Joanna Mytkowska and Andrzej Przywara map out a history of that artist's apartment-studio, inherited from the older avant-garde artist Henryk Stanewski, and how Krasinski's output came to incorporate elements of both artists' work. In the works of all these artists, the private becomes public to a more or less extreme extent, and the contents of their lives may be ordered as libraries and archives. In 'Just Waste', the architects Herzog & de Meuron describe the detritus of their production, which, accumulated over the course of years, has come to include sample materials, sketches and photographs, opened for public exhibition and now available in an organized, curated manner for public viewing.

Facing the World presents texts that illuminate the expansion of the studio concept, particularly from a private to a publicly oriented domain. In 'Start Working', Valérie Mréjen describes the procrastinating events of a morning nominally devoted to work, offering a glimpse inside the potential productivity of unstructured time in one's private studio. Steven Watson's text introduces us to Andy Warhol's fabled Factory in its heyday of the 1960s, an artistic endeavour that involved many participants and a greatly expanded field of activities. In 'A Studio of Their Own' Laura Meyer describes the Fresno Feminist Art Program as it developed its strategies for institutionalized collaboration, focus on gender issues, and more open set of coordinates for thinking about art-making that explicitly rejected 'the modernist paradigm of the autonomous artist/genius creating his work in isolation'. Continuing this story of early feminist art programmes, in a 2003 interview with Judy Chicago, Jane Collings discovers the history of the Woman's Building in Los Angeles, which was initiated by artists in 1973.

In *Seeing is Forgetting the Name of the Thing One Sees*, Lawrence Weschler describes Robert Irwin's re-emergence into the public world after a period of deep contemplation in his studio, producing his line paintings: 'Irwin emerged from his studio after two years, eyes blinking at the daylight ...' to adopt a drastically post-studio practice. In *The Machine in the Studio*, Caroline Jones looks at the 1960s as a time when artists sought to address through their work the post-war conditions of industry and corporate culture.

In 'The Studio of the Street' Jeffrey Deitch describes Jean-Michel Basquiat's emergence in the low-rent, revitalized New York artists' scene of the early 1980s: making no distinction between art and life environments, he drew constantly and everywhere. Jennifer Allen explores the hybridity and utopian/dystopian vision of Atelier van Lieshout's artistic-design-architectural practice, as it creatively explores loopholes in the conditions of globalized capitalism. And in a round table discussion Lynne Cooke, Friedrich Meschede and Sune Nordgren explore the implications of the many residencies offered worldwide, and the now-common practice of artists who, ever-itinerant, use travel and research as primary material for new works. Here the private, local studio becomes a thing of the past, as a series of temporary, international and shared live/work spaces look towards possible alternative futures. As Lane Relyea observes in the essay that concludes this selection, 'The studio is now that place where we know we can always find the artist when we need to, where she or he is always plugged in and online, always accessible to and by an ever more integrated and ever more dispersed art world.'

1   Examples include group exhibitions such as 'Close Encounters: The Sculptor's Studio in the Age of the Camera' (Henry Moore Institute, Leeds, 2001), 'The Studio' (Hugh Lane Gallery, Dublin, 2006), 'Mapping the Studio' (Stedelijk Museum, Amsterdam, 2006) and 'Street and Studio: An Urban History of Photography' (Tate Modern, London, 2008). Notable among the publications is *The Studio Reader*, edited by Michelle Grabner and Mary Jane Jacob (Chicago: University of Chicago Press, 2010). This very useful anthology was published when the present book was at a late editorial stage; while it was decided to repeat several texts, such as those by Daniel Buren and Lane Relyea, that are indispensible to both anthologies, this collection was otherwise revised to ensure a significantly different range of perspectives and voices, so that the two readers can complement each other as resources.

2   For a detailed discussion of both old master and modern period painters in relation to the changing role of the studio, see Svetlana Alpers, 'The View from the Studio', in *The Studio Reader*, op. cit., 126–46; see also the extract from Alpers' *Rembrandt's Enterprise: The Studio and the Market* (Chicago: University of Chicago Press, 1988) reprinted in this volume, 20–24.

3   Svetlana Alpers, *Rembrandt's Enterprise*, op. cit., 58.

Using my body as an extension of my painting-constructions challenged and threatened the psychic territorial power lines by which women, in 1963, were admitted to the

ART STUD CLUB

so long as they behaved enough like the

MEN

Carolee Schneemann, *Eye Body: 36 Transformative Actions* (1963), 2002

Svetlana Alpers
A Master in the Studio//1988

I

[...] There are a number of arguments that could be made against the proposition that Rembrandt's life and the life of his art is (largely) a studio matter. For one thing, the human and historical compass of his art is so great. In choosing to be a painter of historical subjects – considered the noblest kind at the time – Rembrandt turned away from the mundane, visible world of the other Dutch painters. The portraitist's task – condemned to copy after nature – was, in this view, perhaps an economic necessity for Rembrandt, a way to make money, but at a remove from the true ambitions of his art. Surely, it could be said, his works evoke and capture the workings of the human imagination rather than the literal concerns and practical arrangements of a working studio. What, moreover, could be further from Rembrandt's recognition of the essential isolation of the human condition than the hustle and bustle of a workshop scene?

But against such a reading of his art we have the evidence – multiplied because of recent research – of Rembrandt's serious investment of time and energy in being a teacher and the head of a large studio operation. He certainly had over fifty students and/or assistants during the course of his career. And others were attracted to his style. He engendered, nurtured and sold the Rembrandt mode to the Dutch public. To the established description of Rembrandt as a painter who chose the high road of history painting, we must now add that he also chose the life of the studio. There was a marked self-consciousness about this. Among his works and those of his students there are probably more images which record the working operations of the studio – the manner, the accoutrements and surroundings in which models and sitters posed – than there are of any other artist in Europe at the time.

Rembrandt is seen today as one of a crowd – one of a substantial group of artists (students, assistants and imitators) a number of whose works, it is argued, have long been mistakenly attributed to him. The authorship of a surprising number of once canonical paintings is under question – from the *Polish Rider* in the Frick Collection, New York, to the Berlin *Man with Golden Helmet*, to the *David and Saul* in The Hague, to a group of history paintings from the 1650s. The Rembrandt Research Project, which was established in Amsterdam [in the late 1960s] to ascertain Rembrandt attributions, has produced unexpected results: instead of isolating Rembrandt's manner, the team has called attention to its diffusion or spread. From our new knowledge of his studio entourage, we can conclude that for most of his life Rembrandt was not a lone genius but the setter of a certain (and, for a while, fashionable) pictorial style.

This studio habit does not fit our previous notion of the man or of his works. Though studio production was common in Renaissance painting, not all painters were famed, as was Raphael, for example, for being a team player, or, better, the successful captain of a workshop team. While Raphael and Rubens could work with a team, Leonardo and most notably Michelangelo, could not. At some level this reluctance or inability might well have been a matter of personality. The record of Rembrandt's dealings with possible patrons, and actual mistresses, suggests he was not a man who got on easily with others as Raphael and Rubens did. Rembrandt's pictorial personality makes a clear claim to individuality and even separateness. His idiosyncratic application of the paint calls attention to his own hand. His habit was not to work out his inventions in advance through drawings, but rather to invent paintings in the course of their execution. Rather than executing his inventions as was common in other studio workshops, Rembrandt's students had to make paintings like his. What is curious and stands in need of some explanation is that Rembrandt lays claim to a singular authority which he is simultaneously ready to diffuse.

The combination of choosing the high road of history painting and running an active studio had, of course, great precedents. Among living masters in northern Europe, it was preeminently Rubens' way. But unlike Rubens, the world traveller and diplomat, the confidant of kings, and even unlike Bloemaert, Honthorst and Lastman, the more modest masters of studios in the northern Netherlands, Rembrandt stayed home. His studio constituted his world. For most of his life he was not a lone genius but the setter of a particular fashion, but that fashion was, by its nature, of the studio born. Although Rembrandt's ambitions equalled those of any artist at the time, they were manifested more exclusively in this arena. Rembrandt contrived to see, or at least to represent, life in the world as if it were a studio event. [...]

III

[...] At the heart of the entire operation are the painter and his model(s). In Rembrandt's case this was a capacious category. Take a drawing of a beggar, for example [*Standing Man with a Pouch*; Ben. 31, Prentenkabinett, Rijksmuseum, Amsterdam]. The question we are accustomed to ask of such an image is whether or not it was drawn after life, by which we mean was the figure before Rembrandt's eyes when he drew it? This has been taken to mean, 'did Rembrandt go out into the streets and draw beggars?' The general conclusion is that he did not, that he was, instead (as a pair of his etchings after Beham demonstrates) drawing from a repertory of works of art and bringing them to a new appearance of life. But what if another possibility is that the beggar was actually brought into his studio? If this were so, a beggar 'after life' would, in effect, mean working after a studio model. This seems to me to have been a normal working procedure for Rembrandt: the appearance of 'after life' occurs at a characteristic introduction of life into the studio. But just how would this have occurred?

Hoogstraten recounts an amusing incident, repeated by Houbraken, that took place when he and his brother were in Vienna, that offers a possible answer to this question. It seems that his brother wanted to make a picture of the denial of Peter, and he needed a plebian model for his saint. He headed out to the marketplace to find a beggar whom he could persuade to come along with him. The beggar, probably expecting a small handout, followed along without realizing what he was getting into. He arrived at the studio only to get into a terrible state over what he saw. […] The skulls and some headless lay figures, the normal accoutrements of the painter's trade, terrified him. He thought he had been brought into the presence of Death and the Devil himself. He pleaded to be released, and it was only after much cajolery (and promise of cash) that he agreed to stay. The poor man remained, however, in a very shaken state. And so it was that he continued to display his fear and dismay when he came to serve the painter as the model for St Peter. Hoogstraten includes this true-to-life story in his chapter on how to represent human feelings in art. And he ends his account by remarking that the frightened beggar was the perfect model: as fearful and dismayed as St Peter himself.

I take it that the beggar in Rembrandt's fine chalk drawing is one who instead firmly stood his ground. From the swagger of his stance one would gather that he refused to be put off by the new and curious surroundings into which he was brought. His appearance is different; it is a representation of life enacted in the studio.

We took up the beggar's case with the art historian's question: is he drawn after life or not? But the nature of Rembrandt's practice, the beggar serving as a model, reveals an unexpected complexity. For it is indisputable that the 'life' here being drawn after is an enacted life. So the problem would seem to be not whether we consider this drawing to be after life, but what Rembrandt, on the evidence of his practice considered 'life' to be. And the evidence is that Rembrandt got at 'real' life through attending to the acting of it in the studio.

The custom has had a long life. We can compare Rembrandt's beggar to Manet's, who, far from being brought to life in the studio, was treated by Manet as an object to paint [*Rag-picker or Beggar*. Norton Simon Museum, Pasadena]. It is precisely the full or positive sense of an individual caught performing in the studio that is absent. A similar fixity characterizes the violinist in Manet's *Old Musician*. We know that the model was the most famous gypsy in Paris, who was also well known as an artist's model. Here the suspension of life is due to Manet's casting the gypsy in a pose taken from Velázquez's *Bacchus*. Though he shared Rembrandt's affinity for the studio, Manet in such cases could be described as working against the theatricalized model. The role-playing he encouraged otherwise, gives way to painting. Historically, he was at the other end of the studio tradition: while Rembrandt in the studio held out against the established taste for art, Manet held out against the modern taste for the disorderly world outside. [...]

In an etching of c. 1639 known as *The Artist Drawing from a Model*, we are shown the interior of the studio. The disarray of the workplace is evident: clothing, armour, furniture and a bit of sculpture crowd a scene in the midst of which artist and model are face to face. The clutter of objects is uncharacteristic of Rembrandt's works, and our view – an unusual one from behind the model looking back to the artist doubled over at his task – emphasizes what normally was kept invisible. The blank canvas behind the artist and the uneven finish of the plate call attention in different ways to that concentration and transformation necessary to the making of an image. The neutral, undefined surroundings represented by the tell-tale fade-out around the figure in Rembrandt's late paintings distance the sitter from the real activity of the studio and transform it into a place for the presentation of his act.

Nineteenth-century photographic practice is evidence that Rembrandt continued to be understood in this way. Rembrandt's absent but nevertheless implicit studio setting – removed from the world and concentrating on the individual portrayed – had a great appeal for portrait photographers of the nineteenth century. With this description, I think we can see the practical as well as the visual appeal that Rembrandt had. The 'look' of his works was all the rage, and all manner of equipment and effects were dubbed with his name: the Rembrandt portrait; Rembrandt lighting; the Rembrandt process (of printing); Rembrandt accessories of all kinds. And his chiaroscuro technique was recommended as a prime compositional device for a medium with only a limited means at its disposal to hold the viewer's eye. But it is also the staging procedures that led up to the taking of the picture that put one in mind of Rembrandt. The problem was how to get mood into a mechanical image made directly after life. Photographers staged their portraits: sitters were led through reception rooms hung with photographs of past sitters, and finally entered what was known as the operating room, where the portrait was made. Photographers orchestrated the staging of life that was implicit in Rembrandt's studio.

All painting in the seventeenth century was a studio affair. Every painting was a studio production. This in itself was nothing new. But it was at this time that painters addressed themselves to the situation: the relationship between the painter and his model(s) in an interior space was made the subject of art. Though we have a good number of drawings by both Rembrandt and his assistants recording work in the studio, and a number of self-portraits in various media of the artist at work, Rembrandt never made a major painting on the order of Vermeer's *Art of Painting* or Velázquez's *Las Meninas*. Instead, the studio situation is present in the form and in the manner of his late paintings. While Velazquez played host to his royal patrons in the palace, and Vermeer entertained a young woman in domestic surroundings as part of a rich and elusive visible world, Rembrandt painted as if he were the director of his own theatre company. His late works are the equivalent of closet drama rendered in the medium of paint.[...]

Svetlana Alpers, extracts from *Rembrandt's Enterprise: The Studio and the Market* (Chicago: University of Chicago Press) 58–60; 77–9; 82–3 [footnotes not included].

Sarah Burns
Looking in on the Colonies//1996

[...] The centre of art life was the Greenwich Village area, already the locus of an earlier literary bohemia made famous by Walt Whitman's presence at Pfaff's Beer Hall in the 1850s. After the Civil War, the Tenth Street Studio, built in 1857 by Richard Morris Hunt, became the hub of New York's art colony as the young cosmopolitans edged out the older occupants. Other populous studio buildings existed south of Union Square, along lower Broadway, and in the vicinity of Washington Square. Decay and change in the district, brought about by incoming waves of immigrant populations and the departure of the older gentry, resulted in an attractively low cost of living and generated a picturesque ambience of ethnic diversity that was sometimes – as in the case of the French emigré colony of the 1870s – associated with radical politics and subversion. Representatives of the cultural elite, such as Richard Watson Gilder, poet and editor of the *Century*, overlapped and intersected with the art community of the Village proper. Gilder held his literary and artistic salons just off Union Square in 'The Studio', an old stable remodelled for him by Stanford White.[1]

The artists' neighbourhood quickly acquired a distinctive character. Charlotte Adams identified it as the 'artistic colony in New York', which had become a 'recognized factor of the population'.[2] The term *colony* has suggestive connotations. It characterizes discrete and localized groups – prisoners, settlers, nudists – as well as aggregations of animals or other life forms existing as a single unit made up of interdependent parts. Prison colonies, of course, are composed of individuals whose association comes about involuntarily and as a result of the legal process; nudist colonies represent individuals who come together freely in order to pursue common interests, removed and protected from interference and intolerance. In either instance – prisoners or nudists – the group is set apart, contained by superior forces or containing itself. At the same time, it may be the subject of considerable unease or curiosity as the majority outside wonder what goes on inside. By their perceived difference from 'normal' individuals – those who obey the law or wear clothes – the inmates or members assume the function of 'others', deviants of one kind or another against which the parameters of acceptable conduct may be staked out. While nothing so extreme could be said of the New York art colony, such a conspicuous aggregation of painters, sculptors and others in one special area almost automatically proclaimed their common interests and their common differences from the rest of the world.

Unlike prison walls or camp barricades, however, the boundaries of the artists' 'colony' were permeable, inviting observation, inspections, excursions. It was a zone for tourism, locus of diversion, an allowed and allowable space for difference, yet a space that contained that difference, inhibiting its wider circulation. Outsiders and insiders alike appointed themselves tour guides and issued colourful reports of life beyond the border. W.H. Bishop's 1880 article on the lives of young New York artists offered a typical itinerary.[3] Bishop evoked an unstable world of flux and striving beneath the charming, 'happy-go-lucky' surface, especially to be seen and felt in the 'studios of the beginners … a great obscure body, full of aspiration, recognized failures and whimsical vicissitudes of fortune, between the student class and that of established reputation'. Like Jacob Riis eight years later, penetrating the threatening, mysterious slums of New York, Bishop promised to throw a few gleams of light into the obscurity of that elusive and unknowable body. Most of the beginners' studios were on Broadway, where they could be found almost everywhere:

Few of the older business buildings … but would yield to the search some obscure door in the upper regions bearing the title Artist. They are often the dingy quarters, with splintered, acid-stained floors, abandoned by photographers … Disregard of conventional forms sometimes reaches the point of actual squalor. Here in one … three persons are sleeping, two on a lounge – which also serves as a coal box – and one on a shelf conveniently placed at night on trestles. Coffee is drunk from a tomato can. … The collection of dust-covered clothing, old boots and shoes, withered fems, half dry sketches, plaster busts, groceries, books and oil cans, presided over by a battered lay figure in a Roman toga and slouch hat, would do little violence to the idea of symmetry in a rag and bottle shop. It is a veritable *vie de Bohème* that goes on. Such a fellow is said to have reduced to a nicety the art of renovating a linen front with Chinese white instead of sending it to the laundry. Landlords are regarded in an odious light, and if possible locked out. ... Pictures are made a medium of exchange with the butcher and the tailor. If fortune be propitious the bohemian luxuriates at boarding-houses and restaurants, whose walls he becomingly adorns. At other times he takes but a single meal or only mush and milk.[4] [...]

Bishop's tour of bohemia in New York made light of hardship and failure. There was, to be sure, a considerable, undifferentiated clump of mediocrities, but most of the 'beginners' had brighter prospects. This construction of bohemia featured picturesque clutter and temporary poverty, bachelorhood and male fellowship, amusing narratives and anecdotes, and most of all, youth. Whether the bohemia described was historical or contemporary, the stress on being young there was unvarying. The notion of male fellowship also sounded a constant note. The Philadelphia Sketch Club met in a 'garret' on Eleventh and Walnut Streets, where the walls were hung 'in artistic disorder' with sketches, etchings, armour, tapestries, draperies and trophies. There was a huge fireplace where the members smoked their long clay pipes and sipped beer from earthen mugs or mixed toddy from a huge kettle on a crane. They entertained each other with songs and recitations and had a life class on Monday nights. Even though they met in a garret, they were not half-starved weaklings but hearty fellows, each with a 'jovial nature' and a 'strong handshake'. Whether the result of poverty, carelessness, bachelorhood, or careful contrivance, bohemian disorder and clutter connoted freedom from whatever standards of order and regularity certified an individual as a dependable and well-controlled member of America's modern middle and professional classes.

Just as there was no dominant mainstream pattern of artistic identity, however, there was no single version of bohemia. While Bishop's account highlighted the 'beginners', with their lodgings so aromatic and higgledy-piggledy that they might have passed for interiors in low-life genre scenes, there was also the aestheticized and highly calculated bohemia of such artists as William Merritt Chase, with his famously cluttered studio, as well as squalid versions associated with modern, decadent Paris. [...]

1   [footnote 5 in source] See Albert Parry, *Garrets and Pretenders: A History of Bohemianism in America* (1933; rev. ed. New York: Dover, 1960) 62–94; Jan Seidler Ramirez, 'Within Bohemia's Borders: Greenwich Village, 1830–1930', Interpretive script accompanying an exhibition at the Museum of the City of New York, 2–20. Also see Thomas Bender, *New York Intellect: A History of Intellectual Life in New York City, from 1750 to the Beginnings of Our Own Time* (Baltimore: Johns

Hopkins University Press, 1987) 206–22, on overlapping literary 'bohemias' of the period.

2   [6] Charlotte Adams, 'Artists' Models in New York', *Century Illustrated Magazine*, no. 25 (February 1883) 569.

3   [7] W.H. Bishop, 'Young Artists' Life in New York', *Scribner's Monthly Magazine*, no. 19 (January 1880) 355–68.

4   [8] Henry Russell Wray, 'A Bohemian Art Club', in F. Hopkinson Smith, *Discussions on American Art and Artists* (Boston: American Art League, n.d.) 223–7.

Sarah Burns, extract from *Inventing the Modern Artist: Art and Culture in Gilded Age America* (New Haven and London: Yale University Press, 1996) 251–4.

Alexander Liberman
Giacometti//1960

Alberto Giacometti is a wiry man, about five feet ten. His face is that of a *condottieri*; thick, curly brown hair encases his head like mediaeval headgear. The long, straight, noble nose, the deep creases from cheek to thick-lipped mouth, engrave his portrait sharply in my memory.

In the movement of his body there is the weight of gravity. He stands with courage and boldness in front of his easel, in front of his sculpture. His legs, like those of a fighter in the ring, are astride and firmly planted. As he works he springs forward, steps back, scratches his hair.

In his painting everything is reduced to the simplest means of expression: the heads are so small, the nudes and figures so narrow, the brushes so thin. With two fingers he holds a long sable brush at its farthest extremity. He digs it into a tiny layer of grey and white paint. Then, with circular, groping movements, as though in a trance, he shapes a small layer of paint into the suggestion of a face in its minuscule form. His eyes are half closed, his movements rapid. He smokes incessantly. Hundreds of cigarette butts litter the floor. When he sculpts, there is more movement and abandon. He seems to dance around the emerging form. His arms sway wide to add by touch the substance that will be form.

Giacometti lives in an artists' community in one of the sadder parts of Paris. Into a narrow courtyard, some six feet wide and forty feet long, open the doors and windows of various studios. Several garbage cans stand just behind the entrance to the court. On the soot-covered grey stucco walls hang classic bas-reliefs of angels dancing in a frieze, left-overs from more academic inhabitants.

Giacometti has the four small studios on each side of the entrance. On the left is the room in which he works, and next to it his one-room apartment; across the narrow gap are his brother's workshops, where the processing of Giacometti's sculpture is done. He has lived here since 1927.

His studio is a small room, about fifteen feet by twelve. One window takes up a whole wall. Since the studio is on the ground floor and the courtyard is only six feet wide, the light that streams in is grey and dull. The overall impression is of monochromatic greyness. The street outside, the whole quarter, is grey. The walls are grey, the sculpture grey and white, interspersed with the sepia accent of wood or the dull glint of bronze. The walls are scratched and scribbled on as though some cave painter had tried to capture images in this cavern. Under the big window is a long table entirely covered with squeezed tubes of paint, palettes, paintbrushes, rags, bottles of turpentine. Like figures, the bottles stand shrouded in layers of dust chipped away from Giacometti's sculpture. Here sculpture and painting mix intimately. He has painted his recent sculpture in the manner of the ancient Greeks, and on his work table the two media intermingle – turpentine, oil paint, colour-soaked plaster, with clay, wire, stone and bronze.

In the darker corners of the room his long, narrow, life-size figures of white plaster seem like apparitions from another planet. [...]

On the walls of his bedroom are drawings, and the cracked paint on the cupboards reminds one of damaged frescoes. In this room there is a bed with no back, just a mattress with an eiderdown, two pillows and white sheets. An ordinary painted chair, the paint all cracked on its rounded, bent back, serves as a bed table. On it were three or four torn books of poems: Apollinaire's *Alcools* and the poetry of Rimbaud. Like Matisse, Braque and Picasso, Giacometti is a great reader of poetry. But unlike many artists, he reads innumerable newspapers. Behind the bed are an old wireless set, a small lamp, a large, badly painted closet. Next to two jars of instant coffee stand empty jars of yogurt. Diagonally across one corner of the room hangs a string on which clothes and kitchen towels dry. Under the window is a sink, a small two-plate burner, a basin, a pitcher of flowers. The small bouquet that his wife places in their sad, grim bedroom is a spark of emotional relief. Without it this room would seem unbearable.

Giacometti's wife, Annette, is about five feet four, like a slender girl of fourteen. She is not fourteen, she is much older, but her youth, her beauty, a poetic quality of mood are a contrast to Giacometti's sombre brooding. She has the naïve and innocent expression of a child, and laughs often with a girl's laughter. This girl-wife seems made to be the companion who does not distract the artist from his work. They met in 1949. She always says the formal *vous* to Giacometti. He sometimes teases her. Then the wrinkles, the two deep furrows in Giacometti's face crease even deeper, and he beams like a mountaineer enjoying a good joke.

He is a man possessed. Time has no meaning in his daily life; he eats and sleeps as he needs to. There is no specific hour for any activity, only the time to speak, to create. [...]

Alexander Liberman, extracts from *The Artist in His Studio* (New York: Viking Press, 1960) 57; 69–70.

Mary Bergstein
'The Artist in His Studio': Photography, Art and the Masculine Mystique//1995

The Artist in His Studio and *The Artists of My Life*

Critics have long observed that as the twentieth century unfolded the idea of art making as a male prerogative was expounded in representation. The more that masculinity came to be identified as a generative force in artistic creation, the more necessary it seemed for women to assume the foil of alterity – to be cast as natural, passive beings whose role was opposite and complementary to the artistic pursuit.[1] [...]

Around mid century there were several 'cultic' photography books whose production and sale flourished in the United States. Alexander Liberman's *The Artist in His Studio* (1960) seems to have been ubiquitous, especially in its inexpensive paperback edition of 1968.[2] *The Artist in His Studio* can be classified as high modernist reportage. Liberman's rationale for the book was patently modernist: 'I tried to reveal [the] core of the creative act, to show the creative process itself, and thereby to relate painting and sculpture with the mainstream of man's search for truth.' In a foreword to *The Artist in His Studio*, James Thrall Soby asserted that Liberman had 'brought to the work ... a rare capacity for psychological insight'. Until recently the editorial director of Condé Nast, Liberman worked for many years as a *Vogue* photographer and art director; his collected photographs of artists at work represent a project of several decades in which his stated aim was documentary accuracy.[3]

The mystique of the artist's atelier was disseminated in mainstream American magazines such as *Life*, *Vogue* and *Harper's Bazaar*, where Alexander Liberman and Brassaï, among others, represented the artists' lives for public consumption. One of Liberman's early missions had been to bring modernist art to the pages of *Vogue*: interspersed among fine points of etiquette and fashion, these pictures brought the legend of the modernist artist to women within the realm of fashion-magazine fantasy. In this context, it seemed 'natural' for North American women to study a photograph of a model wearing a Dior dress within seconds of having contemplated a photo essay on Picasso in his studio. Fashion and art were glamorous consumer products – out of reach for most readers, but presented as eminently desirable. Liberman is said to have stated that haute couture, with its basis in feminine seduction, had a place within the tradition of Western art 'from Titian and Velázquez to Matisse'.[4] Likewise the tradition of masculine domination and feminine objectification in Western avant-garde art was granted a privileged place in fashion. A persistent interleaving of male artists with women's fashions in magazines like *Vogue* served to reinforce the historical association of masculinity with production and femininity with passivity and consumption.

Liberman's photo essays of artists seemed more intimate and accessible than some of the ideas expressed in actual works of painting or sculpture. Illustrated publications were far more widely replicated and circulated, and thus better known, than the art objects themselves. The experience of poring over books like *The Artist in His Studio* provided people (including photographers, students, and art historians) with a common cultural system. In Liberman's book the artists' biographical sketches consisted of photographic vignettes, accompanied by verbal anecdotes. He constructed an avant-garde modernism of personal legend, inviting the viewer to inspect each image for 'clues' regarding the actuality of the artist's creative experience. This material was packaged in the language of 'documentary' photography.

Many points of connection link the oeuvre of Alexander Liberman with that of the more celebrated photographer, Brassaï. Brassaï photographed the 'artists of his life' in a thirty-year project: some of his photographs first appeared in literary magazines such as *Verve* and *Minotaure*, much of the work was done under the auspices of *Life* and the American fashion monthly *Harper's Bazaar*; Brassaï's *Conversations avec Picasso* (1964) was translated from the French by Francis Price as *Picasso and Company*, with a preface by Henry Miller and an introduction by Roland Penrose (1966). Finally, an art book entitled *Brassaï: The Artists of My Life* (1982), reproduced many of these images of artists with a memoir written by Brassaï to accompany the essentially photographic text.[5] Brassaï's work, like Liberman's, promulgated the legend of masculine domination through representations of studio life.

The artist's studio was an established theme in early twentieth-century painting, and became a prime subject for the documentary photographer. The atelier was perceived as a place of enchantment where the artist's life (real and imaginary) unfolded, as well as being a workshop for the production of art objects. As these aspects of the studio merged in representation, the process of creativity became fused with the artist's personal wishes and gratifications. [...]

Reading the Photographic Material

[...] In *The Artists of my Life* Alberto Giacometti is presented as a major protagonist. And the role of the photographed artist as author looms large: 'Photograph me like this, Brassaï', says Giacometti a few months before his death in 1966.[6] Giacometti's persona and his works in the studio had provided photogenic material since the 1930s. Time and again, Giacometti not only posed but actually performed for various photographers: the resulting images convey an undercurrent of anxious, antagonistic masculinity. Giacometti's stance is articulated in Brassaï's compositions, even those such as *L'Objet Invisible* (1934– 35), spattered with plaster (1948) where the artist's physical presence is omitted. Here, Giacometti's studio is presented as a work of art unto itself. The scribbled-upon walls, inanimate female nude, wood-stove, and crumpled newspapers are all of a piece, touched by the artist's hand with the indiscriminate spattering of plaster and unified through the camera's lens, so that wall, sculpture and stove are given equal value as pictorial components. The medium of black and white photography serves to drain away local colour and suppress incidental extranea. Brassaï compresses Giacometti's studio into a 'pure' Giacometti. The studio is framed as an enchanted place, which is physically inseparable from Giacometti's work process and his ego.[7] [...]

In Giacometti's Studio

Alberto Giacometti was an important subject for Alexander Liberman, much as he had been for Brassaï. The Giacometti spread in *The Artist in His Studio* was again designed to demonstrate a special style of psychological insight expressed by two authors: the modernist sculptor and the documentary photographer. Liberman's strategy was to validate modernist assumptions by means of photographic documentation. He wished to expose the material and emotional factors that were intrinsic to the artist's biography.

Facing pages with a dozen small photographs (labelled A–L) suggest a sequential documentation of a day in the life of Giacometti, from the throes of tormented creativity to exhausted resolution. In this photographic chart, works of art merge with the domestic fabric of the studio, and likewise the personal life and material effects of the artist are inextricable from the studio environment. The strategy of photographic presentation consists of a grid-like mosaic of equal-size mixed-sequence fragments that appear to be excerpted from the continuum of lived reality in the artist's studio. Scanning from A to L, the reader is meant to experience a candid view of the sculptor's kinaesthetic thinking as he forms a clay figure. Similarly, we are permitted to glimpse Giacometti in an apparently private moment of anguished concentration. Annette Giacometti is represented in a distant vignette, reading on a dishevelled couch among her husband's scattered works of art and sketches; she turns away from the viewer into her own private world, and her face and mind are represented as absent to the degree that those of the artist are emphatically present. Liberman's captions accompany the photographic story as follows:

A. The alley that separates Giacometti's studio, right from his casting studio, left, where his brother Diego helps him. / B. The walls of Giacometti's small studio are covered with his drawings. On a shelf are many works in progress. / C. Giacometti working on a bust of his brother Diego. / D. Concentration. / E. Finished and unfinished sculptures, mysterious hieratic forms shrouded in his studio. / F. In his tiny one-room kitchen-bedroom-living room, on a chair by his bed, books of poems by Rimbaud, Apollinaire. / G. Giacometti sculpts standing; he moves around his sculpture. / H. Annette reading in the studio, surrounded by works in progress. / I. In the bedroom, flowers and drawings on the walls. / J. While he works, a cigarette is never out of his hand. / K. When he paints he holds his thin brushes at the very tip, so that his smallest movement is amplified. / L. The artist's family, his wife Annette, brother Diego.[8]

In addition to the set of captions, extravagant prose reiterates the drama expressed in this visual biography. As a kind of modern day Vasari, Liberman thrived on the fantasized details of the artist's personal life, conflating them with his work, as if to quantify that ineffable quality of genius. Liberman described the studio with the apparently impartial but slightly amazed voice of an anthropologist encountering the customs of a distant culture. He then went on to describe the artist's wife, Annette:

Giacometti's wife, Annette, is about five feet four, like a slender girl of fourteen. She is not fourteen, she is much older, but her youth, her beauty, a poetic quality of mood, are a contrast to Giacometti's sombre brooding. She has the naïve and innocent expression of a child, and laughs often with a girl's laughter. This girl-wife seems made to be the companion who does not distract the artist from his work. They met in 1949. She always says the formal *vous* to Giacometti.

And about the Michelangelesque genius at home: 'He is a man possessed. Time has no meaning for his daily life; he eats and sleeps as he needs to. There is no specific hour for any activity, only the time to speak, to create.' Alberto Giacometti is represented as a person of almost unbearable intellect and *terribilità*, whereas his female counterpart is seen as small, graceful, innocent, childlike, submissive, non-distracting, and intellectually absent.

What is 'captured' in Liberman's journalistic images of Giacometti is the hyper-personal atmosphere of the studio, the *Sturm* of activated intellect in the artist's countenance and physical presence, and the contrasting benign cooperation of his wife as passive inhabitant of the studio environment. [...]

Modernist Artists in Yesterday's News

[...] Certain mainstream art journals further amplify and elaborate on modernist legends of masculinity in the creative process. The notoriously glossy American art magazine *Sculpture* in April 1994 published an interview with Alexander Liberman.[9] Here, in conversation with *Sculpture* editor Suzanne Ramljak, Liberman re-articulates his stance towards the image of the artist. 'My book *The Artist in His Studio*, he states, 'was an attempt to find answers to questions of how the great painters of a certain period worked. [...] So my pictures were not a photographer's pictures, they were journalistic documents. [...] I photographed what I was searching for; what was noble in existence. It is always a search for the essence of the best in the world, of man's potential for human achievement.'

With regard to his magazine work (*Vogue*) Liberman asserts that his main contribution 'was to bring the good and noble to American life and American women'. He then posits that whereas 'photography feeds on reality', art feeds on the 'subconscious'. He speaks of the production of art in terms of the male erotic experience, declaring that 'it [art] also has to do with some sort of penetration. Penetration is one of the key forces in the experience of art, along with eroticism. To some people it may sound pornographic or ridiculous, but penetration and eroticism is one way human beings have of leaving this life and going to some superior realm.' And on his own works of large-scale sculpture: 'I do believe in the vertical, the erection.'

When Ramljak leads back into the question of eroticism and *The Artist in His Studio*, Liberman states that the making of [modernist] art requires extensive female suffering: 'That's why I didn't totally plunge into art. I was afraid of making my wife and the women I've loved unhappy. All the lives of women partners of men artists that I have observed have been rather miserable. The real artist is practically a madman, an obsessed man.'

The *Sculpture* interview recapitulates the modernist values that we have seen advanced in the work of Liberman and Brassaï. Namely that photographic images of the artist in his studio served to demonstrate the otherwise invisible essence of masculinity in art. The mystique of artistic production is equated with virility, as in the topoi established by Vasari in the sixteenth century and reshaped in modernity by the Freudian psychologist Ernest Jones. Texts by Brassaï and Liberman continue to encourage a particular response from spectators who have been culturally primed to scrutinize 'documentary' photographic images for traces of the creative process. These representations, which were published in the guise of candid views of the making of art, continue to shape and reinforce abiding cultural imperatives.

1   This phenomenon corresponds to the assumption that whereas the proper identity and habitat of women is found in nature, culture is produced by men; see Sherry Ortner, 'Is Female to Male as Nature is to Culture?', in Michelle A. Rosaldo and Louise Lamphere, eds, *Women, Culture and Society* (Stanford: Stanford University Press, 1974) 67–87. Suzi Gablik, in her *The Re-enchantment of the World* (New York, 1992) 127, articulates the consensus that in a general way, 'modern aesthetics [have] been coloured, structured and controlled by a kind of compulsive masculinity'. The pioneering essay on this subject, written by Carol Duncan in 1973, represents a point of departure for my enquiry: 'Virility and Domination in Early Twentieth-Century Vanguard Painting', *Artforum* (December 1973) 30–39 (reprinted in Norma Broude and Mary D. Garrard, eds, *Feminism and Art History: Questioning the Litany* [New York, 1982] 293–313). For postwar artists see Amelia Jones, 'Dis-playing the Phallus: Male Artists Perform Their Masculinities', *Art History*, no. 4 (December 1994) 546–84.

2   [footnote 3 in source] Liberman, *The Artist in His Studio* (New York: Viking Press, 1968). This paperback reprint was priced at $3.50 [for comparison an issue of the art magazine *Studio International* in that year was $1.50 and the minimum wage was $1.60 an hour; the 1968 edition was also co-published in London by Thames & Hudson]. An informal survey of artists, photographers and art historians who came of age around 1968 confirmed my impression of the popularity enjoyed by the book at that time. Portions of material for the book had already appeared in *Vogue* prior to the first edition published by Viking Press in 1960.

3   [4] See Dodie Kazanjian and Calvin Tompkins, 'In the Right Circles', *Vogue* (August 1993) 270–311.

4   [5] Ibid., 310.

5   [6] Brassaï, *The Artists of My Life* (New York: Viking Press, 1982). Germaine Richier, whose most 'masculine' qualities are visually exploited here, is the only woman included.

6   [27] Ibid., 54.

7   [28] Ibid., 54–67.

8   [42] Liberman, *The Artist in His Studio*, op. cit., 276–80, plates 127–31.

9   [45] Suzanne Ramljak, 'Interview: Alexander Liberman', *Sculpture*, no. 13 (March/April 1994) 10–12.

Mary Bergstein, extracts from '"The Artist in His Studio": Photography, Art and the Masculine Mystique', *Oxford Art Journal*, vol. 18, no. 2 (1995) 45–6; 49–51; 55–6; 57.

Brian O'Doherty
Studio and Cube//2007

[...] The studio as a cultists' club, where a group sets itself up to live, commune with a leader, practice what is unconventional to the popular mind, and manufacture art for the fools who want it, is close to a description of Warhol's ironically named Factory, first located on East 47th Street in New York. There the cult leader, dandified, seemed to hover in idle suspension, a posture refuted by the flow of product to the outside. It would need Roland Barthes to describe Warhol's face, a neutral mask that could accommodate any reading. Warhol's early persona – the silver fetish, silver hair; the walls of silver, light gliding, coruscating, fracturing in an unsettling dazzle – was a marvellous conceit. To work without appearing to work, to be a passive Svengali who held others entranced, so that, nourished by doses of irony and sometimes danger, they believed that everyone outside the group was clumsily comic – that was the quasi-Manson-like character of the artistic cult, which is always a cult of personality. All this ended when the silver carapace was penetrated by the madwoman's bullet. After that, Warhol's cult was different. He could pose as someone already dead, patiently suffering the tedium of the afterlife. Warhol's persona, a brilliant construct, has not been sufficiently appreciated. He made the role-playing of the disco intersect with the studio in a dream of luxury and surface. Advanced art made easy.

We might see the extremes of 1960s studio culture in New York as represented by Warhol and Rauschenberg, contrasting the former's flat ironies with the latter's Whitmanian exuberance. The mystique of Rauschenberg's cult was movement, activity, surfing on the zeitgeist. From 1961 to 1965 Rauschenberg had an omnivorous appetite, as if his studio were a vast stomach digesting twentieth-century media glut. Through the silkscreen, he and Warhol could bring any subject to heel. At that time, Rauschenberg pursued a utopia situated in the 'now'. Like many American constructs, this utopia had an imperfect knowledge of evil, a disbelief in its presence and powers, which survived even the Kennedy assassination in November 1963. The performances, the art and technology wonders, the dancers gliding in and out of the studio, the open house at Lafayette Street (where a huge wooden aeroplane occupied one room), the artist's chronic generosity, urged a generation of dancers and artists on. Remarkably, few of those in his charismatic aura made work that looked like his.

Rauschenberg's studio was a kind of commune, its spirit a radical innocence. It inherited the tradition of the studio as a social centre, a place where ideas about art and dance overlapped with a utopianism like that of Brook Farm, the Massachusetts commune of the 1840s which aimed, as its founders stated, to substitute a system of brotherly cooperation for one of selfish competition. Rauschenberg in his arbitrary, charismatic way joined art, science and dance with collectors, money, business and magazine and newspaper culture, in the amiable promise of immediate gratification. This democratic federation of diverse interests was one of the most extraordinary social creations of the 1960s. At its centre was this kinetic, extroverted creature who seemed to embody Blake's 'Energy is pure Delight'. Money flowed, outer space was being domesticated, the young were dancing to a new beat, drugs and sex promised transcendence, the slogans were peace and love. Altamont was in the future. It seemed as if consciousness itself was being redefined. From Rauschenberg's studio came one work that perhaps summarizes the glorious confusion between art and life: *Bed* (1955). Let us follow that artwork as it tumbles genially between studio and gallery.

There are some profoundly intimate spaces. The inside of a shoe perhaps. Or the mysterious inside of a woman's purse, which calls for its Bachelard. Another is the bed. Like the studio it is soaked with the personal; even when empty it crawls with imprints and residues of identity. It puts on the same horizontal plane the tortures of sex and the ecstasy of dying. The bed is the nocturnal baseline of our vertical endeavours. It seems to exert an extra gravitational pull. Heavy with sleep, we are weighed down into some archaeology of memory and forgetfulness until we are made weightless by dreams or exploded by nightmares. The act of raising this horizontal familiar, like Lazarus, from its prone position to the vertical lets loose on it, in a violent rush, the powerful aesthetic conventions of looking at a picture on the wall. We still pick up shockwaves from this vertical bed. The gesture (it is as much gesture as painting) takes an indispensable part of the studio lifestyle – the bed in the corner, the locus of our nocturnal return – and embalms it in the paralysed time of the white cube. The all-over tactility of the ensheathing bed in the studio is transferred to the exclusively visual, no-touch gallery. The passage from studio to gallery of one of the studio's basics (bed, table, chair, easel, stove) invites comment on the linkage between the loci of generation and display. In 'The Function of the Studio' (1971), Daniel Buren was the first to ponder and write about what he called 'the hazardous passage' from the studio (where he considered the work to be in place) to the gallery/museum, where placelessness isolates and reifies it. Rauschenberg's *Bed*, a kind of sarcophagus, slides both together in such a perfect overlap that it raises the thought of a return journey – back to the studio again, where another bed has now replaced it.

How would Rauschenberg's bed look if it were returned to the studio? How did the painted bed look in the studio both before and after it was attached to the studio wall? It would not be alone. The studio is more or less crowded with artworks, periodically depleted as they migrate to the gallery. Artworks lie around, parked, ignored in remote corners, stacked against the wall, reshuffled with the cavalier attitude allowed only to their creator. As one work is worked on, the others, finished and unfinished, are detained in a waiting zone, one over the other, in what you might call a collage of compressed tenses. All are in the vicinity of their authenticating source, the artist. As long as they are in his or her orbit, they are subject to alteration and revision. All are thus potentially unfinished. They – and the studio itself – exist under the sign of process, which in turn defines the nature of studio time, very different from the even, white, present tense of the gallery.

Studio time is defined by this mobile cluster of tenses, quotas of pasts embodied in completed works, some abandoned, others waiting for resurrection, at least one in process occupying a nervous present, through which, as James Joyce said, future plunges into past, a future exerting on the present the pressure of unborn ideas. Time is reversed, revised, discarded, used up. It is always subjective, that is, elastic, stretching, falling into pools of reflection, tumbling in urgent waterfalls. When things are going wonderfully well it stops in a fiction of immortality. Or it may decay into a tizzy of impotence – as Ingres is supposed to have suffered when precision eluded him – or toss the artist around in a frenzy. In the midst of this temporal turbulence, artworks in the studio have an alertness, no matter how casually thrown around, that they don't take with them when they leave. In the studio, partly as a consequence of this, they are aesthetically unstable. Accompanied only by the artist (and occasional visitors, assistants, other artists), they are vulnerable to a glance or a change in light. They have not yet determined their own value.

That begins when they are socialized on the gallery walls. If the artist is the first viewer, the first stabilizing factor is the studio visitor. The studio visit became a trope in modernism, and remains so. The visit has its etiquette and comic misunderstandings. The studio visitor is the preface to the public gaze. The visitor brings an environmental aura – collector, gallery, critic, museum, magazine. The studio visit can be a raging success or a disaster, a much desired 'discovery' or an intrusion from hell. My favourite is Bernard Berenson's description of his visit to the studio of a barely civil Matisse. There is no better illustration of a sublime philistine (towards modernism) visiting a great modern artist. The art puzzles him. He wonders about Matisse's reserve. His thoughts as he reports them would set any artist's teeth on edge. Matisse says little. Berenson leaves, one of the great art historians – along with Gombrich, Kenneth Clark and Panofsky – to whom the modernist adventure was a wilful and misguided anomaly.

By now, we are aware of the fields of force, as it were, that surround the artist in his studio, whether it is the studio of accumulation or the studio of monastic bareness, which, according to Ernst Kris, descends from Plato through Christian saintliness. Why these extremes? Is it just a matter of housekeeping? If the studio reflects the mind of its occupant, is one mind an attic, the other a prison cell? Does one introduce us to the aesthetics of redundancy, the other to the aesthetics of elimination – the glutinous studio of ingestion and the anal studio of excretion, the fat and the slender, Laurel and Hardy seeing each other in the studio's distorting mirror? Are studios of accumulation indubitably secular? Do studios of elimination have a yearning for some absolute? Does each indicate a temperament and an aesthetic?

A perfect example of the studio as accumulating artwork is Schwitters' Hanover *Merzbau*, begun in 1923. The artist, like some industrious organism, shed his own exoskeleton as the studio progressively evicted him and limited his visitors to one entry at a time. The agent of the process was compressed by his own crowded studioscape. The studio became a proto-museum as Schwitters worked inside, 'wearing' his studio, trying it on for size after every addition or change. Such studios of accumulation have had a didactic, even legendary value with respect to postmodern gallery installations that stuff and insult the white space. As proxies, they take on some of the aura of their creator. Francis Bacon's studio, in a very different way from Schwitters', was a cumulative, living collage, a 'compost heap', as he called it. In *Imagination's Chamber*, Bellony-Rewald and Peppiatt describe 'the floor … ankle-deep in books, photos, rags and other paint-splashed, eye-catching rubble, while the walls have been so thoroughly daubed with trial brushstrokes that they resemble giant palettes'. The small room had one window and one door. It was crammed with accumulated debris: a mirror, slashed canvases, canvases with cut-out centres, encrusted pots of paint, brushes, tubes, patches of bare wood wall (when not covered with photographs), pages torn from magazines, a book on Velázquez, postcards of artworks. No bed, no sink. This version of chaos, however, still had its memory. It was living memory, from which Bacon retrieved the photographs and reproductions that contributed to his paintings. The redundant mess had a reassuring function for the artist. It was a 'womb' within which he could work, perhaps signified in his paintings by the skeletal cubes which trapped many of his figures.

Every studio has to have some traffic with the outside. In Bacon's case it was not only photographs and reproductions. It was words. Magazines and books were ingested and digested in that small room. The processes of reading, looking, thinking, painting, destroying, were superimposed one on the other with the energy of a consumer who tested everything by one criterion: could it be used? Now preserved in Dublin's Hugh Lane Gallery, Bacon's studio carries such a whiff of presence that you can hallucinate the large, restless, reputedly dangerous animal inside as you peer through door and window. What happens to this room when it is frozen in museum time? How does it illuminate Bacon's art? It becomes emblematic, circulating a low-grade energy amongst artist, persona, studio and work, enough to sustain the myth it begot.

Few experiences were as mythopoeic as visiting Mark Rothko's studio on East 69th Street in Manhattan. Easel, a couple of chairs, a scruffy couch where he frequently slept, especially towards the end, huge frameworks, a skylight with adjustable drapery to filter and change the light, racks of drawings and canvases, a table – and the uneasy occupant, the artist himself. Rothko's studio, in contrast to Bacon's and to that of the fascinating nineteenth-century American artist Albert Pinkham Ryder, was bare, functional, puritanical – a *studio povera* indeed. His high seriousness dismissed everyday trivialities and discomforts.

What made a visit so testing was the hypersensitivity of its inhabitant, who was engaged in superimposing, through the finest of micro-decisions, the nineteenth-century quest and the modern void. In that dark studio Rothko seemed as much the victim of his work as its creator. The more he succeeded in his mission, the more he seemed excluded from his own product, as if he could reveal the secret but not share in it. The studio seemed to enfold a great, unmentioned secret. This was a source of irritation and perhaps rage. There was a flow of quiet visitors, many of whom found the experience tense. As they looked at the work, Rothko would fasten his gaze on them. He would decipher, or thought he could decipher, any hint of approval, disapproval, puzzlement, even scorn. One innocent was thrown out because, Rothko said, 'he did not respect the work'. Knowing that respectful young visitor, I was mystified as to how Rothko came to that determination. The high, shadowy studio seemed a preface to transcendence, an ambition easily mocked but, as it turned out, deadly serious. The windows looked out on nothing in particular, but the light from them and from the skylight was coaxed to deposit itself in a crepuscular vibration on the dark canvases. As you sat watching with Rothko, the light slowly waned, its changes barely perceptible, until the edges of the painting blurred into the dusk, something he accepted with pleasure. The gallery's more stable lighting was unwelcome to him since unchanging light deprived his paintings of their variety of moods. The paintings looked better in the studio. Their vulnerabilities echoed Rothko's sensitivities. There was something of Balzac's Frenhofer about Rothko – both artists engaged in an impossible task in the mysterious studios that witnessed their demise.

How different was Duchamp's amiable exhibition of an empty studio, presented in his later years as evidence that, as he announced, he had given up art. Of course, no one knew that in another studio he was finishing his last major work, the *Étant Donnés*. The Duchampian paradoxes are comical. The empty studio, the site of production, is displayed as evidence of non-production, a mask for an activity in process elsewhere. A creative gesture – the invention of an empty studio – is presented as evidence of sterility, the paralysis of the creative act. Duchamp, whom no one saw working, was practising a secretive art in a secret studio – appropriately, since *Étant Donnés*, the work that emerged, reduced the visitor (spy?) to a scopophilic stare through an eye-hole. [...]

Brian O'Doherty, extract from *Studio and Cube: On the Relationship between Where Art is Made and Where Art is Displayed* (New York: Columbia University Press, 2007) 15–23.

Robert Smithson
Studio Conversation with Anthony Robbin//1969

Robert Smithson People who defend the labels of painting and sculpture say what they do is timeless, created outside of time; therefore the object transcends the artist himself. But I think that the artist is important, too, and what he does, the way he thinks, is valuable, whether or not there is any tangible result. You mainly follow a lot of blind alleys, but these blind alleys are interesting.

Anthony Robbin It isn't so necessary for the artist to render this chaos into form so much as to expose the fact that ... ?

Smithson It's there.

Robbin Yes. Not only that it's there, but that he is dealing with it, manipulating it, speculating about it.

Smithson That he is living with it without getting hysterical, and making some ideal system which distorts ...

Robbin Not making an ideal system, but at the same time making *some* system.

Smithson Yes. But even *some* system tells you nothing about art.

Robbin Tentative and transient as it is. It's not enough for him not to do anything.

Smithson I feel that you have to set your own limits ...

Robbin And the self-aware setting of limits is close to the centre of it all?

Smithson Yes. I think the major issue now in art is what are the boundaries. For too long artists have taken the canvas and stretchers as given, the limits.

Robbin The motivation for doing that is not to expand the system. You are not doing it for the sake of the system?

Smithson I'm doing it to expose the fact that it is a system, therefore taking away the vaulted mystery that is supposed to reside in it. The artifice is plainly an artifice. I want to de-mythify things.

Robbin People will be frustrated in their desire for certainty, but maybe they will get something more after that frustration passes.

Smithson Well, it's a problem all the way around, and I don't suspect we will work our way out of it.

Robert Smithson and Anthony Robbin, extract from conversation in the artist's studio: 'Smithson's Non-Site Sights: Interview with Anthony Robbin', *ARTnews* (February 1969); reprinted in *Robert Smithson: The Collected Writings*, ed. Jack Flam (Berkeley and Los Angeles: University of California Press, 1996) 175.

Louise Bourgeois
Statement//1989

I am kind of a recluse, and I do not need to go on and on, faster and faster, and I do not need to show my work, and I do not need to explain it. If the work doesn't talk to you, just relax. Do any of you have to define yourself? It is very difficult to define yourself. It is even more difficult to reveal yourself.

I am not interested in other artists. I do enjoy certain artists immensely, but it's a pleasure that doesn't relate to my work. In fact it's really a holiday for me when I go see a show. I have an open house on Sundays, anybody can come. But I've discovered they want me to criticize their work. Well, this is ridiculous. I rack my brain to criticize, I make constructive criticism, and they cry because they don't want to be criticized – they only want to be loved and encouraged. But that is not possible, you can't encourage everybody. I can spend hours talking about their work, but they can't ask me to love it, and sometimes I do not. I cannot commit myself to saying I love something that I do not love. I do appreciate these afternoons, but at the end of the afternoon I can feel like a failure. I feel that all these people came for something they didn't get. People ask too much; they want me to encourage them to become Picasso – the sky's the limit. This is what I see in the students: they want the show and publicity and the big sale, and there's no end to it. This reminds me of a fairy tale: a child wants to leave home, to forget about home, and he runs in the woods until six o'clock. Then he wants to come home ... but he cannot retrace his steps.

This idea of selling, it's new. In the past, artists made work, they had shows, but then they took the art back home – nothing was sold of course. Naturally that happened to me. A lot of artists gave up, but it was a fantastic experience for the artist to see the work far away from the studio, in exhibition.

I remember when Stuart Davis became successful and had a show at the Modern, he said 'I can never paint again.' And it was true. I don't know what kind of syndrome that is but a lot of artists cannot stand success. But they can't stand failure either, so you might say that art is an addiction you cannot control. [...]

Even though I'm only interested in the work I do tomorrow, I do not destroy my past work. I'm not interested in it, but it lives there all by itself, gathering dust. The dust that has gathered over all this work – we can remove it and say, 'this is a show of the fifties'. It is very nice to face the past. It was not that bad.

The feeling of creating is really your fight against depression. The thing is not to get depressed, which is not interesting at all; the thing that is interesting is to get out of depression, and the way to get out of depression is by having a couple of bright ideas. It really works. Of course it needs discipline, but that is really what is at the back of the work. It's like saying, 'tomorrow is going to be beautiful.' Why say that? It's ridiculous – tomorrow is going to be just like yesterday – but somehow something clicks somewhere, and you think, 'this time I'm going to make it.' But if you are a sculptor you have something. The work is there; it talks back to you.

I have a very tiny life. I am very concentrated; my art is so precise and every day is the same. The discipline, the routine, I do not mind them. I don't take vacations; I don't enjoy them. To go to Europe – there is nothing there. Europe has no wonder for me. What does have wonder is having a challenge that is difficult to meet. [...]

Louise Bourgeois, extract from 'Louise Bourgeois: 11 April 1989. Robert Miller Gallery, 57th Street', in *Inside The Studio: Two Decades of Talks with Artists in New York*, ed. Judith Olch Richards (New York: Independent Curators International, 2004) 75; 76. © Louise Bourgeois Trust.

Iwona Blazwick
On Francesca Woodman//2012

In her short career, American photographer Francesca Woodman created hundreds of photographs staged within the physical confines of her East Village loft. The rooms, cupboards, doorways and mirrors of her studio became an existential world where the camera is a stalking presence, catching glimpses of the artist in a series of fleeting self-portraits. She crouches naked in a glass display case or peers up from beneath a filthy windowsill, like a ghost or mannequin. Woodman becomes both part of the environment of the studio and confined by it. Leaning a door off its hinges between a wall and the floor she choreographs the shadows to create an abstract geometry. In contrast with the rectilinear forms of the studio's architecture, she juxtaposes the softly rounded beauty and vulnerability of her naked limbs and torso. Peering around corners, pressing herself against a wall or hiding beneath a surface, Woodman dissolves into space in an act which is at once a liberation of form and a dissolution of self. Margaret Sundell has commented:

> Rather than a *memento mori*, the indexical imprint of the subject could be viewed as a narcissistic projection perhaps even more fundamental than the expressionistic brushstroke of an abstract painter ... Woodman's contiguity relates the individuation of the body to the seamlessness of its environment, the internal world of subjectivity to an external field that absorbs its uniqueness, so that at a certain point, it becomes impossible definitively to separate self from other ... While there may be a fleeting identification with oneself as an image, the underlying structure of internalized mediation renders this moment highly unstable ...[1]

Woodman's studio is at once a hermetic chamber and a stage set. We are given glimpses of the dramas that unfold there, by virtue of the camera's self release mechanism. [...]

1   Margaret Sundell, 'Vanishing Points: The Photography of Francesca Woodman', in *Inside the Visible: An Elliptical Traverse of 20th-Century Art, in, of and from the Feminine*, ed. Catherine de Zegher (Kortrijk : Kanaal Art Foundation/Cambridge, Massachusetts: The MIT Press, 1996).

Iwona Blazwick, extract from 'An A to Z of the Studio', in *Sanctuary*, ed. Hossein Amirsadeghi and Mariam Eisler (London: Thames & Hudson, 2012).

Jack Goldstein
Helene Winer: Artists Space and Metro Pictures//2001–3

In 1974, after Helene quit her job at Pomona, we went together to New York; after a few years she became the Director of Artists Space. Since graduating in 1972, I had been going back and forth between LA and New York; that continued for another couple of years. Artists Space was a non-profit place where many of us exhibited before we went to commercial galleries. I did my first performances in New York there, as well as showed my films. Irving Sandler was on the board, and Helene used to argue with him; he was an art historian who was extremely conservative in what he considered good art. Even so, it became the most important conduit for the work of young artists until the new commercial galleries opened up. Metro Pictures opened in 1980, and that was the big cut-off point.

Douglas Crimp and Craig Owens would come over to the place where Helene and I lived. They were into post-formalists like Agnes Martin, Robert Ryman and Richard Serra, but slowly they came around to what the CalArts crowd was doing. They formed their careers around our work. It was first defined by Crimp in 'Pictures', which was a show at Artists Space, and an influential article that announced a new sensibility. At first Doug would hardly even speak to me. On different occasions, I showed him a number of my films, but it took a long time before he understood what I was talking about. He slowly accepted the fact that you could borrow and recontextualize images from anywhere, not only popular culture but from political ideologies and history books and fashion magazines.

'Appropriation' became the catch phrase; some did it well, while pretty soon most started copying and repeating themselves. Baudrillard became an art guru for five minutes with his idea of simulation, where what is pictured becomes more important that what you are supposedly representing – it takes on a life of its own apart from any apparent signifier. We learned that we weren't representing anything, or at least nothing stable and fixed. It was just like the television screen.

We were playing with the signs and images of the commercial world, which had formed all of us as we grew up watching television. We were the first generation of 'raised on TV' artists, so the art changed from being something weighty and formal and self-important to art that was more playful and decorative, fast, ironic, even cartoon-like.

Around 1976 I found and lived at the Pacific Building on Santa Monica and Fifth. It was $60 a month; I put an old mattress into the office and slept on it. I went to Santa Monica to shoot films and work while Helene kept the fort in New York. I could make my films and get my props cheaper in LA than in New York.

For example, the barking dog I filmed was found in a special place. He was a trained dog, a TV dog, a star; so was the bird. I hired them. The guy who had the bird and the dog trained all the rats for the movie *Ben*. He used peanut butter to get them to move. The bird going around and around the bone china was done with an animator in LA.

Regina Cornwell, who is a film critic, said that I had to meet a filmmaker named Morgan Fisher. I met Morgan at Pratt, where he was giving a lecture, and he subsequently interviewed me for the Los Angeles Institute of Contemporary Art's *LAICA Journal* where my work was on the cover. When I first met him, I thought he was so pedantic; when you get to know Morgan, he is the nicest guy, but if you don't he is real snooty. I gave Morgan a lot of room just because I thought he was so smart; as an artist, I was always careful to know when to back off. Egos get in the way of being an artist. But it's your superego that is important, not your ego. The superego represents your ideal, and that is what whipped me, that is what destroyed me. I never measured up to what I wanted to be.

During the twenty years I spent in New York, I lived in funky warehouses and sweatshops in all the boroughs. I could never afford to live in Manhattan like my peer group. My first studio was under the Brooklyn Bridge, on the top floor of a building next to the 'Watchtower'. At night it was empty, since all of the sweatshops were closed, so I had my dog Jack run in front of me in case someone was hiding to mug me. The studio was over the water, where the Mafia would drop off dead bodies. The only other artist working nearby was Vito Acconci; sometimes at night I heard the squeaky wheels of his suitcase and I knew he was coming home from a trip.

In the seventies, I spent five or six years living and working there. Troy Brauntuch always ribbed me about living in such strange, out-of-the-way places. He had not hit on hard times yet; they were to come for him, but I was not about to gloat over them. 'You see, it can happen to you as well!'

In 1979 I started painting; by that time I had already made the films and the records. Metro Pictures opened up and I knew I had to make two-dimensional work. Helene would have shown a film here and there, but I knew it would have received very little play. I didn't want to be known primarily as a filmmaker. Collectors don't care about films and wouldn't want to come over to my studio. That's why that work got lost, and that's why it's coming back now. Another reason I started painting was because of David Salle. David and I both were teaching at the University of Hartford; one day when we pulled into the parking lot and he said he was going to stop teaching and devote all of his time to making art, I knew I had to do the same thing.

I stayed on at Hartford for another year and a half because after I quit, the Dean called me back and told me that the students were in an uproar. The students said that if I were gone, they would not be returning. Ed Stein was Dean at the time and begged me to stay; I didn't want him to beg, so I said, 'Okay I'll come back.' The school had to wait a couple of years until the students who were upset graduated, and new students came in who didn't know what they were missing; then the fuss would die down. That is exactly what happened.

The early paintings I made in the 1980s were in black and white because that is how I found them in the history books. Another consideration was that no one since Franz Kline had made large black-and-white paintings. My biggest problem was how to get a flat black background. I went to all of the museums in New York to study the paintings of Ellsworth Kelly, Barnett Newman, Brice Marden and others. When I got up close to their surfaces, they had surface incident. They were not flat at all since they were painted with a paintbrush, while, coming out of California car culture, I was using a spray gun. I always said presentation is everything. That irritated lots of people, but for me content and presentation are inseparable.

I remember calling up Chuck Close, Gary Stephan, even David Salle; no one knew how to create a surface without incident. I finally figured out that when the painting is finished, you need to put down a matte medium. It's a white varnish but sprays on clear. It took me so long to figure that out. I worked from early in the morning until midnight to learn tricks like that. To make the lines in the tracer paintings from World War II, I again turned to car culture and the way pinstripes are made. I used a gravity-fed bottle with a wheel at the bottom; the wheels come in different sizes to determine the width of the line. For the burning city series, I discovered that I could spray paint through cotton to depict smoke.

I directed all of my work; my performances, my sculptures, my records, my films, the choreographed pieces, the burial pieces. When it came to my paintings, I was the one who had to figure out how to make them. I didn't call someone and say, 'Make me a painting and I'll I see you at four o'clock'. I had to figure out all of the methods of making the paintings, not to mention what was going to be painted.

On the other hand, it is also true that I tried to disappear by hiring actors and by hiring others to manufacture my paintings. The movies and performances and paintings became symbolic of my disappearance, just as in my final show at CalArts I was buried. All anyone saw was the blinking light, which was symbolic of my heartbeat.

In the early 1980s, when I went out to CalArts for a lecture, Ashley Bickerton came up to me after the talk; he said he was graduating in a few months and wanted to work for me or Robert Longo. A couple of months later, he knocked on my studio door; he said he had a lot of experience with airbrush and could speed things up for me. The process of making the paintings did speed up, and

I could even turn part of it over to him. He argued continuously with me about using tape and paper templates for the Neo Geo work. He said the work would have a graphic look. I'd reply, 'So what? What's wrong with a graphic look? That's what I want!'

When I received my $25,000 NEA grant, I bought him a car to get to work on time and even found him a loft not far from me. Ashley told me that he used to paint for Pat Steir. I said, 'What?' I couldn't believe it because she is a semi-Expressionist painter. How could you paint for her? She has such a personal style. Pat would tell Ashley that she wanted some lines that 'looked like this' waving in the air. So Ashley would try to paint some lines. She'd say, 'No, I want lines like this' – waving some more in the air – 'lines like this, not lines like this; lines like this'. Ashley would laugh hysterically and I would be rolling on the floor as he related the story with appropriate gestures.

After some time we had too much ego conflict. Besides, Doris and Charles Saatchi started to buy his work; he went to Sonnabend, after a while making more money than I was. From then on I hired people who were not artists, mostly Puerto Ricans, who would work hard and needed the work. They also went with me or went for me to get drugs. They didn't argue with me and they didn't need to know anything; I could teach them airbrush. I could tell by how they touched things, how their nails looked, how clean they were, how they turned the pages of a book and spoke, whether they would be helpful. At the high point in my studios, I had six or seven assistants taping for me; it was like knitting. It took two people a complete day to get all of the tape off one painting. It was like opening a Christmas present: I didn't know what it was going to look like. My colourist mixed the colours in jars; we started taping from the edges. By the time we got to the centre of the painting, it was completely taped. It was like working blind. The results were stunning to me. But I only looked for about a minute and then had them wrapped; I didn't want to become too attached to them. The paintings did not look like anyone else's; as a consequence, no one knew what to think of the work.

Jack Goldstein, extract from 'Helene Winer: Artists Space and Metro Pictures' (transcripts from conversations 2001–3), in *Jack Goldstein and the CalArts Mafia*, ed. Richard Hertz (Ojai, California: Minneola Press, 2003) 89–95.

Ann Temkin
Martin Kippenberger: *Jacqueline: The Paintings Pablo Couldn't Paint Anymore* (1996)//2009

[...] Probably after finishing the *Medusa* paintings in summer 1996, Martin Kippenberger concentrated on what would become ten paintings collectively titled *Jacqueline: The Paintings Pablo Couldn't Paint Anymore*. The departure point for the series was the work of American photographer David Douglas Duncan, who devoted much of his career to documenting Picasso's home and work environment. He published his photographs in the book *The Silent Studio* in 1976, three years after Picasso's death at ninety-one.[1] Duncan, who had been photographing Picasso since 1956, made the book as a memorial to the artist's life at the last of his many residences, the château Notre-Dame-de-Vie in Mougins, France. The book's only texts are Duncan's hagiographic introduction and captions to his black-and-white photographs, worshipful not only of the artist but of every object or spot that he touched. Duncan dedicated his book to Jacqueline Picasso, who had swiftly assumed the role of devastated survivor and secluded her grief-stricken self in Notre-Dame-de-Vie for two years.

In 1988, two years after Jacqueline's suicide, Duncan published a long sequel to *The Silent Studio* titled *Picasso and Jacqueline*.[2] The book enshrined the relationship between Picasso and Jacqueline Roque, whom the artist married in 1961 and with whom he had moved to Notre-Dame-de-Vie that same year. The two had met in 1955, and Jacqueline's visage fills Picasso's canvases of the last two decades of his life. It was she who served as model when Picasso extended his own reach back into art history at the end of his life, whether as the nude in his rendition of Édouard Manet's *Déjeuner sur l'herbe* (1862–65) or as one of the Algerian women in his many versions after the great painting by Eugène Delacroix. Though *Picasso and Jacqueline* includes a few photographs of a despondent Jacqueline taken after her husband's death, most are far more jolly images of the couple romping or relaxing together during the 1950s and 1960s and Picasso's paintings of her.

Kippenberger became interested in *The Silent Studio* during a stay at Michel Würthle's house on the island of Syros; in 1996 he obtained a copy of *Picasso and Jacqueline*. 1996 was already a year during which he was thinking about the kings of modern art in the south of France: in June he mounted 'L'Atelier Matisse sous-loué à Spiderman' in L'Atelier Soardi, a building in Nice that had been Matisse's studio during the early 1950s. The installation recreated a small garret room, its only accoutrements a sink and bare hanging light bulb, lined with paintings in a variety of styles alluding to the major 'isms' of modern art. A wire sculpture of

Spiderman crouched on the floor in the middle of the room, literally embodying the modernist myth of the superhero in the studio.

If Matisse, surely Picasso, too. Kippenberger's fascination with the quintessential modern genius was already evident in earlier paintings that portrayed the master, at once saluting and deheroicizing him. In a 1997 interview, Kippenberger claimed that in making the *Jacqueline* series he was completing Picasso's work, stepping into the shoes of the departed master.[3] The preposterous statement was made in perfect seriousness, and it is exactly this tension between the ridiculous and the earnest that characterizes the *Jacqueline* paintings. One perhaps could argue that the parodic component of Kippenberger's work is latent in Picasso's own paintings: they cannot be considered among his strongest works, for while they inevitably bespeak his painterly magic, they suggest a genius amusing rather than taxing himself.

Kippenberger's paintings look more effortful, but that effort is directed towards resolutely ugly ends. Like the *Medusa* paintings, they feature one figure set against a multicoloured patterned background, usually of stripes. In all of them, Jacqueline is extremely masculine in appearance, as Kippenberger harshly exaggerated her strong features and dark complexion. He drew her with a paintbrush in a naturalistic style, with a pronounced degree of modelling and nuance. Each of the paintings prominently features the initials 'J.P.' in the lower left or right, emphasizing the premise of Kippenberger's enterprise.

Each painting directly appropriates one of Duncan's photographs of Jacqueline, transforming it into something repellent rather than flattering. Those from her days with Picasso show her clowning – trying on an Indian headdress, for example – or looking the part of the regal goddess-muse. But Kippenberger withheld any whiff of seduction from his images – Jacqueline's dissociation from the background and the fractured rendering of her face and torso suggest the lifeless quality of a mannequin. Works based on photographs from her first years as a widow are decidedly grim. In one, Jacqueline looks almost like a bearded Old Testament prophet, bowing her head and covering her face with one hand, letting a loose robe wrap her compressed form and fall onto four-toed bare feet. Only the identical pose proves the painting's source to be a photograph of Jacqueline crouching in the garden, unhappy but still beautiful and stylish. In another she clutches her small dog and gazes listlessly into the distance. Two grey-green stripes are layered over her image, as if to draw a set of blinds between her and the world.

Kippenberger claimed that he was painting the 'things a painter can no longer paint'.[4] This was true on a literal level: Picasso, dead, could not paint them. And the game of pretend did not stop there, for of course Jacqueline was by then dead too, having taken her own life in 1986 in hope of eternal reunion with her husband. But Kippenberger's statement contained more meaning than perhaps even he realized. Today there is no way that a serious male artist can generate interesting work by painting a woman he loves scores of times, as Picasso had managed to do for seven decades. The end of the romance of modern art also dissolved the possibility of making romantic love the non-ironic subject of art. It simply is not a credible exercise – something of which Kippenberger was surely conscious as he painted in his Burgenland studio, kept constant company by the woman he had married only months earlier and who would herself be a widow in less than a year.

So Kippenberger was completing Picasso's work, but he was doing it badly, in works that do not flatter Jacqueline, Pablo, himself, or Elfie. What meaning can be found here? It is not something that can be neatly resolved and certainly does not replicate the transcendent exit of Matisse, with his sublimely and concisely triumphant paper cut-outs. Instead, Kippenberger set in motion a game of mirrors: rather than painting Jacqueline, was Kippenberger painting Picasso, himself, Elfie, or perhaps all three? Whereas in the *Medusa* paintings, there is a plethora of Kippenbergers – Géricault himself and every man on the raft, painted, drawn and printed – here it is not at all clear who or where he is. Even the insistent 'J.P.' inscriptions have the ambiguous potential to serve as a signature – is it Jacqueline who took over Picasso's job and decided to paint herself, or perhaps to portray Martin in drag?

As Edward Said wrote of late Ibsen, these works 'stir up more anxiety, tamper irrevocably with the possibility of closure, and leave the audience more perplexed and unsettled than before'.[5] In an inverse relation to the *Medusa* paintings but in concert with them, the *Jacqueline* series presents the collapse of the possibility of an artist or a model as a whole or single being. By extension, Kippenberger's late work challenges the view of art, or of life, as a unitary comprehensible enterprise.

1   [footnote 19 in source] David Douglas Duncan, *The Silent Studio* (New York: Norton, 1976) 22. Duncan's photographs of the empty studio stemmed from his appointment as the official documentary photographer of the château and its contents, prior to the vast job of sorting out the estate for which Picasso had left no inventory or will.

2   [20] David Douglas Duncan, *Picasso and Jacqueline* (New York: Norton, 1988).

3   [21] Martin Kippenberger, in *'Parachever Picasso/Completing Picasso'*, interview with Daniel Baumann, trans. Fiona Elliott, in *Martin Kippenberger* (London: Tate Publishing, 2006) 64.

4   [22] Ibid.

5   [23] Edward Said, *On Late Style* (New York: Vintage, 2006) 7.

Ann Temkin, extract from 'The "Late Work" of Martin Kippenberger', in *Martin Kippenberger: The Problem Perspective*, ed. Ann Goldstein (Los Angeles: The Museum of Contemporary Art/Cambridge, Massachusetts: The MIT Press, 2008) 277–83.

Sanford Kwinter
Saint Architect of Sodom: Vito Acconci//2001

Vito Acconci masturbates in public, grunting and calling out obscenities to us as he goes about it.[1] He locks himself blindfolded in basements, excoriates us for intruding, menaces us with implements of harm, but ensures that we come.[2] Other days he follows us in the street, anywhere we go, and God knows we can't shake him – not ever! – not, at least, until we arrive at a policed boundary that separates the private *us* from the public *him*.[3] Naturally it pisses us off to have to do this, but how else to rid ourselves of this barely civilized nuisance? Acconci, we tell ourselves, like some latter-day Diogenes, is crazy.[4] We've always said that. Everyone does.

So why is everything in Acconci always opening up and either beckoning or forcing us in? Why does he want everything right in his face – or even further still – *in his orifices*?[5] Why is it all hanging out?

What is the body but a pattern of open and closed patches, and patches that are simultaneously, or alternately, both? If so, this holds not only for the physical, biological body but for the social body and the body politic as well. How and when something is opened and closed determines everything about its life. Making a life – among other lives – is no more or less than a performance, a performance of opening and closing these patches, of performing or composing the patchwork of life. Every act of opening and closing is at once a social, political and sexual act. Each of these acts is a performance not only of opening and closing a patch of space but also of linking the different continuums of bodies (physical, social and political desire) together within the single and same ecstasy – or misery. What are our personal and collective lives but orchestrations of ecstasy and misery, patterns of desire modulated and kept dynamic by an unpredictable system of opening and closing, damming and release?

But damming something up by no means promotes only misery, and ecstasy need not be associated only with release. Ecstasy is derived not simply from the opening but also from the broader, more promiscuous *performing*: from the discovery that the relations of life are plastic and that the world is amenable to manipulation. All performance is the performance of freedom, the freedom to recompose the world-patchwork, to eroticize collective life by opening what's closed and closing what's open, while repudiating the myriad and silent political acts of non-consensual sodomy.

There is a privileged realm from which the concept of performance has been able to take on its broader ecumenical meaning – not sex, not politics, not society alone, but aesthetics. The Marquis de Sade played everything out from within confinement, likewise the great Jean Genet. Each found the incipient plasticity in the closed keep of his jail cell and performed egregious, ecstatic openings with language, imagined deputy selves, even faeces and blood. To this litany of materials Vito Acconci has contributed saliva,[6] sweat,[7] come, taped obscenity,[8] and, of course, humour, always humour. More than anyone else he gave a name and an identity to a practice that had not yet separated itself from the messy business of affirming the primordial drives in the face of their social and political annihilation. Before Acconci we could think of literary manifestations, of speech acts and their perturbing effects on the material world, only as the products of a 'voice', but after him we see the world as a system of performances that we do and undo and that are done and undone despite us. In Acconcian performance, art, desire and activism are one.

Acconci began his career with nothing at all, nothing but a place and his body and its drives and the specificity of those drives being *in that place*. The place was the city, the body was not his own, but rather was his body cast as the first-and-not-yet-formed-body, as an any-body-whatever, 'per'-forming – creating – itself in relation to the existing overtrained, oversubdued bodies of the modern world. When Acconci found himself in the streets of New York in 1969 and began to follow random citizens one by one until he could pursue them no further (because prevented by the consensual boundaries that define private space),[9] he was no different from the adult foundling Kaspar Hauser, who appeared mysteriously on the streets of a small German town one day in the nineteenth century, and to whom all culture, including language, was entirely foreign. Yet bit by bit, though never completely, Hauser became 'naturalized', and his story concerns not so much 'the enigma' – from where he came – but, on the contrary, how he became civilized, how he endured the mortifications and impositions of culture.[10] Likewise, Acconci's early work (from the years conventionally understood as the 'performance period' [1969–72], when he produced almost all the works alluded to above), enacts not only an ontogenesis (genesis of the human individual) but a cosmogenesis as well.[11] For world and self, Acconci has tirelessly shown us, are generated together. This means that the one can always be dismantled through the other as well.

Did re-performing the world in this way make Acconci crazy, or was the craziness presupposed in the first act of placing himself outside the world (as a not-yet-formed-body), ready to be fucked by it for our collective amusement and edification? Acconci does not perform just his own (self) formation but the formation of the world as well as its necessary correlate. In his initial, still parochial art-world view, the world was represented by the gallery, an appallingly clean, white anus definitively sealed off from any public sphere. No wonder

Acconci went deliriously 'dirty.'[12] Like many in those years, he felt compelled to move outside and away from the political and cultural infrastructure of the gallery, yet he remained oriented towards it. In the gallery he discovered the codes and diagrams of a more silent and insidious performance of power, an enforced system of enacted openings and closings. Acconci (alongside Robert Smithson and Daniel Buren) discovered *the wall* as the ambiguous foundation of culture, body and consciousness.[13] His cosmos thus came increasingly to embrace architecture as its final destination and limit case. Architecture is that in relation to which bodies are organized, made and unmade free. Acconci made architecture crazy in a way that no architect has ever been able to. One might say that he seeks to achieve for architecture what Sade and Genet did for literature – to transform the world-prisonhouse into the privileged place from which to conceive and to invent freedom.

The body in Acconci represents both the origin and the end of all things. Architecture, by contrast, represents the ecstasy of the body but also the body's pain. The body is also the architecture of the private self, however, simultaneously the domicile and the performance of the self. Did not Freud teach us this? A body is born, but the self is *that which emerges* as the drives organize on its once promiscuous and polymorphous and – yes, why not say it? – perverse surface. The self emerges like a vortex on an agitated sea increasingly punctuated by blockages, disaggregations, sectoring, and the cumulative peeking that is the inescapable residue of experience. The surface breaks up into organs, or more accurately, we should say that the body's organs become the convenient anchors and way stations of the colonizing self. The body's 'features' become 'organs' only once the self has settled into them, appropriated them into their own landscape of perspective and need. The born body is nothing but mouth: receptive, open, continuous and fluid.[14] World and self have not yet emerged.

Yet the threshold is near. Subsequent development concerns the necessary passage through the anus and no longer the mouth, or rather through that recessed place at the depths of the mouth whose very discovery represents the discovery of unfathomable depth itself and the internal darkness that accompanies it. The oral surface gives way to internal depth, a place not accessible to the light of the world. Self splits away from everything else, and everything else becomes world. As Gilles Deleuze and Félix Guattari once wrote: 'The first organ to suffer privatization, removal from the social field, was the anus. It was the anus that offered itself as a model for privatization'[15] The person or self is formed in the anal stage, Freud tells us, when both the products and functions of this body part must be removed from the social sphere. The dark, interior place is the realm of the private self and its formation, the foundation of private life. But the anal stage must be surpassed in order to arrive at the final or genital sphere. If the anal stage is the scaffold for the formation of the private person, the genital stage is that of the public one. To accede to genital existence, it has been long argued, is primarily to accede to the regime and the domain of the phallus/penis. (Female genitality, as the cliché goes, is an acceding to 'lack' and 'envy', which is a priori an acceding to the phallus.) The double character of genitality allows the penis to remain quasi-private and hidden from view, while the phallus is left free to circulate openly and publicly, to distribute relationships, hierarchies, structures, mores, customs, desires, and the relations among their agents. In a phrase, it literally engenders the social world.

A body's history, quite simply, defines what a body is. Our history is the history of both our personal and our collective bodies, the history of how and when and why and where we permitted this or that patch of our existence to be opened or closed. Our social world, like our personal one, is cleaved in one particular manner rather than another because it is designed to function in the service of calculated ends of which we generally know little. For Acconci the organization and cleaving of the world in *this* manner – a decadently rich private world, on one side, and an impoverished public one, on the other, with none but the most rigid and routinized connection between them – are both arbitrary and unacceptable. [...]

[E]very one of Acconci's performaces is sited in the interface between inside and outside. The development and elaboration of this 'boundary' through extension and transgression is exactly what Acconci is denoting by his frequently used phrase 'to thicken the plot'.[16] All of space and time are the results of scenarios or 'plots' that can be reconfigured through dramatic manipulation, by the insertion of individual performance-plots that initiate new relationships and new becomings: 'A private life makes a deposit into public space.'[17] The typical Acconci project consists of an attack on existing space that always begins with an espousal of that space followed by a reversal and an opening of the closed pathways through the private that lead to it. The craziness of Acconci lies in his capacity continually to 'out' himself before our eyes, shamelessly to flaunt the shameful. It is not so much a critique as a detonation of social space, a setting it *wild* with jokes, mischief, obscenity and dance. Acconci knows that social space is constituted by desire, but a desire that has been muffled, corrupted, made predictable by its relegation to the private sphere. [...]

1   *Seedbed*, performance at Sonnabend Gallery, New York, January 1972.

2   *Claim*, performance with video installation at *Avalanche* magazine office, 93 Grand Street, New York, 1971.

3   *Following Piece*, performance, New York City, 3–25 October 1969.

4   The ancient Greek philosopher Diogenes was known for his public nakedness and onanism, and was commonly said to be mad.

5   *Openings*, performance documented on Super-8 film, August 1970, and *Trademarks*, performance documented in photographs, September 1970.

6   *Waterways*, performance documented on video, 1971.

7   *Runoff*, performance documented in photographs, 1970.

8   *VD Lives/TV Must Die*, installation, The Kitchen, Center for Video and Music, New York, February 1978.

9   'Each day I pick out, at random, a person walking in the street. I follow a different person every day; I keep following until that person enters a private place (home, office, etc.) where I can't get in.' (artist's description of Following Piece.)

10   See Werner Herzog's film *Every Man for Himself and God against All/The Enigma of Kaspar Hauser* (1974), based on this true story.

11   In his seminal 1978 text 'Steps into Performance (and Out)', Acconci recapitulates the aesthetic universe in pure Cartesian fashion from the foundational and primordial 'I' and its capacity to act and enact both the intersubjective and the object-world (in *Performance by Artists*, ed. A.A. Bronson and Peggy Gale [Toronto: Art Metropole, 1979] 26–40).

12   Germano Celant, 'Dirty Acconci', *Artforum* (November 1980) 76–83.

13   Vito Acconci, 'Normal Art in Public Places', course at the San Francisco Art Institute, summer 1983.

14   In *Trademarks* (1970) a naked Acconci bit every part of his body that his mouth could reach to leave deep bite marks that could later be ink-printed. This work performed not only a delirious and ecstatic act of autophagy (mouth incorporates and includes everything) but also generalized and extended the primordial oral opening across the entire surface of his body. This was a kind of architectural regression meant to restore every patch that had been closed to its original oral and open state.

15   Gilles Deleuze and Félix Guattari, *Anti-Oedipus: Capitalism and Schizophrenia* (1972) trans. Robert Hurley, Mark Seem and Helen R. Lane (New York: Viking Press, 1977) 143.

16   [20] See Vito Acconci, 'Some Grounds for Art as a Political Model', in *Art of Conscience: The Last Decade* (Dayton, Ohio: Fine Arts Gallery, Wright State University, 1980) 6.

17   [21] Vito Acconci, 'Steps into Performance', op. cit., 36.

Sanford Kwinter, extracts from 'Saint Architect of Sodom', in *Acconci Studio: Acts of Architecture*, ed. Dean Sobel and Margaret Andera (Milwaukie: Milwaukie Art Museum, 2001) 43-8.

Paul McCarthy
1968–76//2004

Spend the summer digging a continuous narrow trench. *Spring 1968*

Pile dirt on your desk. *Spring 1969*
In your backyard paint the dirt silver. *Spring 1969*
Place dirt in a box or bucket. Paint entire object silver. *Spring 1969*

Invite friends over. Cook them a pot of Vaseline petroleum jelly. *Spring 1971*
Pour equal amounts of water and oil into a bottle, then stir. *Spring 1971*
Buy a minimum of ten new packaged dress shirts. Display the shirts on the floor.
Place them side by side. *Fall 1971*

Use your head as a paint brush. *Fall 1972*
Use your penis as a paint brush. *Fall 1972*

Paint all windows, doors and mirrors in your house black. *Fall 1975*

Consider public masturbation as a true alternative. *Spring 1976*

Paul McCarthy, '1968–76', from *Do It*, ed. Hans Ulrich Obrist (Frankfurt am Main: Revolver, in association with e-flux, 2004).

Ulrike Groos
Paul McCarthy: *Painter* (1996)//2003

In this video, dressed in nothing but a short smock and socks, the artist appears as a painter-clown wearing a wig of curly blond hair, bulbous nose and flap-like ears. Clasping an oversize paintbrush between his giant rubber fingers, he bedaubs – with extravagant gestures, much noise and haste – large-format canvases in various colours, or he clamps the paintbrush between his legs as a symbolic phallus. Paint, which he sometimes mixes with mayonnaise and ketchup, wells from enormous paint tubes on the floor or propped against the walls. Together with other utensils and materials, these paint tubes occasionally take on a life of their own as they dance and move about the room. The painter cuts the tubes open in order to fill them with other paints. Or he uses them, like brushes, to spread paint on canvases. Occasionally, he even crawls into one of them. He pours paint out onto a tabletop and spreads it with an oversized roller. In other scenes, he flings paint at canvases, damages or even perforates canvases by poking a paintbrush handle right through them.

The setting for these events is a wood-panelled room, with plants, a cupboard and mirror, which serves as his studio, plus an adjoining hall and bedroom. Because the painter seems to be imprisoned in this environment, his movements between the various rooms acquire special significance. The hall becomes an extension of the studio. Paint is stirred here in the enormous tubes, over and over again. The artist rolls around on the bedroom floor or climbs into bed, fully clothed. He pees into a big potted plant and indulges his libidinous inclinations. The whole scene increasingly assumes the aspect of a battlefield. For a brief period, his uninterrupted roaming abates: seated, he stabs a knife blade between the fingers of his right hand spread out on the table top, repeatedly hitting the oversize rubber digits. Finally, to the accompaniment of his own hysterical laughter, he hacks at his rubber index finger with a meat cleaver. Fake blood can be seen oozing between the shreds.

The artist is not only hectic. He conducts dialogues with himself, raising and lowering his voice, murmuring invocations and spells that repeatedly describe his own actions, as if he wished to motivate, convince and reassure himself, as he turns in circles: 'I'm a fucking painter … Try to understand your emotions.' He paints noisily in other ways as well. Snoring sounds alternate with a sing-song 'De Kooning'. By naming this painter, generally regarded as one of the chief proponents of Abstract Expressionism, he holds up an irreverent mirror to and satirizes the painterly extravagances of those who practice this style of painting.

Views of the artist's studio alternate with sequences in the office of the woman gallery owner who exhibits his work, as well as in a discussion involving a moderator, a collector couple and the artist. The couple, who hold hands lovingly throughout the discussion, discuss their own collection with naïve pride and enthuse about the artist's excreta, while he sits there in silence.

In the gallery owner's office, a hefty argument takes place between her and the artist. In formulaic repetitions of increasingly hysterical fury, the painter complains about lack of payment and that he is not being looked after properly ('I want you to pay the money. I want all the money, right now … I have shows in Europe with big catalogues'). However, the gallery owner treats him like a child and chides him condescendingly ('You are a spoilt child'). At this, the artist really does throw tantrums, spits, turns sulkily in circles, grunts and moans, crawls around on the floor and destroys supposed works of art in the office.

In the final sequence of the video, a collector appears at the gallery, sniffs around the painter's rear and shows visible satisfaction as he does so. The video ends with the artist giving his 'okay'.

The video sketches a stereotype of the artist genius as a backward, behaviourally-disturbed, infantile eccentric incapable of normal human interaction, who disregards norms and rules since his only means of expression is in the obsessive, impulsive pursuit of his art. However, even the gallery owner fails to take him seriously as a human being, to say nothing of the collectors, who take advantage of his 'wildness' to amuse themselves at his expense.

As in *Bossy Burger*, *Heidi* and *Pinocchio*, *Painter* is exhibited as a single-channel video and shown in conjunction with the theatrical set. However, *Painter* was partially destroyed in transportation to an exhibition because of poor packing. This led to insurance claims and investigation. The results were that letters back and forth between the owners and the venue and the photographs of the damaged piece in the transporting containers are now shown as an installation with the actual recovered, damaged and undamaged parts of the original set. The piece is now a metaphor or fiction between artist, art dealer and collectors, and an actual documentation of interactions within the art world.

Ulrike Groos, 'Painter', in *Paul McCarthy: Videos 1970–1997*, ed. Yilmaz Dziewior (Hamburg: Kunstverein in Hamburg/Cologne: Verlag der Buchhandlung Walther König, 2003) 145–6.

Carsten Höller
The New Perplexity: In Conversation with Hans Ulrich Obrist//1999

Hans Ulrich Obrist You were talking about doubt.

Carsten Höller I was talking about what I call my *Laboratorium of Doubt*. I am not at all desperate but completely perplexed, and I'm thinking about how one could translate this perplexity into a proper form without transposing it into imagery. I am quite grateful for this perplexity. I used to suppress it for a long time because it is associated with uneasiness, which is a totally wrong approach – one should rather try to disengage one from the other and come to appreciate perplexity for what it is. Doubt and its semantic cousin, perplexity, which are both equally important to me, are unsightly states of mind we'd rather keep under lock and key, because we associate them with uneasiness, with a failure of values. But wouldn't it be more accurate to claim the opposite, that certainty in the sense of brazen, untenable affirmation is much more pathetic? It is simply its association with notions of wellbeing that gives affirmation its current status. What needs to be done is to sever the connection between affirmation and wellbeing. [...]

Obrist I'm still wondering how you can manage to find a form, or forms, for doubt and at the same time escape any formalization of the idea. It is a paradox.

Höller I present perplexity as a question so that it won't become formalized as a project: perplexity thus engenders further perplexity. I'd like to give expression to perplexity but it doesn't need to lead to anything. The idea is to put it on public view but first to confront the public in a state of perplexity so that the form may be found in the course of the exhibition ['Laboratorium' 1999–2001], even if that means sitting on a bench and being perplexed. When you give a demonstration you're not really perplexed, since you've already found a form to overcome perplexity. So that creates a certain dilemma.

Obrist Your *Laboratorium of Doubt* is mobile, you move it from city to city.

Höller This is something I've always wanted to do. You know these cars with loudspeakers on the roofs – I'll drive through the city to give expression to my perplexity. It's something that's always been at the back of my mind.

Obrist The laboratory is your white Mercedes which is inscribed '*Laboratoire de Doute*', '*Labor des Zweifels*', and so on, in several languages. But you will not put it in a museum as a readymade but use it every day?

Höller Yes, I'll be driving around in it and eventually drive it to the biennial in Istanbul, where I'll present my diary of doubt. The diary will be entitled *Days of Doubt*. It deals with doubt about my own enterprises and everything surrounding them. Every day I will select a photograph and write a text about doubt. The whole bundle will then be translated into Turkish and published in a small book that will be distributed for free in Istanbul. [...]

Carsten Höller and Hans Ulrich Obrist, extract from 'The New Perplexity', interview in Hans Ulrich Obrist and Barbara Vanderlinden, eds, *Laboratorium* (Antwerp: Roomade/Cologne: DuMont, 2001).

Gabriel Orozco
In Conversation with Wesley Miller//2008

Gabriel Orozco [...] I think one of the important things from my upbringing is that I act with a sense of group work or collective work.

There's one side of me that believes, of course, in an individual approach to things. You have to be very individual in your take on reality and your own experience. You have to be very aware of your own self. But then, when you want to communicate, you need to build up a social engagement and your own community. I think that is something that lies between my Marxist and my Montessori-educated background. It's not just about individual success. It's about the building of situations, experience and exchange.

One of the things I've realized by working with other artists is that some of them were not used to doing this. They were not used to working in teams or used to polemical discussions about some issues. They are afraid sometimes – people are afraid to speak out on politics. And many artists may want to be very political in their work, but I can see sometimes that they make the same mistakes of the 1960s and 1970s by being too straightforward or using one-liners. Well ... I believe they are mistakes, though I definitely make my own mistakes too. [...]

To say 'dialectics', now, it's like 'what's that?' But I do believe in dialectical relationships in nature and in social exchanges. I even think the way I build up my systems of work is often about trying to minimize its capitalistic side, in the sense that I don't own the means of production. I don't have a factory. Now ... I have a *little* one. (*laughs*) But that is another thing we can get into. But I really try not to own the means of production, not to be so exploitative with the people around me, and not to be too into the production line and into reproducing the worst of capitalism.

But of course, on the other hand, it's very hard to believe in the real practice of socialism in relation to art. To be a socialist artist ... if that even exists, how can it be? I'm dealing with all of this. It is for another occasion. We can talk about it if you have any questions.

Wesley Miller This 'little factory' you just mentioned, what's going on there?

Orozco Well, for the Citroën car sculpture, *La D.S.* (1993), I worked with Philippe Picoli, who has been my dear friend and assistant for the special and difficult projects because he knows about everything. And I have my limitations. So when I need help for something I don't know how to do, I call him.

At some point, when I started to do these paintings four or five years ago, I asked him to help me. And he says, 'Uh ... painter? *Ça va.*' Because he's French, and because he was more of a builder and a mechanic. But he said 'Okay', so then he became a French painter. (*laughs*) He starts to look happy. He was normally this serious French guy, and now he's happily chain-smoking.

He's my perfect match. It's this type of relationship where, when you eat, you don't talk. You're working all day and when you're eating, you eat – you don't talk. Once when my wife Maria came to see us we were eating and I *tried* to make conversation. (*laughs*) But when we finished eating, we went right back to work. So he is more than an assistant, he's a friend. And this series of paintings was a long-term project, and we're still doing this project.

He happens to live in a wonderful house by Le Corbusier in Paris, buit in 1924, that used to be the studio of Lipchitz. So suddenly I go from not having a studio to having a Le Corbusier studio in Paris. But it's his house. It's not really my studio; he lives there. So I go to visit my friend and see how he's doing with my work. (*laughs*) So that's very strange – it's a communist factory in this Le Corbusier house.

Gabriel Orozco and Wesley Miller, extract from 'Gabriel Orozco: Samurai Tree', *Art21 Blog* (6 November 2008).

Jori Finkel
In the Studio: Wolfgang Tillmans//2006

It's hard to spend any time in Wolfgang Tillmans' London studio without, if only for a moment, seeing the entire place as a dance club. Look up at the skylight and you will notice the remnants of a party – a mirrored disco ball and a string of Christmas lights hanging from a crossbeam. There's also a pair of turntables in the corner, a reminder that Tillmans made the London tabloids a couple of years ago by spinning at trendy club nights such as *Cock* and *Nerd*.

'I do clear out the studio for a party once in a while, maybe once a year. And you can see my studio in some of the "hangover" pictures', says Tillmans, 37, looking not at all hungover and very clean-shaven. His studio, located in a large warehouse space in London's East End, has all the professional equipment befitting a celebrated photographer – darkrooms, computer stations, a dozen work tables and stacks of supersized prints unrolled on the floor and taped to the walls. Here he likes to play CDs when he works, and talks about the connections between music and his photography, his fashionable life and successful career, openly and without apology. [...]

'I'm the total opposite of a diarist of life', he says, 'My job is to think about the world visually, and I do it best through the camera.' When asked outright whether he even considers himself a photographer, he says he thinks of himself as a 'cultural being' above all else. 'In school I painted, drew, made clothes, made music – all the things an overly expressive and observant teenager would do', he says, 'Photography was the last thing I came to. It is not a necessary medium for me, but it is a great gift.' [...]

Tillmans' first solo show, at the Daniel Buchholz gallery, Cologne, in 1993, was filled with intimate, humble and provocative images. Critics at the time assumed the shots were unscripted glimpses of men and women testing traditional gender roles, but the artist says he often cajoled or guided his subjects and used flash guns for lighting. 'I constructed this world from the start, as much as someone like Jeff Wall', he explains, 'The difference is that I made my staged scenes look as real as possible. Photography never has the same social power when it seems staged.'

Today that show is remembered for its unconventional exhibition format as much as for its content. It was the first time Tillmans hung magazine spreads featuring his pictures along with unframed photographs of varying sizes in salon-style groupings, using adhesive tape and steel pins to hold the works to the wall (the use of binder clips would come later). The goal was to create a nonhierarchical and non-linear visual rhythm. 'Photography very happily sits in a book', says Tillmans, who has designed 19 of his 21 books. 'I'm doing things in galleries that I can't do in books or magazines.' [...]

'There is not a hard line between my portraiture and my abstraction', he says, 'There's an assumption that abstraction is more experimental. But all of my work allows for the mistakes, allows for chance to come into play in a skilled and controlled environment. I have always been interested in the accident, the contingent, the fleeting.'

This sort of mindful channelling of chance extends to Tillmans' work installing his own photographs. He doesn't finalize a display until he arrives at the museum or gallery and can face the actual walls. But that doesn't stop him from trying out (he calls it 'rehearsing') a major installation well in advance. This winter [2005–6], for example, he kept 1:10 scale foamboard models of the Museum of Contemporary Art and the Hammer Museum, Los Angeles, in one corner of his studio, so he could experiment with different arrangements of images.

Visit the studio another time, says his London gallerist Maureen Paley, and you are just as likely to find Tillmans designing a new book, with a maze of page proofs laid out on the floor. Discussing his steady stream of publications and exhibitions, Paley compares his studio with Warhol's Factory. [...]

Jori Finkel, extracts from 'In the Studio: Wolfgang Tillmans', *Art+Auction* (May 2006) 53–4.

Sarah Thornton
The Studio Visit: Takashi Murakami//2008

[...] After a few hours at the Saitama painting studio, two PR women, my interpreter, and I piled into a seven-seater Toyota chauffeured by one of the non-painting assistants, a cool dude in a fedora and vintage fifties glasses, to go to the site of Takashi Murakami's original studio, which he set up with three assistants in 1995. Initially called the Hiropon Factory, in homage to Warhol's Factory and his manufacturing model of art production, it was renamed Kaikai Kiki in 2002, when Murakami reconceptualized his entire operation along the lines of a marketing and communications company. While the Sega Corporation has Sonic the Hedgehog and Nintendo has Super Mario, Kaikai Kiki was named after the mascots that appear on its letterhead and cultural goods. Kaikai is an anodyne white bunny, while Kiki is a wild three-eyed pink mouse with fangs. Both characters have four ears each, a 'human' pair and an 'animal' pair, suggesting that the company is all ears.

Our fifteen-minute journey, which passed modest but respectable homes with bushes pruned like bonsais, ended on a gravel driveway surrounded by a handful of dismal prefabricated buildings, self-seeded trees and weeds. In addition to providing two workspaces, the location plays host to Murakami's archive, two greenhouses containing his cactus collection, and a grand platform of pink lotuses in waist-high ceramic planters. The lotuses were so out of keeping with their humble environment that they looked as if they'd just landed there.

In the first airless building, three studio assistants listened to a Japanese pop-rock radio station, JWAVE, as they prepared to paint a smaller-than-life-sized fibreglass sculpture entitled the *Second Mission Project Ko* (often called *SMPKo2*), a three-part work in which Miss Ko, a manga fantasy of a girl with big eyes and breasts, a tiny pointed nose and a flat, aerodynamic belly, metamorphoses into a flying jet. The work is in an edition of three with two artist's proofs (called APs). The first three editions had already been sold; this first AP needed to be finished in time for the MoCA show. Miss Ko's head, hair, torso, legs and labia were laid out separately on what looked like two operating tables. At one table, two women were cutting tape into precise shapes to cover her for spray-painting. In another part of the small room, a man was testing different shades of white for a Bride of Frankenstein-style lightning streak in her hair. Against her Barbie-pink skin, he examined swatches of creamy white, grey-white, blinding fluorescent white, and a fourth white that lay in between. He chose the two he thought worked best and said. 'Murakami-san makes the final decision.' […]

After a noodle lunch, we headed to Murakami's slick headquarters in a three-storey office block in Motoazabu. It was at least an hour's drive, past more rice paddies and light industrial facilities, over a major river and along an elevated highway engulfed in soundproof fencing to the plush neighbourhood, not far from the designer stores of Roppongi Hills. Once there, we ascended to the studio in an elevator. When the doors drew apart, we faced a stainless steel and glass door for which a fingerprint scan and a four-digit PIN were required. Once we were across the threshold, the swath of bare white walls and well-sanded wood floors initially evoked a gallery back room, but on closer inspection it was clearly a high-security digital design lab. The second floor housed two boardrooms and two open-plan office areas. The third floor was architecturally much like the second, except that's where the real creative work was being done. […]

Murakami roamed the third floor barefoot, evidently happier than he'd been that morning, swiftly answering questions from his staff. His workstation, a sixteen-foot-long table, was situated in the centre of a large room, surrounded by his team of four designers and five animators, all of whom sat with their backs to him, their gazes purposefully directed at their white-rimmed twenty-inch screens. At the hub of his table was a Mac laptop around which were scattered stacks of blank CDs, art magazines and auction catalogues, empty take-out coffee cups, and a box of mini-Kit-Kats. On a counter at the end of the room, a triptych of face clocks told the time in Tokyo, New York and LA Above them were three full-sized colour print-outs of the flower triptych I'd seen in progress at the painting studio.

Had Murakami been sitting in his swivel chair, Chiho Aoshima would have been sitting within reach of his right hand. Although her location would suggest that she was working on one of Murakami's projects, Aoshima was actually putting the final touches on a picture for an upcoming show of her own work in Paris. Aoshima used to run Murakami's design department, but the thirty-three-year-old artist quit to devote herself full-time to her own art. Unlike Warhol's Factory where, in the words of the art historian Caroline A. Jones, women were 'expected to work hard for no pay, suffer beautifully, and tell all', six of the seven artists whose independent careers are promoted by Kaikai Kiki are female.

At the appointed time, Murakami settled into his swivel chair in a half-lotus position, one leg up, the other dangling, ready for a conversation. He offered me green tea and apologized for his English, admitting that even in Japanese, he had 'no power to communicate in words. That is why I twist to the painting.' Nevertheless, he believes in the influence of media coverage and acknowledges that the studio visit is an important art world ritual for promoting art. Murakami told me that he was working on thirty or forty different projects that day. 'My weak point – I cannot focus on just one thing. I have to set up many things. If just looking at one project, then immediately get the feeling it boring.' At the end of last year, Murakami was so exhausted that he spent ten days in a hospital. 'That was very stressful. I bring my computer. Many assistants come to my room. Finally doctor said too much crowd, waste of money, you must go home.'

'What kind of a boss are you?', I asked.

'I am a very bad president', Murakami responded without hesitation. 'I have low technique for driving the company. I don't really want to work in a company, but I have big desire for making many pieces. Operating the people and working on art are completely different. Every morning, I upset people', admitted the unrelenting aesthetic micro-manager. [...]

Sarah Thornton, extracts from 'The Studio Visit', *Seven Days in the Art World* (New York: W.W. Norton & Company, 2008) 191–3; 194–7.

Linda Yablonsky
The Studio System//2007

That myth of a creative genius toiling in solitude is just that. Assistants – whether a few apprentices or a cast of dozens – have long been a mainstay of artistic life, lending support, learning their craft and sometimes even making works for the boss.

Jeff Koons has 87 of them labouring in shifts. Damien Hirst employs several teams, as needed. Jasper Johns has had the same one for 23 years, and Kiki Smith's accompanies her everywhere. Yet John Currin can hardly stand the idea. A studio assistant? 'I'm a terrible co-worker', he says. He prefers to go it alone.

Most artists today depend on at least one extra hand to keep their studios in order and help prime their creative pumps. That could mean anything from mixing paint and cleaning brushes to listening to the boss think out loud. It can also involve making the actual pieces while the artist supplies the vision – the identity for the brand, so to speak. Traditionally, a young wannabe's best entrée into the profession has been to assist an established mentor. Some parlay these jobs into big careers; others may remain in the shadows.

What is curious is how differently the market treats work done by assistants in different eras. Consider how quickly a putative Old Master painting priced in the millions is devalued should new evidence prove it to have been made by other hands. A 1995 exhibition at the Metropolitan Museum of Art, New York, 'Rembrandt/Not Rembrandt', explored this issue by juxtaposing pictures by the master himself with those of his disciples. His studio, it seems, was happy to employ imitators skilled enough to turn out 'Rembrandts' like a machine. Still, it was relatively easy to tell genius from its reflection.

Such distinctions are not always so clear – or so necessary – in the realm of contemporary art. Paintings by Andy Warhol and Jean-Michel Basquiat may require authentication before sale, but no doubts about genuineness haunt artworks by living artists such as Hirst, Koons or Takashi Murakami, whose prices can be astronomical. None of them makes his own paintings or even thinks he should, not when others can do the job better. [...]

It is fair to ask if the art market operates on a double standard that treats certain kinds of 'assisted' works as deceptions while accepting others as unique. For an answer, says Laura Paulson, senior director for contemporary art at Christie's New York, 'we have to go back to Duchamp's readymades and the idea of liberating the artist's hand'.

Duchampian notions of mechanical reproduction reached full flower in the

1960s, when artists like Warhol and Robert Rauschenberg began silkscreening with helpers. 'The idea of art changed to be less about individual brushstrokes and more about the image', Paulson says. 'Mechanical means expanded the artist's product. The studio assistant, who became almost an alter ego, enabled this process.'

'Look at Ronnie Cutrone and Warhol', she continues. 'Andy set up the still life. Ronnie made the photo and the screen. And this whole act has become amplified to an extraordinary level with artists like Koons and Hirst.'

Cutrone, who was Warhol's principal painting assistant from 1972 to 1982 and has retained ownership of the photographs he took for Warhol's paintings, describes their working relationship as almost co-dependent. 'I was born with a duplicate colour sense to Warhol's, Cutrone recalls. 'He would say, 'Ronnie, mix me a green.' And I would attempt to clarify: 'What green?' He would say, 'Up-front green.' And I would know what he meant. But I wasn't going to paint his paintings.' Warhol, he adds, painted for hours a day but also took time to experiment with new ideas – not all of which were his own.

Take the 'Shadows', the 1978 series of 102 abstract panels that Warhol called 'one painting with parts'. According to Cutrone, they were his idea. 'It was Andy's dream to make abstract art, and he could do it fairly well, but people didn't like it', Cutrone explains. 'I said, "Look, you're Andy Warhol. If you want to make abstract art, you have to make something that is but isn't: a shadow." I had this idea for a long time but I was never going to do it. So I mixed all the colours and stretched all the canvases and installed them in Heiner Friedrich's gallery in SoHo. I wasn't jealous. They didn't sell.' (Seventy-two of the canvases from Freidrich's collection are now on permanent display at Dia: Beacon, in upstate New York.)

How should we evaluate an assistant's role in the act of creation? Does it really matter if artists touch their own works, as long as these works are unique and are made in their presence? 'Regardless of the artist's distance from the process', Paulson says, 'there is a nuance that gives it his identity. If there were to be dot paintings generated by someone who used to work for Hirst, you would feel it, and it would not be seen as having any value in the market.'

By helping an established mentor, novices learn first-hand what being a working artist actually involves. The painter Carroll Dunham assisted Dorothea Rockburne off and on from 1970 through 1973 in New York. 'In a way, that was my art school', he says. 'It's important to be involved with the daily operation of a studio and how you organize it both physically and psychologically. But the best part was the incidental talking about art.'

Today many aspiring artists skip this journeyman step. They enter the market while still in school, as collectors buy work from thesis exhibitions and dealers cherry-pick talent for group shows. Not long after graduation, the most promising may be preparing solo debuts and hiring assistants of their own out of the same pool. [...]

Although many artists maintain large studios like those of Murakami and Koons – Matthew Barney and Julian Schnabel are two who combine art-making with film production – others prefer a more personal approach. [...]

Kiki Smith retains two assistants to help her in her studio and one to run her office. 'What I like is that when people show up at a certain time of day, it kicks you out of your own subjectivity and forces you to think in an orderly fashion instead of drifting', she says. 'For self-employed people, that's a big thing.'

What about the impact of such jobs on the assistants? They can reap unexpected benefits – but there are also drawbacks. Painter Carl Fudge, who spent nearly ten years in Smith's employ, says he started out 'grinding glass sperm' but soon found himself becoming part of her life: 'She used me as a barrier against people she didn't know. I sort of protected her.' He also helped install her shows all over the world. 'We went to amazing places and met the most interesting people', he recalls, referring to such travel, however, as 'a great experience rather than a career benefit'. His tenure, which ended in 1998, affected his own identity as an artist as well. 'Even a couple of weeks ago', he says, 'a museum called asking for Kiki.' [...]

Many artists bring on additional people just for specific projects. To prepare 'The Invisible Enemy Should Not Exist', his exhibition last winter at Lombard-Freid Projects, New York, Michael Rakowitz needed plenty of help from his team of six. The show consisted of about 60 small-scale reconstructions – made with Iraqi food wrappers and Arabic newspapers – of artefacts stolen from the National Museum in Baghdad after the 2003 American invasion. Rakowitz intends to remake all 7,000 of the looted pieces.

In this case, the assistants – students, mostly – may make long-term commitments. But how long is too long to stay? Bleckner rotates his helpers out every few years. 'After a certain point, you fear they may hold working for you against you if their career has not happened the way they thought it should', he explains. Dunham concurs: 'If you're ambitious, you have to get out.'

The sculptor Joel Shapiro, who generally works on a large scale, has long relied on assistants, including some who weren't sculptors themselves. Back in the early 1980s, for instance, painter Christopher Wool cut wood for him ('It was the best job I ever had', Wool says). These days Shapiro works closely with Ichiro Kato, a master woodworker, and Patrick Strzelec, an artist who is expert at casting. 'But while they're realizing your work, they sometimes have to suppress their instincts', he says. 'They have a role in the shaping of a piece – but they also have their own art to make. Those who are pivotal to your work stay with you, but it's not necessarily a happy position for that person.'

James A. Meyer's 22 years with Jasper Johns have brought him security. He's been careful, however, to maintain his own painting practice, even though it means he has to get up at 5 a.m. to work for a few hours before starting his day with Johns. 'That way you don't feel like you're not moving ahead', he says. Meyer also points to the dangers of being associated so long with so celebrated an artist. Five years ago, he started working in encaustic, Johns' signature material. 'So my work is perceived as reflective of Jasper's', he says. 'But it's figurative – very different.' […]

On the other hand, John Currin insists that 'it wouldn't help me to have an assistant. I'd end up micro-managing to a degree that there would be no point. That's like hiring someone else to drive a two-seater sports car. Why bother?' Still, he says, he has taken on an artist-bookkeeper who also straightens up.

'My studio looked like Francis Bacon's', he admits. 'Now it's a much more pleasant place to be.'

Linda Yablonsky, extracts from 'The Studio System', *Art + Auction* (November 2007) 192–3.

The Box (2001) turns Paul McCarthy's studio carefully on its side, presenting the viewer with an impossible spatial condition ... floor and ceiling as walls, horizontal window as vertical 'frame', entirely new spaces marked between now vertical table surfaces and walls, video monitors pointing downwards, shelves as floor and ceiling surfaces... the studio only momentarily unoccupied by the artist, his collection of found objects, furniture, half-completed projects, video-editing equipment rendering the picture with such verisimilitude as to force the sense of dissociation, of rupture between the normal and the pathological, back on the viewer

Anthony Vidler, 'Panoptic Drives/Mental Spaces: Notes on Paul McCarthy's "Dimensions of the Mind"', *Paul McCarthy*, The Museum of Contemporary Art, Los Angeles, 2001.

WORKING WITH THE SITUATION

Herbert Molderings
Marcel Duchamp's Studio as a Laboratory of Perception//2007

[...] In terms of their function, the Readymades in Duchamp's studios in New York resembled – to a far greater extent than they resembled traditional works of art – those instruments that in the more recent history of science have come to be known as 'epistemic objects'.[1] These are experimental scientific systems or devices which do not illustrate or symbolize existing knowledge but rather are objects which generate knowledge: they are the unknown, the unclear, the ambiguous. As parts of experiments, these objects provide unknown answers to questions that the scientist still cannot formulate clearly.[2] The kind of aesthetic experiments performed by Duchamp, on the other hand, differed from the aforementioned 'epistemic objects' in that they did not provide answers to questions but rather objectified the process of questioning itself. Thus the Readymades *Bicycle Wheel* and *Bottle Rack* were not three-dimensional visualizations of four-dimensional equations. In this regard, they differed fundamentally from the fascinating mathematical models that were so popular in higher mathematics classes[3] before the First World War and were in all probability known to Duchamp.[4] In a conversation with Arturo Schwarz, Duchamp accurately described the function of the Readymade, using the *Bicycle Wheel* as an example: 'The *Bicycle Wheel* [...] still had little to do with the idea of the Readymade. Rather, it had more to do with the idea of chance. In a way, it was simply letting things go by themselves and *having a sort of creative atmosphere in a studio, an apartment where you live. Probably, to help your ideas come out of your head* [author's italics] To see that wheel turning was very soothing, very comforting, a sort of opening of avenues on other things than material life of everyday.'[5] The Readymades were neither works of art nor scientific demonstration apparatus. They were aesthetic experimental objects, the purpose of which was to generate a creative atmosphere for a speculatively imaginative thought process, the outcome of which was always carefully recorded and preserved. They did not objectify any new, experimentally acquired knowledge but rather the opposite: non-knowledge or, to be more precise, the very fragility of the seemingly so safe epistemic foundations of a modern, scientifically organized way of life.[6]

Just as Duchamp's approach to art had changed, so, too, did the nature and purpose of his studio. What used to be a painter's studio was now a laboratory of experimental perception and theory, a place where thought experiments could be visualized empirically. The living and working areas of the studio were themselves now understood as a real 'image' in the sense of an artistically conceived and created perceptual space.

Evidently Duchamp's intentions behind the installation of his Readymades in his New York studios were bound up, in a playfully humorous way, with questions concerning gravity and the relativity of space. As it would be beyond the scope of this essay to embark upon a detailed explanation of Duchamp's complex theoretical speculations on dimensions and perception that preceded his installations with his Readymades, as later documented in the *Boîte-en-valise*, the following brief summary must suffice.[7]

Completely displaced from their normal positions, everyday objects populate a room, the coordinates of which are upside down. A coat rack 'hangs' on the floor instead of on the wall. A bentwood hat rack has detached itself from the wall and a snow shovel has lifted itself clear from the floor. They are quite literally hanging in mid-air. Even the urinal *Fountain* is performing a different function than in the illustration reproduced a hundredfold from *The Blind Man*, where it is shown on a pedestal.[8] In Duchamp's studio it is hovering in a doorway. Non-Euclidean geometry, much discussed among the Parisian avant-garde around 1910, had shaken not only the Euclidean dogma of the three axes of space but also the notion of an absolute space with fixed coordinates. The great mathematician Henri Poincaré, whose treatises *Science and Hypothesis* (1902), *The Value of Science* (1905) and *Science and Method* (1908) were the chief sources of Duchamp's knowledge of modern spatial geometry, had expounded the theory that it is impossible for an observer in a moving system to tell what is up or down, left or right. Duchamp integrated this theory into his reflections on perception in a four-dimensional space continuum. 'In the continuum, verticals and horizontals lose *their fundamental* meaning (*basic meaning*)', Duchamp noted, '(just as the flat being does not know whether the plane supporting him is horizontal or vertical)'.[9] Thus, in a visual experiment, Duchamp turned the room of his New York studio vertically through an angle of 90 degrees by 'hanging' the coat rack (*Trébuchet*) on the floor instead of on the wall. The Thonet bentwood hat rack, now detached from the wall, suspended from the ceiling and directionally opposed to the coat rack on the floor, reverses our sense of top and bottom, while the directional confusion is heightened by the urinal hovering in the doorway and the snow shovel hanging from the ceiling, and notwithstanding the fact that the latter is the only stable axis, a veritable plumb line, in this now totally disjointed room.

In his treatise *The Value of Science*, Poincaré maintains that geometry is not an empirical science. Thus experience cannot prove to us that space has three dimensions: 'It only proves to us that it is convenient to attribute three to it [...], so that it may have as many as representative spaces'.[10] If one were to class our series of muscular sensations for our senses of sight, touch and movement in four classes instead of three, Poincaré argues, our experience of space would be just as readily explainable with the aid of a four-dimensional model.[11] Poincaré illustrates this theory by describing a thought experiment that seems to have inspired Duchamp's visual experiment with a directionally confusing room:

> Suppose I am enclosed in a chamber between the six impassable boundaries formed by the four walls, the floor and the ceiling; it will be impossible for me to get out and to imagine my getting out. Pardon, can you not imagine that the door opens, or that two of these walls separate? But of course, you answer, one must suppose that these walls remain immovable. – Yes, but it is evident that I have the right to move; and then the walls that we suppose absolutely at rest will be in motion with regard to me. – Yes, but such a relative motion can not be arbitrary; when objects are at rest, their relative motion with regard to any axes is that of a rigid solid; now, the apparent motions that you imagine are not in conformity with the laws of motion of a rigid solid. – Yes, but it is experience which has taught us the laws of motion of a rigid solid; nothing would prevent our imagining them different. To sum up, for me to imagine that I get out of my prison, I have only to imagine that the walls seem to open, when I move.[12]

But whereas Poincaré's thought experiment exists only in the mmd, Duchamp's experiment is an empirically aesthetic one.[13] He transformed his apartment into a kind of experimental room in which the walls, the floor and the ceiling, whilst not being able to disappear, lost their position-defining coordinates by reason of the displaced objects. Thus, even for this exercise, Duchamp had been able to fall back on the inspiring theories of this famous mathematician.

Why do we in fact assign directions to space? Poincaré's answer was thus:

> Space is in reality amorphous and the things which are therein alone give it a form. [...] We should therefore not have been able to construct space if we had not had an instrument to measure it; well, this instrument to which we relate everything, which we use instinctively, it is our own body. It is in relation to our body that we place exterior objects, and the only spatial relations of these objects that we can represent are their relations to our body. It is our body which serves us, so to speak, as a system of axes of coordinates'.[14]

Duchamp's reflections in the *White Box* read like a marginal note on Poincaré's assertion: 'Gravity and centre of gravity make for horizontal and vertical in space. [...] Gravity is not controlled physically in us by one of the five ordinary senses. We always reduce a gravity experience to an auto-cognisance, real or imagined, registered inside us in the region of the stomach'.[15] Since according to Poincaré the three-dimensional geometrical representation of space stems in the final analysis from an association of ideas based on numerous corporeal experiences, such a representation can only be the result of a habit: 'If the education of our senses had been accomplished in a different environment, where we should have been subjected to different impressions, contrary habits would have arisen and our muscular sensations would have been associated according to other laws [to those of four-dimensional geometry, for example – author's note]'.[16]

It is as though Duchamp wanted to provoke this different education of the senses when confronting himself and his visitors with objects so alienatingly displaced as to simulate completely new spatial experiences and relationships. The axial displacements achieved with the aid of the Readymades were intended to jog the imagination, an imagination which, since 1913, was bound up primarily with the idea of something absent, of an invisible fourth dimension. According to Poincaré, this invisible fourth dimension defies representation, for all attempts at imagining a fourth dimension are 'carried back' to our limited, three-dimensional notion and sensation of space. The Readymades served Duchamp to generate a 'creative atmosphere' in his studio, an atmosphere in which space, indeed reality, could be thought of differently: undefined, movable, open. As they themselves wrote in their memoirs, the visitors to his studio at that time had no idea of the theoretical consequences of Duchamp's spatial experiments. They could only sense very vaguely that a new aesthetic was evolving from the 'chaos' and the 'useless objects' that greeted them. It is precisely this aesthetic – an aesthetic in which it is not the objects themselves that are the 'works of art' but rather the room, the ambiance and the experiment, i.e. the paradigmatic action – that was not to be rediscovered and further developed until the advent of the space-related installations and interventions in the 1960s.

1   [footnote 62 in source] Hans-Jörg Rheinberger, *Experimentalsysteme und epistemische Dinge* (Gottingen, 2001) 24 f.

2   [63] Ibid., 22.

3   [64] See Walther von Dyck, *Katalog mathematischer und mathematisch-physikalischer Modelle, Apparate und Instrumente* (Munich, 1892) (Reprint Hildesheim 1994). Martin Schilling, *Catalog mathematischer Modelle für den höheren mathematischen Unterricht*, 7th edition (Leipzig, 1911); Gerd Fischer et al., *Mathematisclie Modelle aus den Sammlungen von Universitaten und Museen* (Braunschweig, 1986); Jean Brette, 'La collection de modèles mathématiques de la bibliothèque de L'Institut Henri Poincaré', in *Gazette des mathematiques*, no. 85, Societé mathématique de France (July 2000) 5–8. On the reception of mathematical models in Surrealism see Gabriele Werner, *Mathematik im Surrealismus. Man Ray – Max Ernst – Dorothea Tanning* (Marburg, 2002) passim, and Isabelle Fortuné, 'Man Ray et les objets mathématiques', in *Études photographiques*, no. 6 (May 1999) 100–117.

4   [65] Duchamp took a course in librarianship at the École de Chartes in the Sorbonne in 1913. The 'Laboratoire de Géométrie supérieure' of the Faculty of Sciences of the Sorbonne had a 'salle des modèles' in which hundreds of such models were displayed in showcases.

5   [66] Quoted from Arturo Schwarz, *The Complete Works of Marcel Duchamp*, 2nd edition (New York, 1970) 442.

6   [67] On Duchamp's critical approach to rationalism and scientism from 1913 onwards, see Molderings, *Kunst als Experiment. Marcel Duchamps 3 Kunststopf-Normalmaße* (Munich/Berlin, 2006). The presence of non-rational knowledge in the culture of modern science is now awakening interest among philosophers to an ever increasing extent. See Wolfram Hogrebe, *Echo des Nichtwissens* (Berlin, 2005).

7   [68] For a more detailed explanation, see Molderings, 'Vom Tafelbild zur Objektkunst. Die Readymades von Marcel Duchamp', in Werner Busch and Peter Schmoock, eds, *Kunst. Die Geschichte ihrer Funktionen* (Weinheim/Berlin, 1987) 215–19; and Molderings, 'Ästhetik des Möglichen. Zur Erfindungsgeschichte der Readymades Marcel Duchamps', in G. Mattenklott, ed., *Ästhetische Erfahrung im Zeichen der Entgrenzung der Künste* (Hamburg, 2004).

8   [69] See William A. Camfield, *Marcel Duchamp's* Fountain (Houston, 1989) 12.

9   [70] Quoted from *The Writings of Marcel Duchamp*, ed. Michel Sanouillet and Elmer Peterson, reprinted edition (New York, 1989) 90.

10   [71] Henri Poincaré, 'The Value of Science' (1902), in Henri Poincaré, *The Foundation of Science*, trans. George Bruce Halsted (Lancaster, Pennsylvania: The Science Press, 1946) 272.

11   [72] Ibid., 99.

12   [73] Ibid., 100.

13   [74] Concerning the notion of the thought experiment in the sciences, see Roy Sorensen, *Thought Experiments* (New York, 1992); James Robert Brown, *The Laboratory of the Mind* (London, 1991); Wolfgang Kienzler, 'Was ist ein Gedankenexperiment', in Günter Abel, ed., *Kreativität*, XX, vol. I. Deutscher Kongress für Philosophie (Berlin, 2005) 447–55.

14   [75] Henri Poincaré, 'Science and Method' (1908), *The Foundations of Science*, op. cit., 417 f.

15   [76] *The Writings of Marcel Duchamp*, op. cit., 87.

16   [77] Henri Poincaré, 'Science and Hypothesis' (1902), *The Foundations of Science*, op. cit., 69.

Herbert Molderings, extract from 'It is Not the Objects That Count, but the Experiments: Marcel Duchamp's New York Studio as a Laboratory of Perception', in *Re-Object: Marcel Duchamp, Damien Hirst, Jeff Koons, Gerhard Merz*, ed. Eckhard Schneider (Bregenz: Kunsthaus Bregenz, 2007) 150–52.

Carolee Schneemann
Eye Body: 36 Transformative Actions (1963)//2002

In 1962 I began a loft environment built of large panels interlocked by rhythmic colour units, broken mirrors and glass, lights, moving umbrellas and motorized parts. I worked with my whole body – the scale of the panels incorporating my own physical scale. I then decided I wanted my actual body to be combined with the work as an integral material – a further dimension of the construction.

In December 1963 I was encouraged by my friend [the artist] Erró when I told him I wanted to do a series based on physical transformation of my body in my work – the constructions and wall environment. I considered that the ritual aspect of the process might put me in a trance-like state, which would heighten the submission of self into materials.

Covered in paint, grease, chalk, ropes, plastic, I established my body as visual territory. Not only am I an image-maker, but I explore the image values of flesh as material I choose to work with. The body may remain erotic, sexual, desired, desiring, and yet still be votive – marked and written over in a text of stroke and gesture discovered by my creative female will.

I wrote 'my creative female will' because for years my most audacious works were viewed as if someone else inhabiting me had created them. They were considered 'masculine', owing to their aggression and boldness, as if I were inhabited by a stray male principle. An interesting possibility, except that in the early sixties this notion was used to blot out, denigrate and deflect the coherence, necessity and personal integrity of what I made and how it was made.

Using my body as an extension of my painting-constructions challenged and threatened the psychic territorial power lines by which women, in 1963, were admitted to the Art Stud Club, so long as they behaved enough like the men, and did work clearly in the traditions and pathways hacked out by the men. (The only artist I know of making body art before this time was Yoko Ono.)

The nude was being used in early Happenings as an object (often an 'active' object). I was using the nude as myself – the artist – and as a primal, archaic force which could unify energies I discovered as visual information. I felt compelled to 'conceive' of my body in manifold aspects which had eluded the culture around me. Eight years later the implications of the body images I had explored would be clarified when studying sacred Earth Goddess artefacts from 4,000 years ago.

Carolee Schneemann, 'Eye Body: 36 Transformative Actions', in Carolee Schneemann, *Imaging Her Erotics: Essays, Interviews, Projects* (Cambridge, Massachusetts: The MIT Press, 2002) 55–7.

Amelia Jones
Yayoi Kusama's Self-Portrait Photographs//1997

There she is [in a self-portrait from 1962, one of a series of photographs set up in her studio] enacting herself as pin-up on one of her vertiginous landscapes of phallic knobs (woman-as-phallus meets phallus-as-sign-of-male-privilege): naked, heavily made-up in the style of the sixties, she sports high heels, long black hair, and polka dots covering her bare flesh. As Kris Kuramitsu has argued, this photograph 'is only one of many that highlight [Kusama's] naked, Asian female body. These photographs, and the persona that cultivated/was cultivated by them is what engenders the usual terse assessment [in art discourse] of Kusama as "problematic"'.[1]

Kusama plays on her 'doubled otherness'[2] vis-a-vis American culture: She is racially and sexually at odds with the normative conception of the artist as Euro-American (white) male. Rather than veil the 'fact' of her difference(s) (seemingly irrefutably confirmed by the visible evidence registered by her body), Kusama exacerbated it. (Intentionally? Would I have 'known' had I been there for her public 'performances' of self?) In a portrait of artists who participated in the 1965 'Nul' exhibition at the Stedelijk Museum, Amsterdam, Kusama sticks out like a sore thumb: there she stands, front and centre – amongst a predictably bourgeois group of white, almost all male Euro-Americans (dressed in suits) – her tiny body swathed in a glowing white silk kimono.[3]

Am I an object? Am I a subject? Kusama continues to perform these questions in the most disturbingly direct of ways, posing herself in 1993, dressed in polka-dotted fabric on a polka-dotted floor in front of a mirror reflecting a polka-dotted wall (her installation *Mirror Room* and *Self- Obliteration*). Now, her pose and garb remove her from us, camouflage shifting her into the realm of potential invisibility ('self-obliteration'). She still can't decide whether she wants to proclaim herself as celebrity or pin-up (object of our desires) or artist (master of intentionality). Either way, her 'performance' takes place as representation (*pace* Warhol, she's on to the role of documentation in securing the position of the artist as beloved object of the art world's desires); she comprehends the 'rhetoric of the pose' and its specific resonance for women and people of colour. The pictures of Kusama are deeply embedded in the discursive structure of ideas informing her work that is her 'author-function'.[4]

Rather than confirming the ontological coherence of the body-as-presence, body art depends on documentation, confirming – even exacerbating – the supplementarity of the body itself. Predictably, although many have relied on the photograph, in particular, as proof of the fact that a specific action took place or as a marketable object to be raised to the formalist height of an 'art' photograph, in fact such a dependence is founded on belief systems similar to those underlying the belief in the 'presence' of the body-in-performance. Kristine Stiles has brilliantly exposed the dangers of using the photograph of a performative event as 'proof' in her critique of Henry Sayre's book *The Object of Performance*. Sayre opens his first chapter with the now-mythical tale of Rudolf Schwarzkogler's suicidal self-mutilation of his penis in 1966, a story founded on the circulation of a number of 'documents' showing a male torso with bandaged penis (a razor blade lying nearby). Stiles, who has done primary research on the artist, points out that the photograph, in fact, is not even of Schwarzkogler but, rather, of another artist (Heinz Cibulka) who posed for Schwarzkogler's entirely fabricated ritual castration.[5]

Sayre's desire for this photograph to entail some previous 'real' event (in Barthesian terms, the *having been there* of a particular subject and a particular action)[6] leads him to ignore what Stiles describes as 'the contingency of the document not only to a former action but also to the construction of a wholly fictive space'.[7] It is this very contingency that Sayre's book attempts to address through his argument that the shift marked by performance and body art is that of the 'site of presence' from 'art's object to art's audience, from the textual or plastic to the experiential'.[8] Sayre's fixation on 'presence', even while he acknowledges its new destabilized siting in reception, informs his unquestioning belief in the photograph of performance as 'truth'.

Rosalind Krauss has recognized the philosophical reciprocity of photography and performance, situating the two as different kinds of indexicality. As indexes, both labour to 'substitute the registration of sheer physical presence for the more highly articulated language of aesthetic conventions'.[9] And yet, I would stress, in their failure to 'go beyond' the contingency of aesthetic codes, both performance and photography announce the supplementarity of the index itself. The presentation of the self – in performance, in the photograph, film or video – calls out the mutual supplementarity of the body and the subject (the body, as material 'object' in the world, seems to confirm the 'presence' of the subject; the subject gives the body its significance as 'human'), as well as of performance or body art and the photographic document. (The body art event needs the photograph to confirm its having happened; the photograph needs the body art event as an ontological 'anchor' of its indexicality.) [...]

1   [footnote 17 in source] Kris Kuramitsu, 'Yayoi Kusama: Exotic Bodies in the Avant-Garde', unpublished paper submitted for Amelia Jones and Donald Preziosi's *Essentialism and Representation* graduate seminar, University of California at Riverside and at Los Angeles (Spring 1996). [...]

2 [18] Ibid.

3 [19] The other artists in the portrait include Jiro Yoshihara, founder of Gutai, Hans Haacke, Lucio Fontana and Günther Uecker. See the labelled photograph in part 2 of the *Nul* catalogue (Amsterdam: Stedelijk Museum, 1965) unpaginated.

4 [20] On the rhetoric of the pose see Craig Owens, 'The Medusa Effect, or The Spectacular Ruse', in his collected writings *Beyond Recognition: Representation, Power and Culture*, ed. Scott Bryson, et al. (Berkeley and Los Angeles: University of California Press, 1992) 191–200. The term 'author function' is of course derived from Michel Foucault's 'What is an Author?' (1969), in *Language, Counter-Memory, Practice*, trans. Donald Bouchard and Sherry Simon (Ithaca: Cornell University Press, 1977) 113–38.

5 [21] Kristine Stiles, 'Performance and Its Objects', *Arts Magazine*, vol. 65, no. 3 (November 1990) 35; Henry M. Sayre's reading of Schwarzkogler's work can be found in *The Object of Performance: The American Avant-Garde since 1970* (Chicago: University of Chicago Press, 1992) 2.

6 [22] See Roland Barthes, 'Rhetoric of the Image', in *Image–Music–Text*, trans. Stephen Heath (New York: Hill & Wang, 1977) 44.

7 [23] Kristine Stiles, 'Performance and Its Objects', op. cit., 37.

8 [24] Henry M. Sayre, *The Object of Performance*, op. cit., 5.

9 [25] Rosalind Krauss, 'Notes on the Index' (1977), in *The Originality of the Avant-Garde and Other Modernist Myths* (Cambridge, Massachusetts: The MIT Press, 1985) 209.

Amelia Jones, extract from '"Presence" in Absentia: Experiencing Performance as Documentation', *Art Journal*, vol. 56, no. 4 (Winter 1997) 14–16.

Coosje van Bruggen
Sounddance//1988

[…] With *Flour Arrangements* and *Composite Photo of Two Messes on the Studio Floor* Bruce Nauman made his first attempt to move away from making static objects. These pieces, which emphasize the remnants of an activity rather than sculptural qualities of objects or artistic photography, were transitional pieces between Nauman's sculptural objects and later works in which the activity itself became the piece. The latter could be arbitrary and absurd – for example, the film *Playing a Note on the Violin While I Walk around the Studio* (1968); in fact, Nauman did not know how to play the violin. The activity could also be more logical, such as 'pacing or rhythmic stamping around the studio'. Nauman remembers at the time telling a friend who was a philosopher that he imagined him spending most of his time at a desk, writing. But in fact his friend did his thinking while taking long walks during the day. This made Nauman conscious of the fact that he spent most of his time pacing around the studio drinking coffee. And so he decided to film that – just the pacing. During the winter of 1967–68 Nauman made four black-and-white films of activities carried out in a studio in Mill Valley that he had sublet from his teacher William T. Wiley, while Wiley was travelling: *Playing a Note on the Violin While I Walk around the Studio*; *Bouncing Two Balls between the Floor* and *Ceiling with Changing Rhythms*; *Walking in an Exaggerated Manner around the Perimeter of a Square*; and *Dance or Exercise on the Perimeter of a Square*. The activities recorded in these films and the videotapes Nauman made in New York during the following winter were originally intended as performances. However, at the time there was no situation in which to perform them. Nauman felt that notes were not sufficient to preserve his ideas, so he made these inexpensive short films (each lasting no more than ten minutes) and hour-long videotapes both as a record of his studio activities and as a form of art.

In the film *Dance or Exercise on the Perimeter of a Square*, Nauman performs a simple dance step: starting from one corner of a square formed by masking tape fastened to the studio floor, he moves around the perimeter. He turns alternately into the square and out towards the wall, with either his face or his back turned to the camera (the back view allows more anonymity). His movements are regulated by the beat of a metronome. In the silent film *Walking in an Exaggerated Manner around the Perimeter of a Square*, a larger square is taped to the floor outside the first one. With great concentration Nauman, shown in profile, puts his feet carefully down on the line of the outer square, one foot in front or in back of the other; at the same time he shifts weight onto a hip in an exaggerated manner. At times a reflection of this exercise in *contrapposto* balance, showing the figure from a different angle, can be seen in a mirror leaning against the back wall. From time to time the performer is completely absent from the screen, because the frame cuts off part of the square; at those times Nauman seems paradoxically to be stressing the artist's isolation within the double entrapment of his studio and the frame. Nauman's method of escape from this imprisonment, stepping out of the picture, also takes him out of reach of the viewer, which creates a strong sense of remoteness. This exaggerated dance exercise was the forerunner of another performance, executed only on videotape in 1969, the hour-long *Walk with Contrapposto*. In this work the artist, his hands clasped behind his neck, walks slowly, with his arms and legs akimbo, towards and away from the camera, along an extremely narrow, 20-foot-long corridor. Nauman's exaggerated movements, mostly taking up lateral space, appear cramped within the narrow corridor. The artist explained: 'The camera was placed so that the walls came in at either side of the screen. You couldn't see the rest of the studio, and my head was cut off most of the time. The light was shining down the length of the corridor and made shadows on the walls at each side of me.' [Interview with Willoughby Sharp, *Arts Magazine* (March 1970) 23]

These three dance exercises are based on a daily activity, walking, but by breaking it up into detached motions they distort its ordinariness. For instance, by emphasizing the hip movement, Nauman lavishly covers space, stressing his presence in the corridor; by turning the step into a balancing act he lifts it out of its everyday context. The disjunction of motion into a series of fragments echoes the multiple frames of Eadweard Muybridge's sequential photographs of people and animals in action, causing tension between movement and rest. The use of the square on the floor is somewhat arbitrary – it could have been a circle or a triangle, or the pieces could have been performed around the edges of the room – but it serves to direct the movements and to formalize the exercises, giving them more importance as dances than they would have had if Nauman had just wandered aimlessly. For instance, in taking one convenient step forward in *Dance or Exercise on the Perimeter of a Square*, Nauman reaches precisely the middle of a side of the square. In *Walking in an Exaggerated Manner around the Perimeter of a Square*, the framing of the image is accentuated by cropping off a part of the square, so that the field of action becomes restricted. The lopping off of the performer's limbs or head serves to objectify the human body.

Nauman practised these dance exercises extensively before filming them. 'An awareness of yourself comes from a certain amount of activity and you can't get it from just thinking about yourself', Nauman stated in his interview with Willoughby Sharp.

> You do exercises, you have certain kinds of awarenesses that you don't have if you read books. So the films and some of the pieces that I did after that for videotapes were specifically about doing exercises in balance. I thought of them as dance-problems without being a dancer, being interested in the kinds of tension that arise when you try to balance and can't. Or do something for a long time and get tired. In one of those first films, the violin film, I played the violin as long as I could. I don't know how to play the violin, so it was hard, playing on all four strings as fast as I could for as long as I could. I had ten minutes of film and ran about seven minutes of it before I got tired and had to stop and rest a little bit and then finish it. [*Avalanche*, no. 2 (Winter 1971) 27]

By reading the psychologist Frederick Perls' book *Gestalt Theory*, Nauman was stimulated to place himself in an unfamiliar situation 'where you can't relax following resistances', and to turn to the root of one's problems as a way to make art. [...]

Coosje van Bruggen, extract from 'Sounddance' in Coosje van Bruggen, *Bruce Nauman* (New York: Rizzoli, 1988) 226–8.

Daniel Buren
The Function of the Studio//1971

Of all the frames, envelopes and limits – usually not perceived and certainly never questioned – which enclose and constitute the work of art (picture frame, niche, pedestal, palace, church, gallery, museum, art history, economics, power, etc.), there is one rarely even mentioned today that remains of primary importance: *the artist's studio*. Less dispensable to the artist than either the gallery or the museum, it precedes both. Moreover, as we shall see, the museum and gallery on the one hand and the studio on the other are linked to form the foundation of the same edifice and the same system. To question one while leaving the other intact accomplishes nothing. Analysis of the art system must inevitably be carried on in terms of the studio as the *unique space* of production and the museum as the *unique space* of exposition. Both must be investigated as customs, the ossifying customs of art. What is the function of the studio?

(1) It is the place where the work originates.
(2) It is generally a private place, an ivory tower perhaps.
(3) It is a *stationary* place where *portable* objects are produced.

The importance of the studio should by now be apparent; it is the first frame, the first limit, upon which all subsequent frames/limits will depend.
      What does it look like, physically, architecturally? The studio is not just any hideaway, any room.[1] Two specific types may be distinguished:

(1) The European type, modelled upon the Parisian studio of the turn of the century. This type is usually rather large and is characterized primarily by its high ceilings (a minimum of 4 metres). Sometimes there is a balcony, to increase the distance between viewer and work. The door allows large works to enter and to exit. Sculptors' studios are on the ground floor, painters' on the top floor. In the

latter, the lighting is natural, usually diffused by windows oriented towards the north so as to receive the most even and subdued illumination.[2]

(2) The American type,[3] of more recent origin. This type is rarely built according to specification, but, located as it is in reclaimed lofts, is generally much larger than its European counterpart, not necessarily higher, but longer and wider. Wall and floor space are abundant. Natural illumination plays a negligible role, since the studio is lit by electricity both night and day if necessary. There is thus equivalence between the products of these lofts and their placement on the walls and floors of modern museums, which are also illuminated day and night by electricity.

This second type of studio has influenced the European studio of today, whether it be in an old country barn or an abandoned urban warehouse. In both cases, the architectural relationship of studio and museum – one inspiring the other and vice versa – is apparent.[4] (We will not discuss those artists who transform part of their studios into exhibition spaces, nor those curators who conceive of the museum as a permanent studio.)

These are some of the studio's architectural characteristics; let us move on to what usually happens there. A private place, the studio is presided over by the artist-resident, since only that work which he desires and allows to leave his studio will do so. Nevertheless, other operations, indispensable to the functioning of galleries and museums, occur in this private place. For example, it is here that the art critic, the exhibition organizer, or the museum director or curator may calmly choose among the works presented by the artist those to be included in this or that exhibition, this or that collection, this or that gallery. The studio is thus a convenience for the organizer: he may compose his exhibition according to his own desire (and not that of the artist, although the artist is usually perfectly content to leave well enough alone, satisfied with the prospect of an exhibition). Thus chance is minimized, since the organizer has not only selected the artist in advance, but also selects the works he desires in the studio itself. The studio is thus also a boutique where we find ready-to-wear art.

Before a work of art is publicly exhibited in a museum or gallery, the studio is also the place to which critics and other specialists may be invited in the hope that their visits will release certain works from this, their purgatory, so that they may accede to a state of grace on public (museum/gallery) or private (collection) walls. Thus the studio is a place of multiple activities: production, storage and finally, if all goes well, distribution. It is a kind of commercial depot.

Thus the first frame, the studio, proves to be a filter which allows the artist to select his work screened from public view, and curators and dealers to select in turn that work to be seen by others. Work produced in this way makes its passage, in order to exist, from one refuge to another. It should therefore be portable, manipulable if possible, by whoever (except the artist himself) assumes the responsibility of removing it from its place of origin to its place of promotion. A work produced in the studio must be seen, therefore, as an object subject to infinite manipulation. In order for this to occur, from the moment of its production the work must be isolated from the real world. All the same, it is in the studio, and only in the studio, that it is closest to its own reality, a reality from which it will continue to distance itself. It may become what even its creator had not anticipated, serving instead, as is usually the case, the greater profit of financial interests and the dominant ideology. It is therefore only in the studio that the work may be said to belong.

The work thus falls victim to a mortal paradox from which it cannot escape, since its purpose implies a progressive removal from its own reality, from its origin. If the work of art remains in the studio, however, it is the artist that risks death … from starvation.

The work is thus totally foreign to the world into which it is welcomed (museum, gallery, collection). This gives rise to the ever-widening gap between the work and its place (and not its *placement*), an abyss which, were it to become apparent, as sooner or later it must, would hurl the entire parade of art (art as we know it today and, 99 per cent of the time, as it is made) into historical oblivion. This gap is tentatively bridged, however, by the system which makes acceptable to ourselves as public, artist, historian and critic, the convention that establishes the museum and the gallery as inevitable neutral frames, the unique and definitive locales of art. Eternal realms for eternal art!

The work is made in a specific place which it cannot take into account. All the same, it is there that it was ordered, forged, and only there may it be truly said to be in place. The following contradiction becomes apparent: it is impossible by definition for a work to be seen in place; still, the place where we see it influences the work even more than the place in which it was made and from which it has been cast out. Thus when the work is in place, it does not take place (for the public), while it takes place (for the public) only when not in place, that is, in the museum.

Expelled from the ivory tower of its production, the work ends up in another, which, while foreign, only reinforces the sense of comfort the work acquires by taking shelter in a citadel which ensures that it will survive its passage. The work thus passes – and it can only exist in this way, predestined as it is by the imprint of its place of origin – from one enclosed place/frame, the world of the artist, to another, even more closely confined: the world of art. The alignment of works on museum walls gives the impression of a cemetery: whatever they say, wherever they come from, whatever their meanings may be, this is where they all arrive in the end, where they are lost. This loss is relative, however, compared to the total oblivion of the work that never emerges from the studio.

Thus, the unspeakable compromise of the portable work.

The status of the work that reaches the museum is unclear: it is at the same time in place and in a place which is never its own. Moreover, the place for which the work is destined is not defined by the work, nor is the work specifically intended for a place which pre-exists it and is, for all practical purposes, unknown.

For the work to be in place without being specially placed, it must either be identical to all other existing works, and those works in turn identical among themselves, in which case the work (and all other identical works) may travel and be placed at will; or the frame (museum/gallery) that receives the original work and all other original – that is, fundamentally heterogenous – works must be adjustable, adapting itself to each work perfectly, to the millimetre.

From these two extremes, we can only deduce such extreme, idealizing yet interesting formulations as:

(1) all works of art are absolutely the same, wherever and whenever produced, by whatever artist. This would explain their identical arrangement in thousands of museums around the world, subject to the vagaries of curatorial fashion;

(2) all works of art are absolutely different, and if their differences are respected and hence both implicitly and explicitly legible, every museum, every room in every museum, every wall and every square metre of every wall, is perfectly adapted to every work.

The symmetry of these propositions is only apparent. If we cannot conclude logically that all works of art are the same, we must acknowledge at least that they are all installed in the same manner, according to the prevailing taste of a particular time. If on the other hand we accept the uniqueness of each work of art, we must also admit that no museum ever totally adapts itself to the work; pretending to defend the uniqueness of the work, the museum paradoxically acts as if this did not exist and handles the work as it pleases.

To edify ourselves with two examples among many, the administration of the Jeu de Paume in Paris [in 1971 a museum of Impressionist art] has set Impressionist paintings into the museum's painted walls, which thereby directly frame the paintings. Eight thousand kilometres away at the Art Institute of Chicago paintings from the same period and by the same artists are exhibited in elaborate carved frames, like onions in a row.

Does this mean that the works in question are absolutely identical, and that they acquire their specific meanings only from the intelligence of those who present them? That the 'frame' exists precisely to vary the absolute neutrality of all works of art? Or does it mean that the museum adapts itself to the specific meaning of each work? We may ask how it is that, seventy years after being painted, certain canvases by Monet, for example, should be recessed into a salmon-coloured wall in a building in Paris, while others in Chicago are encased in enormous frames and juxtaposed with other Impressionist works.

If we reject propositions 1 and 2 above, we are still faced with a third, more common alternative that presupposes a necessary relationship between the studio and the museum such as we know it today. Since the work which remains in the studio is a non-entity, if the work is to be made, not to mention seen in another place, in any place whatsoever, one of two conditions must apply; either

(1) the definitive place of the work must be the work itself. This belief or philosophy is widely held in artistic circles, even though it dispenses with all analysis of the physical space in which the work is viewed, and consequently of the system, the dominant ideology, that controls it as much as the specific ideology of art. A reactionary theory if ever there was one: while feigning indifference to the system, it reinforces it, without even having to justify itself, since by definition (the definition advanced by this theory's proponents) the space of the museum has no relation to the space of the work; or

(2) the artist, imagining the place where his work will come to grief, is led to conceive all possible situations of every work (which is quite impossible), or a typical space (this he does). The result is the predictable cubic space, uniformly lit, neutralized to the extreme, which characterizes the museum/gallery of today. This state of affairs consciously or unconsciously compels the artist to banalize his own work in order to make it conform to the banality of the space that receives it.

By producing for a stereotype, one ends up of course fabricating a stereotype, which explains the rampant academicism of contemporary work, dissimulated as it is behind apparent formal diversity.

In conclusion, I would like to substantiate my distrust of the studio and its simultaneously idealizing and ossifying function with two examples that have influenced me. The first is personal, the second, historical.

(1) While still very young – I was seventeen at the time – I undertook a study of Provençal painting from Cézanne to Picasso with particular attention given to the influence of geography on works of art. To accomplish my study, I not only

travelled throughout south-eastern France but also visited a large number of artists, from the youngest to the oldest, from the obscure to the famous. My visits afforded me the opportunity to view their work in the context of their studios. What struck me about all their work was first its diversity, then its quality and richness, especially the sense of reality, that is, the 'truth', that it possessed, whoever the artist and whatever his reputation. This 'reality/truth' existed not only in terms of the artist and his workspace but also in relation to the environment, the landscape.

It was when I later visited, one after the other, the exhibitions of these artists that my enthusiasm began to fade, and in some cases disappear, as if the works I had seen were not these, nor even produced by the same hands. Torn from their context, their 'environment', they had lost their meaning and died, to be reborn as forgeries. I did not immediately understand what had happened, nor why I felt so disillusioned. One thing was clear, however: deception. More than once I revisited certain artists, and each time the gap between studio and gallery widened, finally making it impossible for me to continue my visits to either. Although the reasons were unclear, something had irrevocably come to an end for me.

I later experienced the same disillusion with friends of my own generation, whose work possessed a 'reality/truth' that was clearly much closer to me. The loss of the object, the idea that the context of the work corrupts the interest that the work provokes, as if some energy essential to its existence escapes as it passes through the studio door, occupied all my thoughts. This sense that the main point of the work is lost somewhere between its place of production and place of consumption forced me to consider the problem and the significance of the work's place. What I later came to realize was that it was the reality of the work, its 'truth', its relationship to its creator and place of creation, that was irretrievably lost in this transfer. In the studio we generally find finished work, work in progress, abandoned work, sketches – a collection of visible evidence viewed simultaneously that allows an understanding of process; it is this aspect of the work that is extinguished by the museum's desire to 'install'. Hasn't the term installation come to replace exhibition? In fact, isn't what is installed close to being established?

(2) The only artist who has always seemed to me to exhibit real intelligence in his dealings with the museum system and its consequences, and who moreover sought to oppose it by not permitting his works to be fixed or even arranged according to the whim of some departmental curator, is Constantin Brancusi. By disposing of a large part of his work with the stipulation that it be preserved in the studio where it was produced, Brancusi thwarted any attempt to disperse his work, frustrated speculative ventures, and afforded every visitor the same perspective as himself at the moment of creation. He is the only artist who, in order to preserve

the relationship between the work and its place of production, dared to present his work in the very place where it first saw light, thereby short-circuiting the museum's desire to classify, to embellish and to select. The work is seen, for better or worse, as it was conceived. Thus, Brancusi is also the only artist to preserve what the museum goes to great lengths to conceal: the banality of the work.

It might also be said – but this requires a lengthy study of its own – that the way in which the work is anchored in the studio has nothing whatsoever to do with the 'anchorage' to which the museum submits every work it exhibits. Brancusi also demonstrates that the so-called purity of his works is no less beautiful or interesting when seen amid the clutter of the studio – various tools; other works, some of them incomplete, others complete – than it is in the immaculate space of the sterilized museum.[5]

The art of yesterday and today is not only marked by the studio as an essential, often unique, place of production; it proceeds from it. All my work proceeds from its extinction.

1   I am well aware that, at least at the beginnings of and sometimes throughout their careers, all artists must be content with squalid hovels or ridiculously tiny rooms; but I am describing the studio as an archetype. Artists who maintain ramshackle workspaces despite their drawbacks are obviously artists for whom the *idea* of possessing a studio is a necessity. Thus they often dream of possessing a studio very similar to the archetype described here.

2   Thus the architect must pay more attention to the lighting, orientation, etc., of the studio than most artists ever pay to the exhibition of their works once they leave the studio!

3   We are speaking of New York, since the United States, in its desire to rival and to supplant the long lamented 'School of Paris', actually reproduced all its defects, including the insane centralization which, while ridiculous on the scale of France or even Europe, is absolutely grotesque on the scale of the United States, and certainly antithetical to the development of art.

4   The American museum with its electric illumination may be contrasted with its European counterpart, usually illuminated by natural light thanks to a profusion of skylights. Some see these as opposites, when in fact they merely represent a stylistic difference between European and American production.

5   Had Brancusi's studio remained in the impasse Ronsin, or even in the artist's house (even if removed to another location), Brancusi's argument would only have been strengthened. (This text was written in 1971 and refers to the reconstruction of Brancusi's studio in the Museum of Modern Art, Paris. Since then, the main buildings have been reconstructed in the Place Beaubourg opposite the Centre Pompidou, which renders the above observation obsolete – author's note.)

Daniel Buren, 'The Function of the Studio', written in 1971; first published, translated by Thomas Repensek, in *October*, no. 10 (Fall 1979) 51–8.

Daniel Buren
The Function of the Studio Revisited//2007

The function of the studio is absolutely, basically, the same as it always was. The studio as I defined it in 1971 has not changed, although perhaps more artists are escaping their studios today than when I wrote 'The Function of the Studio'. Artists have a much looser idea of what constitutes a studio than they did in the early 1970s. However, I think it is still the main place of work for the majority of artists.

The function of the studio is the making of a work of art for an ideal place, a work which may be endlessly manipulated. If you work most of the time in a studio you produce works that are destined to be installed somewhere else. That was the key point of my text – in a studio you produce work to be shown anywhere – whether in a gallery, museum or private collection – and you must work with a preconceived idea of what these rooms might be like, as the final destination of the work is totally unknown.

It is a different case when the artwork calls on the specifics of its location for its identity and completion and cannot be installed or seen in another place. This returns us to the idea of the site as an integral component of the work whereby it can only be understood at that site, which is in turn transformed by the artwork, forever or for the time that they are together. If the work is created thus there is a break from the idea and the idealism of the studio.

When the studio becomes a place to work on something that will be visible only at a particular site, then the spirit of production is entirely different. But the function of the studio as I defined it a long time ago is exactly the same even if the work seems to be different. A studio obliges a certain type of work even if you are just using it to prepare a plan. Today, of course, you have many more variations of the studio, yet that which I defined in the text is still completely valid in the majority of cases. The system still prescribes the result under the same restrictions.

The studio process creates objects that complement our society of exchange and market value. The market value of an artwork that is produced in the studio is directly influenced by exchangeability and critically relies on an eternal nomadism, not of the producer but of the artwork. Needless to say, I reversed that habit. The art market barely existed in 1971. It is a hundred times more prevalent now than when I wrote the text. Then it existed for historical art rather than for any young working artist, and it would have been a dream to even survive by selling work. Today, if you start out as an artist at twenty years of age you cannot imagine that you are not going to make an adequate living from your work. If you cannot, you simply do not do it. In the 1980s, although it was a little provocative, there were artists who would say, 'If I'm not commercially successful in two or three years I'll go back to the stock exchange and stop what I'm doing.' The most surprising thing is that some of the people who said that succeeded with their art, such as Jeff Koons. Not that he represents the majority, as obviously it was and still is very hard to survive on artistic production. Today artists are much more aware of the market than was the case thirty-five years ago, reinforcing even more the idea of objects that are absolutely born of the studio. [...]

In 1971 my standpoint was unusual because, to the best of my knowledge, Brancusi was the only one who saw the contradiction between the work and the way that the work was shown. In leaving his studio to the French state he decided to keep the very lively aspect of the artist in the studio where the work was most comprehensible. He wanted to show that it is this site where the work is most readily understood. It is where you speak with the artist and see the environment where he creates. In the case of the Brancusi studio, in its first incarnation, you had a conceptual totality as designated by the artist rather than a reconstruction that was never requested by him, as happened later when the studio was reconstructed outside the Centre Pompidou in 1977 and again, and even worse, in 1997. From this history two perspectives are presented that define contrasting attitudes: criticism or analysis.

For me, analysis leads to criticism and criticism leads to action. In 1968, when I decided to quit the studio, I hadn't realized all of the implications. Many familiar doors were immediately closed to me, although luckily others opened that I hadn't even been aware of. To not have a studio, as well as to have a studio, automatically implies the production of a certain type of work. I can see that the day when I cannot move or travel any more, as I have done over the past forty years, I will either stop working or my work will be different. The only thing that I can imagine helping to keep it going in its present form might be my long experience of moving and looking at different places. Perhaps with documentation I could still work, but I would miss those little details that you can only see when you are there, when you meet people. My work would be completely different and certainly, as far as I tell from my viewpoint today, would revert to more traditional aspects. I prefer not to think about it!

Daniel Buren, extracts from 'The Function of the Studio Revisited', conversation between Daniel Buren and the curators/editors Jens Hoffmann, Christina Kennedy and Georgina Jackson, in *The Studio*, exhibition catalogue (Dublin: Dublin City Gallery The Hugh Lane, 2007).

Briony Fer
Studio//2004

[...] By September 1967 Eva Hesse was working with latex on *Schema*. Dorothy Beskind's film of Hesse in her studio shows her placing the little cast hemispheres in lines on the latex mat. The way she set them down in lines on the mat (they are not attached) follows those straggling chains and changes of direction in the circle drawings [on graph paper, 1966–67]. The grid is made up of uneven 'intervals' between the bumps. We see more than one arrangement: early on there is a glimpse of *Schema* with the latex hemispheres arranged close together, touching each other; then she later arranges it, more spaced out with a narrower border. This suggests that even this piece was intended to be expandable and adaptable. At another moment in the film Hesse is shown puncturing with a screwdriver and threading rubber hose through little latex hemispheres like the ones in *Schema*, though whiter. This suggests that she was in the process of working on even more variations on this format than now exist. Originally the smooth latex mat of *Schema* was translucent, and the orange colour of the rubber (it was never clear) was shiny and almost tacky in its texture. Her title *Schema* cuts against the sheer materiality of the thing. As Anne Wagner put it, Hesse's work 'floats on a sea of language'.[1] Here the language of her title intervenes – at the same time as it seems to invoke a logic of series – the logic of series that for Hesse consists of drawing, puncturing, cutting, threading, moulding and casting. The word *schema* – one of the few words not from the thesaurus that she used for a title at this time – also playfully invokes Dan Graham's work of the same name from 1966, a work made of words and numbers and holes between words and numbers, a game of ellipses and absences and substitutions, understood as a linguistic operation. Graham gave Hesse a copy.[2] It was one of the works photocopied in Mel Bochner's 'Working Drawings' show [of the same year, at the School of Visual Arts, New York].

That artists are friends does not, of course, mean that their work shares a common ground. Nonetheless, this was one of the contexts for Hesse's own thinking about her work. The differences are illuminating. Graham's piece was one of his works that would be cited in the pages of magazines, outside the space of the gallery. Placed in different magazine situations, Graham's schema would be filled in dependent entirely on its context. As he put it later, 'the work is composed as it decomposes into the constituent material elements of its context. Its place pertained to both the work's internal grammatical structure and to the external physical position it occupied.'[3] He talked about making a kind of Pop art 'that was more literally disposable'.[4] Little of this strikes a cord with Hesse's work at first. But on reflection some of the terms gel as those which describe precisely the radical configuration of art at that moment: composition and decomposition, played out by Hesse through a dereliction of sculpture, and then the maybe more surprising idea of disposability – surprising in relation to Hesse, that is. But that is one way of describing the adding and extracting and remaindering that is the main drive of her serial logic. From this point of view, these two iterations of 'decomposition' can be seen as flipsides of the reconfiguration of art at this moment.

In her statement for the 'Art in Process' show [Finch College, New York, 1965–66], Hesse asked herself 'How to make by not making?'[5] This was a question very much of its time. We could imagine Bochner or Graham or LeWitt asking it. Given what I have described as Hesse's intense physical involvement with her work, even when she had it made by fabricators, it seems an odd question for her to ask. Certainly for Hesse, making something, physically making the work, was not so easily dispensable as it was for some others. Duchamp had asked the question 'How to make a work that is not "of art"?' Hesse's answer was not, as it had been for Duchamp, the ready-made, although she certainly worked with ready-made materials. Nor was it to make art out of language, although her trawling through the thesaurus, once she got it, certainly leaves its traces in her notebooks in lists of words alongside sketches. What she did with all of this, in the studio, is the point.

Hesse asked herself 'How to make by not making?' It's hard to catch her thought, and even harder to catch her answer: 'It's all in that/ it's not new. It's what is not yet known, thought seen touched.'[6] She seems to be saying that it's all in the future, after all, making is making what has not yet been made. Alex Potts has referred to a kind of modernist utopian strand in Hesse, compared with, say, Smithson's dystopian vision.'[7] The ready-made becomes the never made, the never before made. This is not Smithson's vision, but it is her own kind of high-risk scrambling of the temporal order of things. Then, as we read on, just when we think we might have caught her drift, she seems to discard it all by saying it is simply a matter of 'what is not'.[8] Suddenly the 'thought seen touched' is jettisoned in favour of a negative, less a resounding 'no' than a quick reversal which she brings out of the hat at the end of her thought. If, as I suggest, her thought was a string of twists and turns and reversals all along, then it is worth allowing the thrown away phrase 'thought seen touched' to resurface. It is a constellation of terms, after all, that suggests that Hesse's way of thinking could not be contained within prevailing modernist preoccupations with opticality and the appeal to eyesight alone, where the material existence of things is sublimated in a vaporous, immaterial web of optical effects and nuances. A dynamics of sight might not have been entirely redundant but it certainly had to be reimagined in relation not only to sculpture (as opposed to painting) but a new way of thinking about making.

One of the earliest and certainly one of the best attempts to characterize Hesse's sculpture was that of her friend Robert Smithson. It was 1966, at a pivotal moment for her. Though Hesse's work has since been interpreted in a number of different ways, this was certainly one that provided a groundwork. It reads as a conversation with the works. Words are traded. One of the most vivid words Smithson used to describe her work was 'vertiginous', and her *Vertiginous Detour* was one of her works that he talks about. He talked brilliantly about its qualities of 'dereliction', the 'emptiness' at its centre. These are all words that describe what happens to sculpture at this moment. It is not just a description of the look of the object but a dereliction of viewing itself, where prevailing ideas of what a sculpture was no longer held. This may sound prescient of the materials she would go on to use that would actually decay, like latex, but this was nothing to do with Smithson's point. He wrote that they were destined for a funeral chamber but, on this he is adamant, there is no anthropomorphism and he says, 'No evidence of human decay'.[9]

I don't think there is much that is funereal about Hesse's work. That says much more about Smithson's imagery. And he got this image, it is pretty clear, from George Kubler, whose strange and quirky book *The Shape of Time* had been published in 1962. Smithson referred to Kubler at several points throughout the article in which the discussion of Hesse appeared, 'Quasi-Infinities and the Waning of Space', published in *Artforum* in 1966. Looking again at Kubler, what he had to say about tombs and funeral chambers was not about death (or not principally) but about what kind of a space a tomb was in ancient cultures. The thing about placing objects in tombs was that it was a way of both discarding and retaining things at the same time. Kubler contrasted this with a modern understanding of obsolescence[10] – the kind of obsolescence that is necessary for capital continually to accumulate and so to renew itself; where things have to become obsolete, to be thrown away, in order for new things to be consumed. Art can become a tomb-space because it is a place where things are retained, kept, collected. We are reminded of Claes Oldenburg's *Bedroom Ensemble*, understood as a kind of pharoah's tomb to commodity culture.

Discarding and retaining at the same time: this taps into something in Hesse's work, but from a different angle. Thought of like this, her materials are never entirely exempt from a commodity culture – but locked into its logic in a radically subversive way. They certainly dramatize feelings and anxieties that we collectively share about the lives of objects and things, reflecting upon ideas of obsolescence without ever succumbing to its economy. Smithson once told Lucy Lippard that he saw Hesse making psychic models.[11] Discarding and retaining become twin functions of psychic as well as material and cultural life, where the 'petrified', to use another of Smithson's words, is absolutely alive to change. Discarding and retaining, saving and leaving, is also the economy of the studio. The studio is not exempt in that sense. This may be true of many artists' studios, but particularly so of Hesse's, especially given her habit of reusing discarded materials from one work in the making of another. Photographs of her studio bear witness and indeed are part of this circulation: ropes and strings piled in heaps or hanging in works, polythene drop-cloths in and out of use, arrangements and rearrangements of things she made.[12]

The pastry cases that she made seem to me to crystallize what I want to call Hesse's studio economy. The story goes that Sol LeWitt first put the collection of little test-pieces that Hesse had given to him as gifts in a display case from a cake shop, similar to the kind that Oldenburg had used. Apparently, Hesse liked the idea and began to collect her little experimental test-pieces together in the same glass cases. Bill Barrette refers to pieces in *Untitled, 'Douglas Glass Case'* as a plaster and latex 'sandwich' or a latex 'pie crust', making them seem even closer to the cakes and fancies that Oldenburg favoured.[13] She went on to exhibit the glass cases that she assembled herself, which suggests that they were works in their own right. I think the glass cases also function a little bit like notebooks, or rather commentaries on her work as well as works. Her notebooks are full of visual inventories of her works, lists of drawings of the things she made. In the glass cases she grouped together widely disparate materials and shapes and textures in a way that echoes the way she worked in series. Each shelf makes a series of bizarre connections. On the top, a latex bucket sits next to a little concertina-type arrangement of transparent tubes (test-pieces for *Repetition Nineteen* and *Accretion* respectively) and a wire-mesh sleeve; in the middle, a cast latex hemisphere sits on a grey foam rubber sheet punctured by a grid of threads waving in every direction; and on the bottom shelf, itself covered all over with metal grommets, are placed more pieces, including a grid of metal numbers embedded in plaster and encased in the latex 'crust' Barrette mentioned. Ready-made elements such as the metal number tabs used by glaziers, or the tubing, or the metal grommets, were bought by Hesse from a hardware store. But they are transformed by sinking them in plaster, or cutting, or tightly rilling them into the shape of a grid. There is a string of techniques – casting, moulding, embedding, puncturing, threading – that are used in various conjunctions. And there are any number of combinations of materials – cheesecloth, wire mesh, latex, plaster, fibreglass – that sit side by side. The connections are both horizontal and vertical, almost like a three-dimensional thesaurus. These make for much stranger thing-scapes than Oldenburg's. As test-pieces, in which she tried out techniques, they are remnants of her process of making, which are kept and displayed and recycled. The small pieces with which Hesse experimented were highly provisional, yet they come to look like leftovers, especially, of course, as some of the materials, like the latex, have decayed. The display cases, found on the Bowery, are remnants of shop fittings, which are also reused and recycled.

The glass cases also dramatize something about looking at her work. Part of their strangeness is that the spectator is invited to peer in, to look close. This almost totally reverses the logic of viewing Hesse's sculpture – which expands to occupy a whole room. Here you have to look close-up in order to see the textures, which as a result come to be magnified. This gives us another perspective on Hesse's work as peculiarly made things in a world of things, fabricated things in a field or fabric of things. Hesse once said how much she liked Warhol because 'he and his work are the same',[14] but for me the correspondence with Warhol is here: in repetition and manufacture and in a dynamics of viewing and obsolescence. The glass cases, from this point of view, are almost an uncanny double of the commodity form. [...]

1   [footnote 13 in source] Anne Wagner, 'The Life of Language: How Words Matter to Hesse's Art', talk given at the symposium held to coincide with the Eva Hesse retrospective at San Francisco Museum of Modern Art in 2002.

2   [14] This was a typewritten copy, now at the Eva Hesse Archives, Allen Memorial Art Museum, Oberlin College, Oberlin, Ohio.

3   [15] Dan Graham, 'My Works for Magazine Pages: "A History of Conceptual Art" 1965–69', in *Dan Graham*, ed. Gloria Moure (Barcelona: Ediciones Poligrafa, 1998) 65.

4   [16] Ibid.

5   [17] Hesse, statement for 'Art in Process', in *Eva Hesse: Sculpture* (London: Whitechapel Gallery, 1979) unpaginated.

6   [18] Ibid.

7   [19] Alex Potts, 'Eva Hesse' review, *Burlington Magazine*, vol. CXLV, no. 1200 (March 2003) 238.

8   [20] Hesse, statement for 'Art in Process', in *Eva Hesse: Sculpture*, op. cit.

9   [21] Robert Smithson, 'Quasi-Infinities and the Waning of Space', *Artforum* (1966) in *Robert Smithson: The Collected Writings*, ed. Jack Flam (Berkeley and Los Angeles: University of California Press, 1996) 37.

10   [22] George Kubler, *The Shape of Time* (New Haven: Yale University Press, 1962) 77–8.

11   [24] Lucy R. Lippard, *Eva Hesse* (New York: Da Capo Press, 1992) 6.

12   [25] Hesse's drawing table was in her apartment below her studio space on the Bowery. Beskind's film is mainly shot in her apartment, giving the sense that the boundary between the two spaces was blurred. Certainly the larger scale work was done upstairs, certainly the messy work in latex or fibreglass; it seems Hesse would then bring it down and arrange it in the apartment.

13   [26] Bill Barette, *Eva Hesse: Sculpture* (New York: Timken Publishers, 1989) 144.

14   [27] Hesse, interview with Cindy Nemser in *Art Talk: Conversations with 15 Women Artists* (New

York: Harper Collins, 1995) 196. She also picked out Oldenburg, who she said 'is one of the few people who work in realism that I really like – to me he is totally abstract – and the same with Andy Warhol.'

Briony Fer, extract from 'Studio', *The Infinite Line: Remaking Art after Modernism* (New Haven and London: Yale University Press, 2004) 129–34.

Lawrence Weiner
In Conversation with Hans Ulrich Obrist//2003

Hans Ulrich Obrist Could you tell me about the history of collaboration in your practice?

Lawrence Weiner Okay, but I have to personalize it. My own praxis is based on my relationship to materials. It's a studio practice. The studio might be the North Sea, but it's still a studio praxis. There's no difference between a landscape painter carrying their easel out into the landscape or staying inside and looking at a photo – it's the same for me. It's very good for contemporary artists when you are trying to have a conversation with the world as it is – not as it was – to work with other people. You can't make music, you can't make film – you can't even make a book without working with other people who have skills that are on the same level as yours. And I like that. It takes you out of the ivory tower. I'm also in the position where I have a reasonably good life, but I don't have a lot of extra money, so if somebody is working with me on a project, they're not going to be making a lot of money. I have to entice them. I have to make it worthwhile for them to take their skill and put it with my content, or else they're not going to do it. By the time you walk away, you walk away with a book. When you open it up, all the credits are there. When you see a DVD you know who handled the computer, and every one of those things determines how that project is done. It's no longer a matter of the artist being the Hollywood auteur. It doesn't work. You have to accept that there is a division of labour. One of the things that you do in that division of labour is accede to another person's concept of context, because if your work cannot exist within their context, then it cannot exist as a universal that you claim it can when it goes into another world. I see context and content as inherently different. I used to believe that aesthetics were ethics, but the more I've worked, the more I've realized that this is the reason for a lot of the political malaise that we have. In fact, aesthetics are not ethics; aesthetics are aesthetics. Ethics seem to be something that can cross aesthetic lines, and I'd like to have an aesthetic that can cross ethical lines. [...]

Obrist Another issue I'd like to discuss with you is the fact that you describe yourself as a studio artist.

Weiner I have always been a studio artist. I am a materialist, and I am not a conceptual artist. The people whose work has continued to have value and use within our structure are all materialists, from Robert Ryman to Daniel Buren – he is involved in the material of history. But his reference is always to history. I like to have a practice that doesn't have to refer to history. That's the difference.

Obrist What about context and site-specificity?

Weiner No, I don't see it. Site-specificity. I don't understand it. If someone says to me 'Lawrence, we have a city and we'd like you to deal with it', then that's a context. So I'll say, 'Look, this is what I am working on at the moment; this is what I can do best right now, because it's the thing that is closest at hand, so I'll place it within your context. Let's go for it.' And I try to do the best job that I can. I try to find out all I can about drainage, city planning and things like that, for that site, and I'll put the work in, but I'm not going to change the work for them. There's no reason why I should, and I don't think people expect it, although they like to think it's special for them. No, it's special after it's made. Then it becomes something else. But it's not site-specific; it comes out of a studio practice. [...]

Lawrence Weiner and Hans Ulrich Obrist, extract from conversation during the 'Utopia Station' project curated by Obrist, Molly Nesbit and Rirkrit Tiravanija (2003), in *HAVING BEEN SAID/WRITINGS & INTERVIEWS OF LAWRENCE WEINER 1968–2003*, ed. Gerti Fietzek and Gregor Stemmrich (Ostfildern-Ruit: Hatje Cantz, 2004) 422–3.

Bruce Nauman
In Conversation with Michael Auping//2001

Michael Auping So what triggered the making of this piece [*Mapping the Studio I (Fat Chance John Cage)*], and how long did you think about it before you actually began to make it?

Bruce Nauman Well, I was working on the Oliver [collection's] stairway piece (*Untitled*, 1998–99) and I had finished up the *Stadium Piece* (1997–99) in Washington and I was trying to figure out what the next project would be. I was trying to come up with something out of those ideas, thinking about where those ideas might lead me next, and I really wasn't getting anywhere. Those pieces had pretty much finished off a line of thought and it didn't make sense to try and extend it. So a year or so ago I found myself going in the studio and just being frustrated that I didn't have any new ideas to work on. What triggered this piece were the mice. We had a big influx of field mice that summer, in the house and in the studio. They were everywhere and impossible to get rid of. They were so plentiful even the cat was getting bored with them. I'd be sitting in the studio at night reading and the cat would be sitting with me and these mice would run along the walls and the cat and I would watch. I know he'd caught a few now and then because I'd find leftover parts on the floor in the morning.

So I was sitting around the studio being frustrated because I didn't have any new ideas and I decided that you just have to work with what you've got. What I had was this cat and the mice and I did have a video camera in the studio that happened to have infra-red capability. So I set it up and turned it on at night when I wasn't there, just to see what I'd get. At the time, I remember thinking about Daniel Spoerri's piece for the book *An Anecdoted Topography of Chance* (1966). You know, he would photograph or glue everything down after a meal so that what you had were the remains. For the book, a friend of his did the subtext, writing about the leftovers on the table after Spoerri had preserved them. He wrote about every cigarette butt, piece of foil, utensil, the wine and where it came from, etc. It made me think that I have all this stuff lying around the studio, leftovers from different projects and unfinished projects and notes. And I thought to myself why not make a map of the studio and its leftovers. Then I thought it might be interesting to let the animals, the cat and the mice, make the map of the studio. So I set the camera up in different locations around the studio where the mice tended to travel just to see what they would do amongst the remnants of the work. So that was the genesis. Then as I got more involved I realized I needed seven locations really to get a sense of this map. The camera was eventually set up in a sequence that I felt pretty much mapped the space.

Auping So the final piece is six hours long? How did you decide on that length, as opposed to eight hours or two hours?

Nauman Well, it felt like it needed to be more than an hour or two, and then I thought if it's going to be that long then it should be … well, it just felt like it needed to be long so that you wouldn't necessarily sit down and watch the whole thing, but you could come and go, like some of those old Warhol films. I wanted that feeling that the piece was just there, almost like an object, just there, ongoing, being itself. I wanted the piece to have a real-time quality rather than fictional time. I like the idea of knowing it is going on whether you are there or not.

Auping It seems to me this relates to that early pacing the studio piece [*Pacing Upside Down*, 1969]. Do you see that?

Nauman Somewhat. It generally goes back to that idea that when you don't know what to do, then whatever it is you are doing at the time becomes the work.

Auping In that sense, it also relates to your last video, *Setting a Good Corner.*

Nauman Yeah.

Auping So the fact that you've done two in a row means that you don't have any more ideas.

Nauman (*laughter*) I guess there's nothing left.

Auping Tell me about the subtitle. I think the reference to Cage is fairly clear in terms of the open-ended character of the piece, but why the words 'Fat Chance'?

Nauman Well, when I chose the seven spots, I picked them because I knew there was mouse activity, assuming that the cat would occasionally show up too. So the given area that I would shoot over a certain period became a kind of stage. That's how I thought of it. So, when nothing was happening, I wanted it to still be interesting. These areas or stages, if you will, tend to be empty in the middle. So that became the performance area and the performers are the bugs, the mice and the cat. So the performance is just a matter of chance when the performers are going to show up and what is going to happen.

'Fat Chance', which I think is just an interesting saying, refers to a response for an invitation to be involved in an exhibition. Some time ago, Anthony d'Offay was going to do a show of John Cage's scores, which are often very beautiful. He also wanted to show work by artists that were interested in or influenced by Cage. So he asked if I would send him something that related. Cage was an important influence for me, especially his writings. So I sent d'Offay a telegram that said 'FAT CHANCE JOHN CAGE'. D'Offay thought it was a refusal to participate. I thought it was the work, but he didn't get it, so ...

Auping So along with the debris in the studio, you're re-using an earlier work in the title as well.

Nauman Yeah.

Auping Let me ask you about the issue of cutting and editing for this piece. You refer to Cage, which is about indeterminacy and chance, and you do the piece with that kind of inspiration, and then you go in and cut and edit it ...

Nauman No. I didn't. It's all real time. The only thing that comes into play in regards to what you're saying is that I only had one camera and I could only shoot one hour a night. So it's a compilation. There's forty-two hours altogether. So it's forty-two nights. The shooting went from late August through late November or early December. I didn't shoot every night. Before I went to bed at night I would go out to the studio and turn the camera on and then in the morning I'd go out and see what had happened. And I'd make a log of what happened each night.

Auping But you have flipped or reversed and then colonized some of the scenes.

Nauman Right. There are two versions of the piece. In the first version, nothing has been manipulated, no flips, reverses or colour changes. In the second version, there are colour changes and flips and reverses. Then there is also a third. I'd show the piece to Susan [Rothenberg] and she'd get really bored with it and say 'Why don't you cut out all of the stuff where nothing is happening?' And I'd say, well, that's kind of the point of the piece. And then she said 'Well, obviously that's what you should do then', precisely because it is contrary to the piece. So I did do a kind of 'all action' edit. So the six hours gets cut down to forty minutes or an hour.

Auping How did you decide what colour to use and when to reverse or flip an image? Was it generally a matter of composition or highlighting certain scenes?

Nauman Both. In terms of the colours, I wanted to run through the rainbow, but it ended up having a kind of quiet colour. It changes from a red to a green to a blue and then back to red over fifteen or twenty minutes. But it changes at a very slow rate. You can't quite see the colour changing. In each of the seven images it's changing at different times so you have a lot of different colours at any given moment. It's a quiet rainbow. The flips and the flops are fairly arbitrary at about fifteen minutes apart. It's a way of keeping the eye engaged, to give the whole thing a kind of texture throughout.

Auping In terms of reading this symbolically, were you thinking of the cat as a surrogate for the artist, chasing mouse/muse?

Nauman Not really. I was interested in the relationship between the two of them, but more in a psychological way. Their relationship exists as a sort of a paradox between a joke and reality. They've been cartoon characters for so long that we think of them as light-hearted performers, but there is this obvious predator-prey tension between them. I wanted to create a situation that was slightly unclear as to how you should react. I think there are parts that are humorous and there are parts that are not at all. But those are glimpses that you might or might not catch. The overall effect is ambiguous, maybe a little anxious. Then you can hear the dogs barking once in awhile and the coyotes howling now and again. So there is also an element of what's going on inside and what's going on outside, which I like. There are also two locations on the tape of the different doors in the studio. One door goes into the office and two doors go outside and most of the time during the taping I could keep those doors open because it was still warm. Sometimes you can see the reflections of the cat's eyes outside through the screen door. The mice also go inside and outside because there is a hole in one of the screens and they could come and go. Throughout the piece there is an outside-inside dialogue that deals with being in the studio with all this activity going on, and then being aware of a larger nature going on outside that space.

Auping What kind of emotion do you associate with this piece? If you had to assign it an emotion, what would it be?

Nauman I don't know about an emotion. What I've felt in watching it is almost a meditation. Because the projection image is fairly large, if you try and concentrate on or pay attention to a particular spot in the image, you'll miss something. So you really have to not pay attention and not concentrate and allow your peripheral vision to work. You tend to get more if you just scan without seeking. You have to become passive, I think.

Auping There's a kind of forlorn beauty about the piece, almost a pathos. This may sound, well, you just turned sixty so you are now making what curators and art historians call 'the late work'. Is there any thought here in regards to reviewing yourself?

Nauman (*laughter*) I guess it's late work. I hope it's not too late. Maybe in the sense that there's ten years of stuff around the studio and I'm using the leftovers, but I've always tended to do that anyway. Pieces that don't work out generally get made into something else. This is just another instance of using what's already there.

Auping Well, I was also thinking about the fact that the camera is an extension of your eye. In the primary sense, you are the observer. We are following you watching yourself.

Nauman That's true. There are times when I 'see myself', as you put it, and times when I don't. There are times when I just see the space, and it's the space of the cat and the mice, not necessarily my space. On the other hand, I've had to re-look at all of this stuff before it finally gets put on the DVDs – and I'd forgotten that I'd done this, but the spaces that I'd shot, because I wasn't shooting every night, every hour the cameras move just a little bit. The image changes a little bit every hour regardless of any action that's taking place. I was working in the studio during the day all that time. I would unconsciously move things around. Maybe organize a few things – what you do in a studio when you're not supposedly making art. So the areas that I was shooting tended to get cleaner or have fewer objects in them over the period of the six hours. I thought that was kind of interesting. It didn't occur to me when I was doing it, but then I went to SITE Santa Fe and saw Ed Ruscha's film *Miracle*. In the garage as he gets more precise, the garage gets cleaner and cleaner and he gets cleaner as the film goes on. The film made me think that I had done the same thing unconsciously.

Auping Since I haven't seen the final cut, I'm curious how the piece ends.

Nauman It ends pretty much how it starts. It begins with a title and a few credits, and then basically it just starts and then it ends. No crescendo, no fade, no 'The End'. It just stops, like a long slice of time, just time in the studio.

Bruce Nauman and Michael Auping, curator, conversation before the exhibition of *Mapping the Studio I (Fat Chance John Cage)* at the Dia Center, New York (9 January – 16 June 2002), in *Please Pay Attention Please: Bruce Nauman's Words: Writings and Interviews*, ed. Janet Kraynak (Cambridge, Massachusetts: The MIT Press, 2003) 397–404.

Phillip Zarrilli
The Metaphysical Studio//2002

[...] The studio ... a location where words count less. Where something comes of nothing; sound from silence. Action from impulse. To speak at all of the 'studio', in the studio, other than in the metaphors of practice, may be to speak too much. So I speak first, now, in action and through metaphor. Two working metaphors. Two hypotheses for exploration, for this studio:

How is it possible 'to stand still while not standing still'?[1] How is it possible to work precariously between balance and counterbalance, to be poised and counterpoised 'on the edge of the breath'?[2]

The elephant pose: external gaze moves from a point ahead to the hands above the head and fists, and then travels down with the fists, to return to the point ahead. Animal forms where breath animates form, animating awareness towards its dynamic possibilities, outward into space above (through the top of the head), behind, to the sides, and simultaneously inward and down into the earth through the feet.

A short sequence of t'ai chi ch'uan, Wu style: each movement phrase coordinated with breath – with inhalation or exhalation. Both these psychophysical processes allow the participant to explore these seeming paradoxes ... of how one might begin to 'stand still while not standing still', or to be poised and counterpoised 'on the edge of the breath' ... ready. The impulse, originating in that place between in-spiration and ex-piration, on the 'edge of the breath'. Both in-breath and out-breath derive from the Latin *spiritus*: spirit, breath; *spirare*: to breathe ... As Hollis Huston reminds us, 'the breath of life; the animating or vital principles giving life. [...] Sentience itself is readiness, and readiness appears at the top of the breath.'[3]

But the problem with inspirations is that we too often aspire to being inspired. As soon as we aspire, the breath is mis-spent, and we die a thousand deaths. And how much performance work today is about aspiring, rather than in-spiring? The gap between the desire and the inhabiting is uncrossable without a descent to the bottom of the belly, with each breath. A location and place of constant erasure of all the marks of 'obvious meaning and acquired skill'[4] ... and therefore of creating an opening, a space ... that place necessarily left open for the audience ... otherwise, self-indulgence.

The studio – a location where words 'count' less ... but where ideas, intellect and the imagination are forged through an embodied practice where the words must 'speak' unseen, or be purposefully shown and displayed, to have an edge where they can cut with precision. The studio ... a place of hypothesis, and therefore a place of possibility ... where something can come of nothing. Sound from silence. Light from darkness. Therefore, a liminal place, between. ... As a place between, a location without coordinates or answers. A place to map, temporarily, space-time along some continuum, but only momentarily, in that moment of performance. A place that can never be definitively mapped because the marks of its mapping disappear as they appear. Therefore, a place of erasure, risk, loss, and always, as anyone who steps on the stage knows, potential failure.

In this setting, within the studio, can this be a place where failure means more than 'success'? A place where, at times, failure, and its risks, should not only mean more but count more than 'success'.

The studio ... a 'liminal' place between ... a place dedicated or set apart. ... A place to explore the relationship between the doer and the done. A place of fundamental paradox. Implicit in any paradox is ambiguity, change ... the potential for transformation. A place to explore such fundamental paradoxes as

(1) how to make the complex simple, the simple complex;
(2) the relationship between space and time; between absence and presence; here/there; now/then; if/when;
(3) the embodied relationship between in-spiration and ex-piration;
(4) the relationship between the said and the unsaid, or the must-be-said;
(5) the relationship between 'self' and 'others' – the other 'selves' that inhabit me; those I might wish to inhabit; the other as 'character'; the interpersonal you-as-other; the action/the doing/the saying, as 'other'.

The studio ... a site to explore and develop the ability to modulate between union and separation ... the drawing near to, or keeping a distance from. A provisional place where there can be no absolutes. A place of propositions, not givens; a place to practise dialectics, not ends or goals; a premise, not a decision; a possibility, not a fact. That place where preliminary psychophysical training, having educated one towards an embodied intuition, gives way to application of principles in structured improvisations – the known in the un-known.

The studio – a place that can never be completely sure of itself, where foundations will always be shaken, expectedly, at any moment. If we try to stand firm on this ground, it will always be loose beneath our feet – the disaster waiting to happen; the rug about to be pulled out; the pratfall waiting to happen; the 'shit' that happens. The studio reeks of the possibility of failure and loss. It cannot have the hubris or self-assurance of facts or answers, of 'faith' or 'belief'.

The studio ... a place of how, and 'what if', of make-believe, of what anthropologist Victor Turner so aptly identified as the 'subjunctive mood'[5] – the 'as if' of possibility and play ... the space between, where failure awaits us

... In that place on the edge, we meet the works of Beckett and perhaps confront ourselves in a self-reflexive mode. What Lao Tzu calls 'the space between heaven and earth'.[6]

As Mark Napier explains, the skill of make-believe depends on paradox, 'the acceptance of what empirically is not'.[7] In science this becomes hypothesizing. In the practice of masking is the art of hypothesizing 'what we are not': I am not that, yet I can 'be' that. 'Pretending is basic to our apprehension of change.' Masking is the most widespread form of disguise, and entering masking to experience and understand its conventions can tell us a lot about the notion of pretence, make-believe and paradox since it involves the masker very clearly in 'transformation': am I 'this' or am I 'not this?' This is so because masks, unlike make-up, are not only illusory but also simple and uncompromising devices for analysing the relationship between illusion, on the one hand, and the recognition and integrity of a face on the other. Masks are hypothetical and make-believe. They are paradoxical.[8] As Napier explains:

[D]isguise is the foremost example of how we articulate the problems of appearance in the context of change. The potential for ambiguity remains fundamental to change. The use of disguise is thus conducive both to make-believe and to changes of state that are imputed to be real.[9]

As a realm where paradox reigns, the studio is necessarily a site for philosophical exploration ... a site where, when you put on and embody the 'mask', you might be said to be practising 'philosophy in the flesh'. *Philosophy in the Flesh*, the title of the jointly authored book by philosophical linguists and cognitive scientists George Lakoff and Mark Johnson, in which they explain how

Living a human life is a philosophical endeavour. Every thought we have, every decision we make, and every act we perform is based upon philosophical assumptions so numerous we couldn't possibly list them all. We go around armed with a host of presuppositions about what is real, what counts as knowledge, how the mind works, who we are, and how we should act. Such questions, which arise out of our daily concerns, form the basic subject matter of philosophy: metaphysics, epistemology, philosophy of mind [and consciousness], ethics, and so on. Metaphysics, for example, is a fancy name for our concern with what is real. Traditional metaphysics asks questions that sound esoteric: What is essence? What is causation? What is time? What is the self? But in everyday terms there is nothing esoteric about such questions.[10]

Perhaps 'we are all metaphysicians' whenever we attempt to 'make sense of our experience' since it is 'through our conceptual systems that we are able to make sense of every life'.[11] All too often, as we all know, in our ' every dayness' we defer any attempt at 'making sense' of experience. As a paradoxical place where it is impossible to hide, and where our experience and our 'selves' are always reflected back to us, the studio offers a place for the unremitting examination of such everyday questions of experience. Perhaps our task, then, in the studio, is to 'practice metaphysics', i.e., thoughtfully to tease out in our specific modes of embodiment the assumptions and presuppositions about the body, mind, 'self' and 'action' that are at 'play' there, informing what we do and how we do it. That means systematic exploration of the nature of the bodymind, our consciousness and our 'selves', not as an empty 'academic' or intellectual exercise, but as an active experience 'on the edge of the absent' – that place where we 'risk' losing our craft and our selves.

The Polish theatre director Jerzy Grotowski provided one model for pursuing the rigours of what might be called the 'metaphysical studio' when he said, 'One cannot work on oneself [...] if one is not inside something which is structured and can be repeated, which has a beginning a middle and an end, something in which every element has its logical place, technically necessary.'[12] The psychophysical exercises I use in training performers provide one structure through which such an exploration can begin. There are many others, such as Stephen Wangh's process, involving a series of Grotowski-based exercises, that would allow the performer to pursue the issues and phenomena discussed here.[13]

In the metaphysical studio, one of the most fundamental questions to explore is how to discover what is 'necessary' in the performative moment. The 'necessary' is not a decision of the mind, but one of learning how to embody a sedimented decisiveness in space, through time; the how of that embodied relationship as it happens. [...]

1   Robert L. Benedetti, 'What We Need to Learn from the Asian Actor', *Educational Theatre Journal*, no. 25 (1973) 464.

2   Herbert Blau, *Take Up the Bodies* (Urbana: University of Illinois Press, 1982) 86.

3   Hollis Huston, *The Actor's Instrument* (Ann Arbor: University of Michigan Press, 1992) 27.

4   Koen Tachelet, 'Displaced Consciousness: Tracing the Blind Spot of Our Perception', *Performance Research*, no. 5 (2000) 87.

5   Victor Turner, *The Anthropology of Performance* (New York: PAJ Publications, 1986) passim.

6   A.C. Scott, unpublished lecture, University of Wisconsin–Madison (10 October 1979) 6.

7   Mark Napier, *Mask, Transformation and Paradox* (Berkeley and Los Angeles: University of California Press, 1986) 3.

8   Ibid., 3–4.

9   Ibid.

10 George Lakoff and Mark Johnson, *Philosophy in the Flesh* (New York: Basic Books, 1999) 9.

11 Ibid., 10.

12 Cited in Thomas Richards, *At Work with Grotowski on Physical Actions* (London and New York: Routledge, 1979) 2.

13 Stephen Wangh, *An Acrobat of the Heart: A Physical Approach to Acting* (New York: Vintage, 2000).

Phillip Zarrilli, extract from 'The Metaphysical Studio', *The Drama Review*, vol. 46, no. 2 (Summer 2002) 159–65.

Aimee Chang
Edgar Arceneaux: Drawings of Removal//2004

Edgar Arceneaux is interested in the relationship between artistic processes, most often drawing and psychology, physics and philosophy. His explorations – in the form of room-sized installations incorporating sculpture, drawings and ephemera – favour a non-linear and non-objective logic, paying attention instead to unintended connections, interstitial spaces and 'a different way to construct relationships between things'.[1] In early works he placed portraits of famous figures – *Star Trek*'s Mr Spock and Tuvoc, and rapper Tupac in one work, the nineteenth-century thinker Ralph Waldo Emerson and twentieth-century author Ralph Waldo Ellison in another – on single sheets of frosted vellum, delighting in alliteration and association while simultaneously probing the fundament of our culture. In keeping with his open-ended approach to information and with the way in which we receive information in our day-to-day lives, no distinction is made between fictional characters and real people, high and pop culture. More recent works – *Drawings of Removal* (1999–), *The Trivium* (2001), *Rootlessness* (2002), and *Lost Library* (2003) – take over entire rooms, allowing for more points of contact, an increased field of consideration, and deeper associations.

In 1998 Arceneaux and his parents took a road trip to his father's hometown, Beaumont, Texas. The artist was there for the first time, and his father had not been there in more than twenty-five years. They arrived in Texas and found the city practically unrecognizable. Recalling the trip, Arceneaux said: 'The house [my father] grew up in is completely gone, [the site] is just a grassy field with a tree stump. The geography itself had changed. They'd put in new streets – literally reconfiguring the landscape.'

Soon after, Arceneaux began working on *Drawings of Removal*, an ongoing exploration of memory through the medium of drawing. Consisting of layered sheets of drawings, some cut out and erased, and an on-site studio, the installation embodies the mnemonic process, displaying a conflation of theme and form that is emblematic of Arceneaux's work. His drawings stand in for processes and exist as metaphors. They are not so much representation as event, process made manifest. 'Memory', wrote Charles Gaines, a mentor to Arceneaux, 'has the structure of catachresis. And as such we understand how memory is a faculty operating in the present and not in the past. As a catachresis it is a misstatement that produces a paradox: the attempt to recover a moment in the past that is unrecoverable. The person who returns to a childhood neighbourhood finds him [or her]self not in the objects remembered from youth but in the empty space between that time and the moment of remembering'.[2] *Drawings of Removal* takes on this paradox and adds another one of its own. Time based and essentially unstable, the piece is, in the artist's words, 'literally active – something is being built and something is breaking down'. New pages replace old ones, and the layers build, reflecting the expansive process of memory itself. Images are also cut out, erased and scattered – fragments forgotten or barely remembered. Glancing through the cut-out holes, one can see additional drawings or sometimes the blank surface of an underlying sheet of paper or wall. The work, like memory, is cumulative.

Begun in 1999, *Drawings of Removal* has no foreseeable end. Also like memory, the work is bounded by space rather than by time. It contains all aspects of its own being and is created only within the makeshift studio that is a part of it. The tube in which the drawings are shipped from location to location stands in a corner, its mailing labels recording the work's itinerary. The tools – pencils, pens, rulers – that create the work are scattered about. Joining them are snapshots, exhibition announcements, books and clipped articles. The artist appears from time to time, changing elements, adding, subtracting. Gallery becomes studio becomes installation – the work is not so much something to see as somewhere to be. Like memory, it is a creative space separate from the place remembered. The presence of mirrors, new to this version of *Drawings of Removal*, is both an evocation of mirrored walls in the artist's own childhood home and a new and continuing motif in Arceneaux's work. Echoing the dislocation of memory, mirror images are as close as we can come to seeing ourselves, yet what we see is never the 'real' thing. Placed opposite each other, mirrors are also an intimation of the infinite – the flow of time and the unending mirroring of memory back upon itself. Throughout his work, Arceneaux has shown an interest in systems. A recent installation, *Library as Cosmos*, tackled the library of Alexandria, different forms of cataloguing, and the history of cartography. As a part of his larger body of work, *Drawings of Removal* traces a more organic organizational system. A chart of a lost landscape, it is perhaps also a shifting map of synaptic thought and an attempt to catalogue, in Arceneaux's signature open-ended way, a specific memory, shared across time and space.

1   All quotations from the artist are from a conversation with the author (30 January 2003).

2   Charles Gaines, 'Memory and the Sublime: Looking for the Jersey Devil', in Edgar Arceneaux, *107th Street Watts*, ed. Franklin Sirmans (Frankfurt am Main: Revolver/Archiv für aktuelle Kunst, 2003) unpaginated.

Aimee Chang, 'Edgar Arceneaux', *Hammer Projects, 1999–2009* (Hammer Museum, Los Angeles: 2009) 200–205. © 2009 The Regents of the University of California.

Manthia Diawara
The 1960s in Bamako: Seydou Keita//2001

[...] It is important to understand that at the time they were taking people's pictures in Bamako, neither Malick Sidibé nor Seydou Keita considered himself an artist. It is also important to understand that the types of photos each took and the perfection they both achieved in their work were a condition of the demand that existed at their respective times. Photographers in Bamako were no different than the barbers or tailors – they all beautified their clients or provided them with styles for the visual pleasure of people in Bamako. Their success depended on word of mouth, which contributed, as French sociologist Pierre Bourdieu would put it, to increasing their symbolic capitals. They only became artists by first pleasing their customers, by providing them with the best hair styles, dresses and photographs. Seydou Keita's photography was both enhanced and limited by the economic, social and cultural conditions prevailing in Bamako between 1945 and 1964, when he had to close his studio and become a civil servant for the socialist government in Mali. The people he photographed in his studio were from the middle class. They were from traditional Bamako families – businessmen and their wives, landlords and civil servants (schoolteachers, soldiers and clerks for the colonial administration). As a photographer, Seydou Keita's role was to make his subjects look like they belonged to the bourgeoisie and middle class of Bamako, to make them feel modern and Bamakois. The women were very beautiful, with their hair braided and decorated with gold rings, and their long dresses with embroidery at the neck. The men wore European suits or traditional boubous, and they exhibited their watches, radios or cars. Seydou Keita produced artifice through studio *mise-en-scène* and make-up to ensure that every one of his subjects looked like an ideal Bamakois, a bourgeois nobleman or woman, or a civil servant invested with the authority of the colonial administration.

When independence arrived in 1960 and the colonial administration had to cede its place to the new government of Mali, people's relation to photography, as to many other things in Bamako, began to change. Civil servants were no longer content with their intermediary roles between whites and Africans; they were now competing with the traditional leaders for control of the country. They no longer wanted to mimic the colonial administrator in Seydou Keita's studio; they wanted to be seen occupying the colonial master's chair at the office, his house, and his places of leisure. As these patterns of life changed in Bamako, new structures of feeling emerged and studio photography became devalorized as something conservative and artificial. Soon the studio's customers would be largely composed of people who needed passport and identification photos and visitors from rural areas. Seydou Keita's reaction to the changes was also conservative: not only did he have problems with the new socialist government, but he also found women in pants, mini-skirts, and Afro hairdos to be neither beautiful nor religiously acceptable in a predominantly Muslim country.

Thus, the change in power from a colonial system to an independent state brought about a profound transformation in people's sense of aesthetics in photography. Young people especially began to look upon studio photography as old-fashioned or as something reserved for people who were pretending to be Bamakois. To be photographed in the studio was associated with being a fake and a powerless pretender. In other words, studio photography was seen as unreal, whereas realism had become the criterion for defining the new aesthetics of Bamakois photography. By insisting on realism, people were demanding a new photography that portrayed them as actors in situations, a photography that was neither a studio re-enactment nor an imitation of something previously done. The new Bamakois wanted to be filmed while he or she took the centre of the action that was unfolding. Photographers therefore had to come out of the studio and follow the action wherever it was taking place. It was these limitations of studio photography – a genre fostered by colonialism – that led to Malick Sidibé's emergence as the photographer of the young generation. While maintaining his studio – largely for passport photos and camera repair – Sidibé took his camera to where the youth were and photographed them there. [...]

Manthia Diawara, extract from 'The 1960s in Bamako: Malick Sidibé and James Brown' (2001), in *Arts Culture and Society*, The Andy Warhol Foundation for the Visual Arts (www.warholfoundation.org)

Frances Richard
Seydou Keita//2006

Seydou Keita, 'the Bresson of Bamako', died in 2001, leaving a body of work specific to the postcolonial, urban Mali of the 1950s and 1960s. [...]

The photographs still speak about their sitters and about the artist who helped them to represent themselves as cosmopolitan individuals held in a matrix of familial, tribal, national and symbolic relations. As Manthia Diawara has observed, 'To go before Keita's lens is to pass the test of modernity.' To stand before his pictures now is to take the test again. How do we recognize this quality called 'modern'? How do we distinguish it from 'traditional'? The same questions apply to related pairings: sophisticated/naïve; African/Euro-American; collective/individual; authentic/inauthentic. [...]

Like all photographic portraiture, Keita's images conjure a threefold reality, comprising the sitter's manner, the historical moment, and the photographer's vision. Over the past decade, critics have repeatedly observed in Keita's work an opposition between African and Western, old and new. It's time to move past this either/or reading. Yes, his photographs are tessellated signs in which West African markers of status (scarifications, jewelry, fabrics) interlock with markers of urban chic and buying power (a radio, a watch, a handbag). But it's the interlocking, not the opposition, that is at stake. Keita's work captures the energy of the unique body – the crook of this one's elbow, the tilt of that one's chin – and in so doing secures the individual, separate (read: modern) subject in a web of contextual (read: traditional) relations.

This connective mesh is literalized in surface patterning and in the repetition of details. The same watch, the same lacy backdrop, the same foot-on-a-chair pose appear in many of these shots. Partly this reveals Keita as a businessman, repeating successful formulas. But it also realizes compositionally his understanding that such portraiture is neither innocent of commercialism (gangster movies, fashion magazines), nor separate from European high art (Matisse, the French Symbolists), nor detached from African kinship structures. Why, after all, should such things be disconnected? The fact that global audiences and competing impresarios now figure in the equation shouldn't surprise us either. Keita's art is both intensely local and totally adaptable to displacement. That's modernity for you.

Frances Richard, extract from 'Seydou Keita: Sean Kelly Gallery', *Artforum* (April 2006).

Hans Ulrich Obrist
A Rule of the Game//2008

[...] Science never really played a role for me at the beginning. I was completely ignorant about science. I didn't grow up with a scientific background, I didn't study it, and I didn't auto-didactically work on it. Then in 1993 I got a phone call from Christa Maar, who at that time was just about to set up the Academy of the Third Millennium with Hubert Burda. She had read an article about my unusual exhibitions on aeroplanes and in hotel rooms, and she thought it would be interesting to invite me to these meetings.

I went to Munich, and the first couple of times I was completely lost, because I had never met scientists before, I had never read science, and there were people there like Wolf Singer and Ernst Pöppel. After not saying anything during the first meetings, I then started to read systematically. And it was really through these experiences at the Academy of the Third Millennium that I began to build bridges with scientists. In the meantime I had started to work as a curator at the Musée d'art moderne in Paris, and each time a well-known scientist visited Paris, Christa would ring me and say, 'Show him your museum.' I started to walk with biologists and neuroscientists through the Rothko exhibition at our museum and that was really the beginning of how this whole bridge with science began.

A very interesting next step somehow happened. In a certain way, all my work in terms of curating, and expanding the notion of curating, has never been a priori defined, because it's almost like a long walk. It's a sort of *flânerie*, to use the French term. It's almost like strolling – a promenade. And chance plays a very big role. It's a sort of controlled chance but it's always about how to allow chance to come into the process.

Out of our conversations in 1995, Christa then invited me to do an exhibition for her first big conference in Munich, 'Mind Revolution', which was about the connection between the computer and the brain, between neuroscience and the computer. Bruce Sterling was there. It was the first time I met him. A lot of scientists were there, neuroscientists. But I felt intuitively that somehow it would be wrong to get artists to illustrate a scientific conference, and I also felt the conference wouldn't be the right place for an exhibition to take place, so, instead, I suggested to Christa, and to Ernst Pöppel, that we could invite artists to Pöppel's KFA in Jülich – artists from Douglas Gordon to Matt Mullican to Rosemarie Trockel to Carsten Höller.

Ernst was located near Cologne in Jülich, Germany's biggest science centre, which has hundreds of labs. He is a leading neuroscientist who is also part of

Edge [http://edge.org]. We thought we'd do a conference there, but then talking to Ernst Pöppel, we actually realized that this was again wrong, because to some extent why would we do a conference with artists and scientists who had never met, and who would feel put on the spot. Instead, we decided that the most important thing would be to create a contact zone, which wouldn't put people on the spot, where something could happen, but nothing had to happen.

I feel very often with my projects that we cannot force things. One cannot engineer human relations. One can set the conditions under which things then happen. For that reason, we decided, a few hours before the event was supposed to take place, to cancel the conference and to just do a 'non-conference'. It had all the ingredients of a conference – badges, tee shirts, bags with all the speakers' CVs, a hotel where all the people would stay, a bus to pick them up in the morning and bring them to the science centre, people at the airport picking the guests up, all of the logistics – but the conference no longer was there. It was just a coffee break. It was the invention of this idea that we should just do a coffee break. And it was my first project with art and science.

This came from that observation that obviously at a conference the most important things happen in the coffee break. Why do the rest? We'll just do the coffee breaks.

The most important things happen in interstitial spaces, they happen in between, and they happen when we least expect it. Incredible things happened. The artists visited the science labs they were interested in. At the end we made a little film, and everybody spoke about his or her impressions. We published a set of postcards. It was the first conference as a coffee break, of which we did many afterwards.

Just as Cedric Price talks about the 'non-plan' in urbanism, this was the 'non-conference'. That was the inspiration. As a curator, conferences and symposiums are not my main activity. But I felt it was a very interesting thing, because in exhibitions almost every single rule of the game has been invented. The whole twentieth century is a permanent invention of new ways of doing exhibitions. Almost every radical gallery gesture has been tested, from the full gallery, to the empty gallery – everything. Yet somehow with conferences and symposiums very little has been shifted in terms of rules of the game. It is always the same kind of protocol: there is the table, there are speakers, there is a speech by everyone, then there is discussion, then there is a Q&A, and then, maybe, there is a dinner. I think there is a huge potential to change the rules of the game.

Then we did 'Bridge the Gap?', which was in Japan with Akiko Miyake and CCA Kitakyushu, and it was again art and science, and we paid homage to Francisco Varela, who had just passed away. Varela was a very important person for me, a mentor, a great inspiration in the few meetings we had. We made a homage to him, so we invited a lot of his friends. At the same time, we also had scientists and artists and architects. We thought we'd do it in a remote house, on the outskirts of Kitakyushu. Guests would fly to Tokyo, and then there would be an internal Japanese flight, and then an hour-long car ride. Finally they were brought to this very old Japanese house so remote that once they were there, they couldn't get away anymore.

The idea was for three days to bring into the house all these incredibly busy people, who would usually immediately run away after their lecture and have meetings. We had rooms that were for official meetings, and then, inspired by online chat rooms, we had rooms where people could retire and have their own self-organized chats. There were a lot of rooms in the house, rooms for Hosts, Guests and Ghosts, to quote Marcel Duchamp.

There were about 30 or 40 speakers, all in one big house. There was a Japanese garden, so people could also stroll outside. And we had all the books by all the speakers inside, so there was a reading room that was a big success. The speakers went from Rem Koolhaas to Marina Abramovic, to Gregory Chaitin. Anton Zeilinger came with a little suitcase and made one of his teletransportation experiments.

The whole event was also about what the artist Paul Chan calls 'delinking'. That was also a conference that had to do with how we can delink very linked people.

Curating is my primary activity, even while experimenting with these different types of conferences, I always wanted to bring it back to the exhibition, which is my main medium. So, even though my whole venture into science actually started out with actually refusing to do an art and science show, I then, in 1999 with Barbara Vanderlinden, brought science back into the exhibition, and we did 'Laboratorium', which investigated how studios and labs are more and more interrelated. And we investigated the notion of the laboratory in the late twentieth and early twenty-first centuries. 'Laboratorium' was a transdiciplinary project searching the limits of the places where knowledge and culture are made. It started as a discussion that involved questions such as:

What is the meaning of 'Laboratorium'? What is the meaning of experiments? When do experiments become public and when does the result of an experiment reach public consensus?

We installed many laboratories all over the city:

A laboratory of doubt; a cognitive science laboratory; a highway for choreographic investigation; an existing artist's studio; the first laboratory of Galileo, etc. ...

We invited Bruno Latour to curate the theatre of proof, a series of demonstrations, a lecture series aiming at rendering public what happens in the laboratory. At the same time we declared the whole city of Antwerp a lab. And we found out that actually labs are very often invisible, part of the invisible city.

People were saying, 'You're crazy to do a show in Antwerp about labs. There are no labs in Antwerp.' But we had a whole group of researchers mapping every lab, and there were dozens of world-leading labs in Antwerp; people just didn't know about them. They're invisible. So, we had an 'open lab' day so people could visit the labs throughout the whole city. And then the museum became a place for all the artists' 'labs'.

The city got behind it. And we had full support from Antwerpen Open. It was really about the idea of the citywide lab exhibition, and then the museums. 'Laboratorium' showed me that the most effective thing for the issue of art and science is really this idea of doing something together to produce reality. [...]

Hans Ulrich Obrist, extract from talk for 'Experiment/Marathon/Reykjavic', curated in collaboration with the artist Ólafur Elíasson, Reykjavic Art Museum (15 May – 17 August 2008); first published by *Edge* (www.edge.org)

Caitlin Jones
The Function of the Studio (When the Studio is a Laptop)//2010

Brooding, solitary and usually male, the trope of 'the artist in the studio' has existed in multiple iterations throughout the history of art. From Rembrandt's workshop to the twentieth-century Parisian studios of Picasso, Braque and others, to Warhol's Factory, the studio contains within it an evolving narrative, albeit one that remains focused on a specific physical site of artistic production. In a particularly damning critique of this romantic construct, Daniel Buren posited in a 1971 essay, 'The Function of the Studio', that the studio has a 'simultaneously idealizing and ossifying function',[1] a state of 'purgatory' that grants artists limited agency in the production and dissemination of their own work and culture at large. Buren's essay is a concise example of the postmodern conception of 'post-studio' practice – a practice cultivated by the likes of Robert Smithson, who came to reject the confines of the physical studio as a site of production in favour of the unconfined natural landscape, or by John Baldessari's infamous 'Post-studio Art' class at CalArts, in which students were encouraged to 'stop daubing away at canvases or chipping away at stone'[2] and embrace a wider framework for art production. The influence of these artists is clearly evident in a range of contemporary artistic practices that continue to question traditional modes of production and dissemination.

The legacy of 'post-studio' art is amplified for artists working with digital forms and online environments. Generally these types of practices are less an overt negation of the 'ossifying' element of the studio and more a reflection of how the digital has changed cultural production at large. What happens when the studio in question is simply a laptop in the artist's kitchen or the local coffee shop? When the studio exists in a network space and is linked to countless other studios, shifting the studio experience from ossifying to dynamic? Or when the site of the studio is the same as that of exhibition and distribution?

Portraits of the 'Post-Studio' Laptop Studio
We write, communicate, relax and create on our computers, and our minds and bodies have become completely and seamlessly integrated to the form – the keyboard an outlet for language and the screen an extension of our eye. New York-based artist Erin Shirreff's *Shadow, Glare* (2010) brings the screen, with its smudges, spots and glares, quickly back into consciousness. Available for download from the online journal *Triple Canopy*, this work digitally simulates the effect of light and shadow moving across the screen, its movement and patterns simultaneously subtle and distracting. (http://canopycanopycanopy.com/9/shadow_glare) *Shadow, Glare* is a response to the increasing ubiquity and transparency of our computer screens and the moments when that transparency is broken. Or as the artist states in the introduction to the work, 'in my living room the light will shift and suddenly I'll be looking at all the dust on my computer screen or the splotches of light. That will really jar me back into my chair.' From an artist who works in both traditional and digital contexts, *Shadow, Glare* reads as a meditation on the lingering physicality that surrounds digital space. It is also a revealing portrait of the artist in her studio – capturing moments of distraction, focus and the areas in between.

The artist Petra Cortright provides a more traditional example of studio portraiture and illustrates the 'post-studio' laptop condition through a series of self-portraits. In her work *vvebcam* (2007), Cortright takes a customary position in front of her computer's webcam, the bluish glow of the monitor reflecting off of her unexpressive face. Her pose calls to mind the convention of the candle-lit self-portrait that heavily populates art history, but in this version the artist is in her bedroom and found graphics like pizza slices, tennis balls and lightning bolts move across the screen. *VVebcam* and other works by Cortright, including *cats spirt spsit spit* and *SSSSSSSSSSSSSWWWWWRRRRRLLLLLL* (both 2008; all works viewable at http://petracortright.com), refer more specifically to a contemporary mode of self-portraiture seen in abundance on YouTube in which legions of young women (or men) sit in their bedrooms performing for their webcams and, by extension, the world. The 'artist' in this case is still alone in the studio but has immediate access to a broader community. Cortright's repeated takes on this genre are emblematic not only in their content but also for the self-contained mode by which they are produced and distributed.

The emergence of the Internet accounts for probably the largest divergence between a physical studio and the laptop studio. There is the distraction factor (ready access to email, Facebook, YouTube, etc.), the easy research factor ('What painter wrote that essay about post-studio practice?'), but most importantly, it provides access to an unprecedented platform for sharing and collaboration. The image of the solitary artistic genius is replaced by a more collaborative mode of production. This collective spirit and its effects on online studio practices can be seen in a number of so-called surf clubs. Nasty Nets, Spirit Surfers, Loshadka and Double Happiness have generated, shared and provided commentary on a lot of content in the past four years. (http://nastynets.com, www.spiritsurfers.net, www. loshadka.org, http://double-happiness.org) Nasty Nets, one of the earliest and best known of these clubs, is a flexible affiliation of artists, academics and designers. Although they have never published any form of manifesto or general statement of purpose, they have continued to post links, sketches for works and ideas specific to this loose and collegial collective blog. The subject of much debate as to its place in the art world, Nasty Nets was described by contributor John Michael Boiling, in a particularly testy comments thread from October 2007, as a place 'where "art" often happens, but just as often as "not art" happens'. This lack of any concrete internal definition is part of what has made Nasty Nets so exciting to follow, as projects or inspirations that will likely never see the inside of a physical gallery find a perfect home online. Artist and contributor Kevin Bewersdorf, who is also founder of the more overtly art-specific surf club Spirit Surfers, referred to Nasty Nets (in the aforementioned comments string [no longer accessible]) as 'a public record of our hang out zone (HOZ), critics didn't used to be allowed in the HOZ or MUD (multi-user dungeon, domain or dimension). Now they can see it all'.

Always under Construction
Constant change, in the form of beta testing and perpetual updates, is integral to the World Wide Web. In her 2006 essay *The Vernacular Web*, artist Olia Lialina expounds upon the changing nature of the Web – from an amateur to a professional space – and devotes a considerable amount of discussion to the once ubiquitous 'under construction' sign. (http://art.teleportacia.org/ observation/vernacular/) These yellow and black graphics took multiple forms. Images of construction, such as hazard tape, construction workers and hard hats (in still, sparkling and blinking forms), were some of the most easily understood signs on the Web: 'work was everywhere and everywhere there was something that wasn't ready … "Always under Construction" didn't mean the site would

never work but actually the opposite. It informed users that there was somebody who was always taking care of the site so it would be interesting to return to again and again ... Even the mainstream press wrote that the web was always under construction so, after a while, people stopped putting it everywhere.'[3]

Without delving too far into a technologically determinant argument, many artists working online or with digital forms embrace forms of art production 'under construction' or 'in process' as a principal mode of engagement.

Oliver Laric is one of these artists. In both his Internet-based and gallery-based practice he has consistently drawn on ideas of construction and process, most recently in his work(s) *Versions* (2009). Comprised of sculpture, digital stills and video, *Versions* is an open-ended and ongoing meditation on the idea of completeness in an era when any 'original' image is instantly and constantly copied, remixed, retouched and circulated. Inspired in part by the missile-launch photographs doctored by the Iranian government in 2008, *Versions* follows a trail of image manipulation from Iran through Disney to hardcore pornography. (http://oliverlaric.com/versions.htm) Multiple iterations of the video portion of *Versions* exist with invited interpretations by artists, including Momus, Guthrie Lonergan and Dani Admiss. And as amplification of the open-ended nature of Laric's work, an unknown artist uploaded their own version to YouTube unbeknownst to Laric – a practice the artist has encouraged in other projects. Versions stands out as a clear example of the conflation of production and dissemination occurring within the site of the computer. Researching, viewing, compiling, production, post-production, exhibition and distribution double and triple back on themselves in a way that renders their separation untenable, and possibly even undesirable.

In a recent project for the online conceptual fashion magazine *DIS*, artist Ryan Trecartin makes the process of production giddily visible. Trecartin was invited to create a photo spread for the high-end fashion magazine *W* (November 2010) and responded with a hyperactive yet completely accurate vision of consumer culture and social networking. As a postscript to the *W* magazine spread, the *DIS* piece, titled *Web 1.0*, lays bare the shot list for the *W* photo shoot. (http://dismagazine.com/dysmorphia/9844/ryan-trecartin-w-magazine/) *Web 1.0* illustrates a dizzying range of influences and requirements for hair, makeup and items to be procured, such as these two samples:

2. The Hair Style:: I want to take an **Ed Hardy Hat**

And cover it Mostly with **White Out** (Crusty and some what see-through): One will still be able to tell it's a Hardy dump
The White Out bottle will then be
Hooked to a **Belly Chain**, It will

hang off the Hat to the side of the
Head above Ear

On the Rim of the hat I want to
create a 'Belly Button' situation by
finding a Plastic Button or making
one in **Post** that looks like Either a
'**Internet Mail Button**' or a '**Computer Power Button**' [...]

In Post I want to **Merge the Home
Depot logo with the Mexican Flag,** And
Have it look like it's Transparently yet
richly printed into the clothing. OR at least
fused in some way ...

Trecartin's treatment of 'accessories', such as Marc Jacobs bags, software
application icons and car steering wheels, reflects a vision of a hyperactive
contemporary consumer culture where status and meaning are conferred by
nearly everything around us. In juxtaposition to the high production value of the
images in the luxury-concerned *W*, *Web 1.0* feels more like a snapshot of the
Internet – an equalizing space where professional and DIY, luxury and banality,
high and low coexist in gleeful harmony.

This notion of cultural levelling is also the subject of Aleksandra Domanovic's
Biennale (Dictum Ac Factum) (2009) (http://aleksandradomanovic.com/
dictumacfactum.html) A collaborator (with Oliver Laric, Christoph Priglinger and
Georg Schnitzer) in the online curatorial project *VVork.com* (www.vvork.com),
Domanovic, similarly to Trecartin in *Web 1.0*, investigates how cultural products
– art, cinema, music, commercials or politics – are read differently when viewed
through the frame of our computer screens. The speed and ease with which one
can search Google, YouTube or Wikipedia for information, music and film has
radically altered our understanding of the process of research, and *Biennale
(Dictum Ac Factum)* takes this shift as its subject.

Made as part of the Internet Pavilion project (http://manetas.com/
padiglioneinternet/) at the 2009 Venice Biennale, Domanovic's work, a single
website composed with embedded images, audio files and YouTube clips, was
originally inspired by both Lars von Trier's stripped-down set for his film *Dogville*
and the inclusion of the BitTorrenting site The Pirate Bay (http://thepiratebay.
org) in the same pavilion. Domanovic uses von Trier as her starting point, the
filmmaker himself inspired by Bertolt Brecht's idea of *verfremdungseffekt* (a
theatrical device used to distance the audience from the action or character on

stage) and the song 'Pirate Jenny' from *The Threepenny Opera*. Combined with her own personal influences, dreams and anxieties, Domanovic creates a work that makes visible the endless paths and circuitous routes of influence and appropriation – always under construction and always close at hand.

All Together Now

Thus the studio is a place of multiple activities: production, storage and finally, if all goes well, distribution.[4]

These words by Daniel Buren were originally meant as a critique of the traditional studio system, but the quotation in fact offers a prescient description of art production today. For many artists the notion of the studio does not present a problem to be dismantled or deconstructed. The laptop studio serves simultaneously as the tool, the space, the product and the frame. This conflation of the studio's many functions is the goal, and quite often the meaning of the work.

The 'post-studio' laptop studio has other meaningful implications for contemporary art production. The concept of access transforms significantly within this notion of the studio. Access to (virtual) studio space, public access to artists' work, artist access to materials – each of these transactions is enhanced in the shift. Traditional 'open studio' conventions are rendered obsolete as, by its very nature, the laptop studio can always be 'open'. The 'post-studio' laptop studio also significantly disrupts the temporal process of the traditional studio – moments of research, production and dissemination are continually evolving and reorganizing.

In these ways, post-studio practice in a contemporary sense could be understood less as a reaction against established norms of production and distribution and more a reaction to expanded cultural platforms writ large.

1   Daniel Buren, 'The Function of the Studio' (1971), trans. Thomas Repensek, *October*, no. 10 (Fall 1979) 55; reprinted in this volume, 83–9.

2   John Baldessari, 'Oral History interview with John Baldessari', 4–5 April 1992, Archives of American Art (Washington, D.C: Smithsonian Institution) (http://www.aaa.si.edu/collections/oralhistories/transcripts/baldes92.htm)

3   (http://art.teleportacia.org/observation/vernacular/uc/)

4   Daniel Buren, 'The Function of the Studio', op. cit., 53.

Caitlin Jones, 'The Function of the Studio (When the Studio is a Laptop)', *Artlies*, no. 67 (Fall/Winter 2010) (www.artlies.org).

THERE
IS NOT ANY
PAPERWORK
IN EVIDENCE,
ONLY

BOXED MUSICAL
and
RECORDING EQUIPMENT,
and
A SINGLE OPEN BOOK
ON THE COUCH.

Yet the various objects and furniture in the image do indicate potential activity: the book, musical equipment,

AN ASHTRAY AND
A CASE OF BEER

Ian Wallace, *Corner of the Studio* and *El Taller*, 2005

Francis V. O'Connor
Hans Namuth's Photographs of Jackson Pollock as Art-Historical Documentation//1978

Hans Namuth's photographs and films of Jackson Pollock document the physical environment and painting technique of one of America's most famous and controversial artists at the peak of his career: 1950 to 1956. Just as Daguerre's famous 1839 view of a boulevard in Paris documents facts about early nineteenth-century chimney pots, roof carpentry and shoeshine boys before it assumes its status as a turning point in Western visual culture, Namuth's images of Pollock are visual records before they are works of art. What a photograph says in itself and what others can say about it produces a subtle triangulation between (1) the physical record of what light etched at a given moment on a given chemical emulsion; (2) the meaning of that data relative to an art historian's inevitably selective and usually subjective purpose; and (3) the role of the image as a cultural 'icon'. It is a tribute to the strength of Namuth's technical and visual sensibility that his images of Jackson Pollock not only record the artist at work but in certain instances have come to symbolize the aesthetic roots of an entire school of American painting.

Namuth made two films and approximately 500 still photographs of Pollock between 1950 and the end of the artist's life. Both films, and the great majority of the still photographs, show the artist in the act of painting. The remaining stills record the studio at East Hampton, several of Pollock's most important exhibitions, and his changing appearance during the last years of his life.

About Pollock's studio, the photographs tell us that it was a converted barn with numerous chinks between the wall boards. This primitive construction reduced painting, for Pollock, to a seasonal occupation, though he occasionally worked in winter, using dangerous kerosene stoves for heat. Only in the very last years of his life could he afford to insulate his studio for year-round work. Fortunately, at East Hampton the weather is relatively mild into the early winter and spring can be early. But painting was, for Pollock, in many ways determined by the cycle of nature.

The photographs also reveal that Pollock was constantly surrounded by his earlier work. As with insulation, there was no 'stack' space built into the studio until late in his life. His life's work lined the walls of the studio and was kept face up so he could engage in a constant visual dialogue with his origins and achievements. Other photographs of 1951 show how many of his famous 'black and white' paintings of that year were painted on long strips of canvas 'in series' – to be cut apart and stretched later. These photographs will prove invaluable when someone comes to study Pollock's 'iconography' in terms of the juxtaposition of images revealed. The positioning of human heads next to less 'representational' configurations will shed light on the meaning of such major works as *Portrait and a Dream* (1953). One can also find in these photographs at least one 'underpainting' – that for *Number 1* (1952).

But above all else, Namuth's photographs and films make explicit Pollock's famous and seriously misunderstood painting technique. First of all, they reveal that when a very large painting was in process, its area reduced Pollock's work space to just a few feet around its edge. The flat plane of the canvas – a literal recreation of the uninhabited plain of Tanguy or Dalí, or the empty plane of Miró – had to be reached without entering. The painting process therefore became an ongoing tension between the edges and the centre of the canvas and Pollock's gestures of bending, kneeling, stretching and straddling corners constituted an intense and awkward struggle against relentless, self-imposed limits. After the very early stages of laying in the initial design, he could not step into the canvas; he was remanded to the periphery of the four sides of the canvas, painting towards the centre in an intense, mandalic dance which is most dramatically revealed in the films.

The films also help to redefine what is commonly, and imprecisely, described as Pollock's 'drip' technique. He began to utilize this method in earnest in 1947 and developed endless variations on it over the years. While Pollock himself once spoke of preferring 'dripping fluid paint', and of how it is possible 'to control the flow of the paint', he never specifically characterized his technique. Unfortunately, the English language does not contain one word which comprehensively describes the full complexity of his famous method.

'To drip', according to the *Oxford English Dictionary*, means 'to let [a liquid] fall in drops' and is totally unsuited to describe a process of painting which was intended to produce a predominantly linear effect. 'To flow' is essentially an intransitive verb which attributes too much agency to the medium itself and implies a flooding, planar effect foreign to Pollock's work. Other verbs, such as 'to splatter', 'to splash', 'to dribble', 'to trickle', etc. connote a capriciousness of intention similar to the implications of 'to drip'. The one word which comes closest to describing accurately both the artistic results and the kinetic realities of Pollock's technique is the transitive verb 'to pour'. The OED defines 'to pour' as 'to emit in a stream; to cause or allow [a liquid or granular substance] to flow out of a vessel or receptacle; to discharge or shed copiously'.

Pollock's method ought, therefore, to be called the 'pouring technique'. It must, however, be further defined in terms of the varied physical situations encountered in actually painting a picture – situations for which Namuth's films constitute primary evidence.

In general, the films show liquid paint propelled across flat canvases of varying size. As the paint traverses the air it enters trajectories that are recorded instantly and accurately when the paint lands on the surface. Thus the paint, forming itself in space as it travels in time over a predetermined area, sets down an accurate picture of the force – either gentle or violent – which initially impelled it. As can be seen in Namuth's colour film of Pollock painting, the speed and rhythm of this process were functions of the size of the work and the complexity of its execution. *Number 29* (1950), filmed from below as it was painted on glass, was slowly and carefully poured over collage elements. The other painting created on the ground in the colour film (on canvas – and later destroyed by the artist), was poured out with a quicker weaving, tossing, rhythmic gesture required by its larger scale. The short black-and-white film, which reveals Pollock's technique more explicitly than the colour film, shows the artist beginning with a studied pouring out of an elegant black 'drawing' over the entire surface of a long, narrow ground. He then proceeds to develop this initial drawing, carefully countering its formal elements (some of which are suggestive of figures) with an ever more dense and complex interweaving of strands of paint. In doing so he picks up speed, entering into the momentum of the process until he is working furiously around the four sides of the painting. Thus, by speeding up or slowing down the pouring process, and by employing different kinaesthetic gestures – a thrust of the arm, a flick of the wrist – varied effects are obtained: elegant delicacy, complex linearity, feathery calligraphy, intricate density. None of these dynamic effects are adequately described by the idea of 'dripping'; all find either literal or figurative definition in the human process of 'pouring out' which Namuth's films so dramatically document. [...]

Francis V. O'Connor, extract from 'Hans Namuth's Photographs of Jackson Pollock as Art-Historical Documentation', first published in French in *Hans Namuth, L'Atelier de Jackson Pollock* (Paris: Macula/ Pierre Brochet, 1978) 11–15; reprinted in *Art Journal*, vol. 39, no. 1 (Fall 1979) 48–9.

Barbara Dawson
7 Reece Mews: Francis Bacon's Studio//1998

[...] Situated on a quiet cobbled lane in South Kensington, London, this modest mews was Bacon's home for the last thirty years of his life. He moved in during the autumn of 1961 and lived there until his death in 1992. [...]

Steep wooden stairs approached the accommodation on the first floor. A ship's rope handrail secured to the wall helped the ascent. The small studio, measuring 8 x 4 metres was to the right at the top of the stairs. To the left was a kitchen-cum-bathroom. In stark contrast to the studio, these rooms were ordered and tidy.

This studio at Reece Mews was just a stone's throw away from Bacon's other famous studio at 7 Cromwell Place, where he lived from 1943 to 1951. [...] Indeed, Bacon was a creature of habit and all of his studios were within about a two-mile radius of each other. Although he bought several other properties, he never strayed from the Chelsea and Kensington area.

The chaos of his Reece Mews studio became famous. Vying for floor space amid the boxes and slashed canvases were art catalogues, hundreds of photographs, creased and torn, books on wildlife, male anatomy, cricket, Egyptian sculpture and the supernatural. Such diversity suggests the range of material he consulted.

After Bacon's death John Edwards, his longtime companion and heir, concluded that his studio should be preserved in an appropriate location where it could be on public view. When he decided to donate it to the Hugh Lane [the city gallery in Bacon's birthplace, founded by Lane in 1908], the gallery at once brought together the necessary expertise to excavate the studio and bring the contents to Dublin. [...]

An increasing familiarity with the Reece Mews studio revealed a method in the chaos. The easel placed to the right of the door was positioned to best benefit from the morning light which filtered through the skylight. The naked bulbs hanging from the ceiling, which appear in so many of Bacon's paintings, were the only lights, and the sole blue bulb provided additional daylight effect. The two windows facing west were blocked out by mosquito nets brought back from one of Bacon's many visits to Tangier in the 1950s. Large canvases stacked up facing the walls and blocking the windows towered like sentinels over the mounds of source material strewn around.

The area around the easel was relatively clear, allowing the artist to manoeuvre around the canvas. The table of paintbrushes was within easy reach and his source references lay on the ground nearby. It was also possible to pick out the path that cut through the books, catalogues, photographs, illustrations and boxes to the table and shelves at the east end of the room where a circular mirror dominated the wall. Heavily oxidized from the paint toxins, it could possibly be one of the mirrors which feature in *The Studio* article of 1930 [surveying a modernist studio created by Bacon when he was also an interior designer]. However, although he used mirrors as spatial devices in his paintings, a circular-shaped mirror never appears.

On the shelves in front of the mirror, Libby's Orange Juice and Bachelor's Peas tins were crammed full of used brushes. To the left of the mirror was a table supporting an incredible diversity of materials. The table was removed to the Hugh Lane in one piece. [...] It was found to contain approximately 600 items, many of which were not used since the early 1960s.

Piles of books, fallen in a heap, had obviously been stacked on the shelves behind the table at some stage. A small easel stood abandoned to the right of the door beside a cane-backed chair, probably the one used for *Portrait of John Edwards* (1988). Behind the main easel was the dumping area where empty boxes for Krug, Tattinger and Château Petrus lay discarded. No palette was found in the studio. Instead Bacon seemed to prefer to use the walls, the door and small canvases. He referred to the beautiful paint-splattered walls as 'my only abstract paintings'. The heavily impasted wall to the left of the mirror is a magnificent explosion of pure colour, and the other walls continue this vibrancy. Both sides of the door were used for paint tests, indicating that Bacon painted when the door was open as well as closed. [...]

Barbara Dawson, extract from 'Francis Bacon's Studio: A Stimulating Solitude', in *7 Reece Mews: Francis Bacon's Studio* (Dublin: Dublin City Gallery The Hugh Lane, 1998).

Albrecht Barthel
Brancusi's Studio: A Critique of the Modern Period Room//2006

Constantin Brancusi (1876–1957) was a pioneer of abstract sculpture. In 1907, the Romanian-born sculptor briefly worked in the atelier of Auguste Rodin, but left, claiming that he needed his own space. Nothing grows in the shade of large trees, he would later say.[1] Brancusi eventually broke with academic tradition, preferring to work in stone with no intermediary plaster model. Within a few years, he had developed nearly all the main themes of his abstract sculptural work. He became close friends with Henri Rousseau, Marcel Duchamp, Erik Satie and Man Ray. Ray taught Brancusi photography, which became an important documentary and artistic medium for him. In 1916, Brancusi began to live and work in the cité d'artistes in Montparnasse, a mews of humble studios consisting of thin stone walls and wooden frameworks. He would spend the rest of his life in impasse Ronsin No. 11. Brancusi gradually enlarged the studio by renting adjacent rooms; he used two spaces for his living and work quarters, and connected three additional spaces to form a large showroom, where he displayed his past and ongoing work.

Judging from the numerous photographs of the space, most of them taken by the artist, as well as contemporary descriptions, Brancusi's studio must have possessed a captivating aura. Paul Morand compared the space to a Gothic cathedral of endless columns.[2] For Man Ray, entering Brancusi's studio was like 'penetrating into another world'.[3] The studio was described as a sacred forest, an enchanted or mythical place where every object, even the tools, seemed to 'vibrate with a supernatural presence'.[4] The material substance of this sanctuary showed all signs of wear and tear, among them the oft-repaired glass slates, the cracked walls, the rough-timbered wooden frames and the raw concrete floor.

By the mid 1940s, Brancusi had arranged his sculptures in their final positions. As his productivity began to fail, he became a curator of his own studio and welcomed visitors on his premises, most of them American. By 1946, a threat arose when the neighbouring Hospital Necker demanded that the cité d'artistes be demolished for its expansion. Protracted negotiations ensued to safeguard the studio as long as Brancusi was alive, but its future after his death remained uncertain. In a joint effort, the curators of the Musée d'art moderne and the Musée Rodin tried to persuade Brancusi that his studio should be transferred to one of Rodin's studios at Meudon. Given that Brancusi had left Rodin's 'shade' to go his own way, his refusal came as no surprise.[5] Brancusi persisted with the hope of keeping his studio intact until April 1956, when fatigue and serious illness forced him to bequeath the space and his sculptures to the French state. Brancusi died in March 1957. Sculptor Henryk Berlewi led the last protest against the studio's demolition immediately before Brancusi's death, stating, 'Brancusi's studio may not be demolished … The preservation of this studio, which is absolutely intact, in which everything should be left in the order or disorder it is presently in, is self-evident.'[6] He argued that Brancusi's bequest could only be interpreted as mandating the preservation of the studio *in situ* as an entity of the historic building and its contents. Alternatively, Jean Cassou, chief curator of the Musée d'art moderne, and fellow conservators saw the building, decaying from the lack of maintenance, as an irretrievable cracked shell. It was a threat to the valuable contents inside and should be removed without delay.[7] From a curatorial standpoint, this stance may have been accepted protocol, but it failed to recognize that Brancusi had lived and worked within the studio for nearly thirty years, exposing himself and his creations to the building's decay. Therefore, its very substance was an integral part of the works of art that had taken shape within its confines. The building also contained manifold information that, apart from historiographic interest, bore immediate witness to the artist's everyday life. The 1961 demolition irrevocably destroyed Brancusi's studio. Three subsequent reconstructions of the studio would fail to recapture what had been lost in the demolition, even though they would display Brancusi's sculptures in their original configuration.

Palais de Tokyo (1962–77)

With the artist's prior consent to exhibiting some of his sculptures, a Brancusi sculpture gallery was inaugurated in early 1962 in the Palais de Tokyo, at that time the site of the Musée d'art moderne. Chief curator Jean Cassou would later pronounce the partial anastylosis of Brancusi's former showroom as a 'reconstruction of the studio'.[8] In fact, most of the sculptures were arranged in their exact original positions, but their new setting did not bear any resemblance to the historic studio. The ceilings were low, and some of the larger pieces could not be exhibited. The confining surfaces were neatly painted walls and a parquet floor. The original studio had been flooded with daylight from its clerestories; here, there was no natural light at all.

The excision of his *orphelins* – or 'children' as Brancusi used to call his sculptures – from their original context also encouraged intrusions on the artwork itself. Conservators involved in the latest restoration have reported that art historians at the Musée d'art moderne made alterations to the pedestals of the sculptures in violation of the artist's intentions.[9] These transgressions included smoothing and repairing what were perceived as irregularities. The ideal of an immaculate, timeless presentation of the highly valued works misguided curators into eliminating traces of wear and tear that could have been preserved. Conservators, too, erased irregularities caused by Brancusi's manual craftsmanship. In the shelter of the original studio, such assaults to the integrity and authenticity of the sculptures perhaps would not have taken place. During Brancusi's lifetime, the studio's decay and his readiness to adapt the art to its aura went hand-in-hand.

As early as 1958, Carola Giedion-Welcker published a book of 86 photographs taken by Brancusi of the original studio and of individual sculptures.[10] Alexander Liberman followed in 1960 with his book *The Artist in His Studio*, which features photographs capturing the roughness of the studio and its sculptures.[11] The photographs illustrate the dense atmosphere of the studio and its context: the leaves that filtered the sunlight over the walls and sculptures, as well as the intimacy with neighbouring workspaces and the street. Both publications gained wide recognition and proved the inadequacy of the installation in the Palais de

Tokyo, prompting a reconsideration of how accurately to display Brancusi's artwork to the public.

The First Reconstruction (1977–90)

In the late 1960s, discussions began for the creation of a new museum of modern art, the Musée national d'art moderne (Mnam) at the Centre Georges Pompidou. Initially, the plan was to integrate the studio into the complex, which would have limited any naturalistic qualities of its reconstruction. In April 1976, Pontus Hultén, the new director of Mnam, and Robert Bordaz, the president of the Centre Pompidou, agreed to reconstruct the studio as an identical clone of the original building, adjacent to the Centre. The scale of the two buildings was completely disproportionate; the Centre dwarfed the studio with its sheer mass. The Centre presented itself as a high-tech-art-exhibition machine, displaying its vast technical entrails in bright colours, while the reconstructed studio celebrated crude naturalism.

Hultén's praise for 'the moving and significant evocation of the conditions the artist creates and lives in at the foot of the most ambitious of cultural programmes' sounded false to the majority of those who had first-hand experiences with the original studio and Brancusi.[12] They could not match the replica to their own memories of the studio. The marks of transitoriness and the density accumulated by the imprints of time were associated with Brancusi's presence, a quality that *a priori* could not be replicated. The painter Jacques Herold perceived the reconstruction as 'something fabricated', which did not 'exude the same power, the same intensity. Brancusi's studio was very old, the ground only soil, the walls partly damaged and dissolving'.[13] The sculptor François Lalanne was 'certain that Brancusi would not have his studio reconstructed; that is absolutely ridiculous and not in his sense. … Brancusi himself never thought of reconstruction. He wanted his studio to remain on its original site … that there would be an artistic colony, with his studio as the centre.'[14] Lalanne describes an essential aspect of authenticity relating to context: the studio *in situ* would have had the potential to retain its *raison d'être*, not to be fossilized in a museum and preserved ad infinitum. The studio would have served as an agent for further artistic production: preservation, presentation and production augmenting one another.

The reconstruction suffered severe construction and curatorial deficiencies. After heavy rains, the replica, which had permitted visitors to enter the studio replica on a small-cordoned lane, was closed in June 1990. Considering that the original studio was more than amply documented, it is remarkable that the Mnam has never published plans or photographs of either the reconstruction or the installation in the Palais de Tokyo.[15] There seems to be a reluctance to have a visual comparison of the exhibit to its predecessors.

The New Studio Brancusi (1997 – present)

Aware of the sculptures' ever-increasing art-value, curators wanted to eliminate any further hazards to their security and conservation. After an intermediary exhibition at the Centre Pompidou, the director of the Musée national d'art moderne, Dominique Bozo, responded to curator Jean-Paul Ameline's desire to provide a new, dignified building of the highest curatorial standards to equal Brancusi's bequest.

Designed by the Renzo Piano Workshop and inaugurated in early 1997, the new building combined the highest architectural standards with optimized curatorial conditions for displaying Brancusi's sensitive sculptures. The building was modelled after the original studio in its volume, shape and wooden framework, but naturalistic imitations were avoided. The new studio is surrounded by an ambulatory, and separated by ceiling-high glazing that offers an unimpeded view of the sculptural installation within but no physical access. From the outside, solid walls separate the ambulatory, with only a view upon an enclosed garden, or *hortus conclusus*, that evokes the idyll of the impasse Ronsin.

At an early stage of planning, visitors were supposed to view the studio through unglazed openings that would have represented the original windows and door of the studio, but these were considered 'insufficient for easy viewing of all works, as well as impractical, especially if several visitors were to crowd an opening'.[16] The unglazed openings were also considered problematic in creating the ideal conservation setting. Although quasi-naturalistic, this concept would have upset the parameters of the original studio, as it placed the sculptures and the visitors in separate spaces. Yet it still represented the studio as a volume defined by solid walls. The problems of convenience in presentation might – at least to some extent – have been resolved by working on approaches that would not have disturbed the spatial integrity, such as restricted access or prolonged opening hours. But again, curatorial concerns outweighed other considerations. A majority of the solid walls were replaced by glazing, a tremendous deviation from the original space, dissolving the volume of the studio into the surrounding ambulatory.

The glazing affected the spatial dispositions of the sculptures. The background of solid walls is no longer there to support them and they are exposed to views from places that Brancusi never intended them to be seen. Thus, the visitor finds him or herself confronted with an analytical representation of the studio that, although everything seems to be in place, does not consider distance. This perception is intensified by the 'invisible' glazing, as Peter Buchanan, a historiographer for the Renzo Piano Workshop, concedes: 'The glass as usual betrays the promise of its transparency and seems to distance the artworks as much as render them visible'.[17]

Brancusi's sculpture arrangement was focused towards the studio's centre, allowing his visitors to encounter each sculpture individually in a dialogue that, besides mere visual perception, included kinaesthetic qualities of close sight. On the contrary, what is true for most museum period rooms applies to the present curation. Jeremy Aynsley states, 'In terms of representational strategies, the orthodoxy of the museum period room is to look onto the interior, as if the fourth wall were removed. … In this sense, the experience of looking onto a naturalist setting of an unpeopled room is not totally removed from viewing its representation on the published page.'[18] Or, in the words of Amelia Cidro: 'The logic of a museum – to expose – cannot reconstruct intimacy with the sculptures, this certain tendency to hide, to reveal themselves bashfully, like the *più bella*, a statue of Giacometti's that wants to be discovered, to be noticed, but not be blandly smashed into the spectator's face.'[19]

The inaccessibility of period rooms can be vexing, since the space is distanced as much from the present onlooker as it is from its original purpose. But in the case of three-dimensional art, exclusiveness and stasis become fundamentally problematic as the sculptures are divested of their immanent artistic dimension to provoke contact.[20] Sequestered, artworks are reduced to relics, to be admired with an uncritical attitude of reverent appreciation – a cult based on humbling distance.[21] The installation also evokes the ostentation of precious goods, pristine for the sake of market value, as much displayed as guarded in their showcase, a capital that may not be consumed. This logic does not follow innate dimensions of artworks, and in overriding the artist's intentions the present curation is not free from an exploitative connotation.

Failures of Conservation and Reconstruction

The first phase of the studio's curation since Brancusi's death – which encompassed the destruction of the original studio, the partial exhibition at the Palais de Tokyo, and the studio's reconstruction adjacent to the Centre Pompidou – was distinguished by the loss of the material substance of the studio. The attempt to reconcile that loss with an uncritical substitute proved elusive and even harmful to the artwork. In despite of its defects, the exhibition at the Palais de Tokyo at least attempted to retrace part of the studio's narrative and was anchored in historicity in the arrangement of the sculptures in their original geometric positions. The most recent trial is a radical reinterpretation of Brancusi's studio, dwelling and artwork. It casts the installation as something timeless, as far removed from its origin as from its decay. In this iteration, there are no intrusions on substance, but Brancusi's artistic intentions are rendered null, since he never intended for his sculptures to be viewed from an outside ambulatory.

Conservation theorist Alois Riegl contended that age-value 'turns most forcefully against having a monument uprooted from its organic context and confined into a museum, although exactly there it would most certainly rise above necessity of restoration'.[22] While the latest design provides an optimized conservation setting, providing uninterrupted views of the spaces, it lacks a coherent depiction of Brancusi's life as an artist.

If the original building and artwork had not been dissociated, any interventions on Brancusi's sculptures or their presentation, such as the removal of walls for a 'better' view, would have met fierce resistance, since the studio would have remained a coherent manifestation of Brancusi and his sculpture. In such a context, even the replacement of originals with exact replicas to grant access to the studio space would not have been unfeasible. The artwork was not the sole referent of the studio's authenticity, but it is the only authentic record of Brancusi's studio that remains.

1   Michel Seuphor, *Die Plastik unseres Jahrhunderts. Wörterbuch der modernen Plastik* (Cologne: Neuenburg, Ed. du Griffon, 1959) 241.

2   Marielle Tabart, *L'atelier Brancusi* (Paris: Centre Georges Pompidou, 1997) 197.

3   Man Ray, *Self-Portrait* (New York: Little, Brown and Company, 1963).

4   Dorothy Dudley, 'Brancusi' (1927) in Friedrich Teja Bach, *Constantin Brancusi: Metamorphosen plastischer Form* (Bonn: Dumont, 1987) 321.

5   Ibid., 252 (Interview Jean Cassou).

6   Germain Viatte, 'Une longue marche pour l'atelier de Constantin Brancusi', in Tabart, *L'atelier Brancusi*, op. cit., 14.

7   Ibid., 14. [...]

8   Friedrich Teja Bach, op. cit., 252. [...]

9   Chantal Quirot, Juliette Lévy et Astrid Lorenzen, 'L'atelier de Brancusi au Musée national d'art moderne', in *Revue du Louvre*, no. 2 (Paris, 1996) 77–86.

10   Carola Giedion-Welcker, *Constantin Brancusi* (Basel and Stuttgart: Schwabe & Co, 1958).

11   See also Alexander Liberman, *The Artist in his Studio* (New York: Viking Press, 1960).

12   Pontus Hultén, quoted by Germain Viatte, in *Tabart*, op. cit., 17.

13   Bach, op. cit., 260.

14   Ibid., 263. Lalanne stands for a couple of other artists cited in Bach's interviews.

15   See Tabart, op. cit.

16   Peter Buchanan, *Renzo Piano Building Workshop, Complete Works*, vol. 4 (London and New York: Phaidon Press, 2000) 29.

17   Buchanan, op. cit., 29.

18   Jeremy Aynsley,'The Modern Period Room – a contradiction in terms?' in *The Modern Period Room: The Construction of the Exhibited Interior 1870–1950*, ed. Penny Sparke, Brenda Martin and Trevor Keeble (London and New York: Routledge, 2006) 14.

19   Amelia Cidro, 'Atelier: Brancusi, Giacometti, Bacon', *Golem-l'indispensabile*, no. 1, January 2002,

http://www.golemindispensabile.it: [...]

20 See Michael Gubser, *Time's Visible Surface: Alois Riegl and the Discourse on History and Temporality in Fin-de-Siècle Vienna* (Detroit: Wayne State University Press, 2006) 208/ [...]

21 Gubser, op. cit., 209. [...]

22 Alois Riegl, *Der moderne Denkmalkultus, sein Wesen und seine Entstehung* (Vienna 1903), transl. K.W. Forster and D. Ghirardo, *Oppositions*, no. 25 (Fall 1982) 41.

Albrecht Barthel, 'The Paris Studio of Constantin Brancusi: A Critique of the Modern Period Room', *Future Anterior*, vol. III, no. 2 (Winter 2006) 34–44.

Jon Wood
The Studio in the Gallery?//2005

Close Encounters

[...] The exhibition 'Close Encounters: The Sculptor's Studio in the Age of the Camera' (Henry Moore Institute, Leeds, 2001–2) focused on photographs of sculptors' studios in Britain and France from the late nineteenth to the mid twentieth century and spanned a range of avant-garde and academic, well known and less known sculptors.[1] Among the curatorial questions we asked ourselves during its planning were: How can we create or re-evoke the sculptor's studio in the gallery, in an informed historical way, without resorting to mock-ups with tools, stone and sawdust, or creating an overly didactic presentation about sculptural techniques and methods? How could we articulate the studio's importance in the history of twentieth-century sculpture and show how photographs of the studio (as much as written accounts) were crucial to this history? How could we re-enact a kind of studio visit, across a range of fifty or so studios, for the gallery visitor? How could we show 'the studio in the gallery' without seriously compromising or misrepresenting either place? And how would the exhibition address the fact that many such spaces functioned – and for today's artists often still do – as exhibition sites in their own right?

At the Henry Moore Institute there is a suite of three main galleries. The first is long (20 x 6 metres), the second is large and lofty (10 x 8 metres, and 7 metres high) and the third is smaller (6 x 6 metres) and windowless. This sequence of differing spaces is excellent for the display of varying forms and scales of sculpture. We were, however, careful to avoid the sense of beginning, middle and end that this trajectory might suggest. Instead, we devised different ways of encountering the studio in each gallery, while drawing out both a conceptual development and a synchronicity between them, so that the rooms functioned in tandem with each other.

In the first gallery we showed over 60 framed archive photographs. Half were from our own collections (the Leeds Museums and Galleries collections are particularly rich in studio photographs), half on loan from elsewhere. They were arranged in a sequence that began with close-up photographs and progressed to panoramic views, rather than being organized by historical period or genre. We started with photographic representations of the hand of the sculptor and ended with more hands-off, hands-free, studio photo arrangements and ensembles, in which the sculptor him or herself did not figure. The idea here was to evoke, or re-enact, a kind of studio visit (or rather a journey around a number of studios) in which the point of view of gallery visitors was implicitly and poetically allied to that of studio visitors. In this way it was hoped that the idea of the studio would gradually open out as visitors progressed through the gallery.

The exhibition was thus about ways of looking and representing, rather than social or biographical histories of the studio. As an interrelated group, the photographs selected (and their subjects, scenarios, compositions and formats) shared secrets, told stories and subtly shed light on the studio's status and function as well as the ways in which relationships between sculptor, sculpture and studio were constructed in this period. Viewers could compare photographs taken in Jacob Epstein's studio, for example, with others from the studios of Ossip Zadkine, Constantin Brancusi or Henri Gaudier-Brzeska; or images by professional photographers with those taken by the artists themselves. On one hand such photographs provide a 'behind the scenes' view of the studio; on the other, they are highly staged and self-consciously artificial images, overlaying factual documentary with varying levels of fiction.

The studio photograph series that Brassaï published in 1933 in the surrealist journal *Minotaure* represents an extraordinary moment in the genre's history and was the subject of the second gallery display. In this room a sculpture by each of the six artists included in Brassaï's series (Constantin Brancusi, Charles Despiau, Alberto Giacometti, Henri Laurens, Jacques Lipchitz, Aristide Maillol) was positioned in front of large prints of the studio photographs in which the same work appeared.[2] The sculptor had disappeared altogether and viewers were faced with a quite different experience: an imaginary, composite studio – an impossible studio, in the sense that it could never physically be frequented, only envisioned and imagined through this encounter with object and photograph.

The dimensions of the large second gallery were perfect for this, corresponding with the typical scale of an established modern sculptor's studio. Its roof lights are also studio-like and these were used as the principal light source. The walls were painted a tone of grey that echoed the ambiguous time of day evoked in many of Brassaï's photographs and brought the ambience of the gallery closer to a studio's more intimate environment.

This installation also provided visitors with the opportunity to compare materials such as clay or plaster from the original studio with the bronze or other fine materials of the finished sculptures. One could also reflect on the play of different scales between original and copy, and between the sculpture in the photograph and the actual sculpture displayed under the gallery's lighting conditions. One could walk around a sculpture depicted in a nearby photograph and by extension imagine, in an embodied sense, being in the studio. We thus tried to map the studio onto the gallery in a 'poetic' rather than 'archaeological' or accurately reconstructed sense. This conceit was taken further in the final room, titled 'The Studio without Walls'. Here small sculptures by Jean Arp, Barbara Hepworth, Henry Moore and William Turnbull were displayed in 'mini-studio' formations: sculptural ensembles seen as studio ensembles; the studio floor or the table top serving as the sculptures' horizontal base. The kind of framing, miniaturization and (trans)portability of the sculptor's studio that could be achieved in a studio photograph was, in turn, taken up by the sculptures themselves in three dimensions.

In retrospect, this exhibition can be viewed in terms of two perspectives on the presentation and representation of the 'studio in the gallery' which pull in different directions: one is historical, the other contemporary; one retrospective, the other anticipatory. The first focuses on the historical and museological problems of reconstructing an artist's studio after the artist's death. The second centres on the ways a number of contemporary artists self-consciously deal with the question of restaging their own studios in the gallery setting – both as material environment and as a metaphorical shorthand for a way of working and thinking. Both of these manifestations of 'studios in the gallery' have gradually emerged since the late 1960s, attracting wider attention from the early 1990s onwards.

Studio Reconstructions: Brancusi and Bacon

On the problems of studio reconstruction in the gallery I will base my observations on two examples: the reconstruction of Francis Bacon's studio at the Hugh Lane Gallery, Dublin, which opened in 2001, and that of Brancusi in Paris, redesigned, after earlier replications, by Renzo Piano Workshop in 1997, and sited opposite the Centre Pompidou at the Place Beaubourg. I limit my scope to what is at stake here with the material conditions of display and what is afforded the visitor, and will not deal with the complicated legal conditions of these acquisitions and bequests.

From the outset it should be said that both these reconstructions are also relocations. Place was, as it were, sacrificed for space – or at least seen as secondary to it. Bacon's studio was moved from its London address at 7 Reece Mews in South Kensington to Dublin, and Brancusi's studio at 11 impasse Ronsin, a quiet cul-de-sac off rue Vaugirard in the 15th arrondissement, was moved in 1977 (superceding a partial reconstruction in the Palais de Tokyo, 1962–77) to the Place Beaubourg site. Whatever the curatorial and museological strategies later adopted, the original social, economic and geographical contexts of these studios were immediately erased. The studios, dislocated from the fabric and contingencies of their previous urban lives, would from now on belong to the art world.

In both cases, the gallery/studio visitor is not able to enter the studio but invited to look into it (to different extents) from behind glass. In the case of the Bacon studio, visitors approach it via the Hugh Lane's main galleries.[3] Before they reach it, they have to go through an introductory foyer in which is shown, on a continuous loop, the broadcast presenter Melvyn Bragg's South Bank Show interview with Bacon in the Reece Mews studio. Visitors then progress to the studio room itself, painstakingly reconstructed with archaeological precision and immaculately transported across the Irish Sea. Where there was a door there is now a glass window. The visitor can look in from this threshold, examine the mess and clutter in all its authentic/inauthentic glory, and marvel at the superhuman effort and brilliance that has gone into creating this 'unique copy' in homage to one man's working quarters. Bragg's film prefacing the display might tempt us to imagine Bacon here in this reconstructed studio, but it is such an extraordinary sight in its own right that we don't really need or want to. Walking around the studio anti-clockwise, we then get a chance to view the insides again from different vantage points – first looking through a peep-hole close to the wall and then through the first-floor studio's window. Visitors are then led into the 'micro gallery', which is set up with interactive technology that enables us to click onto information about the artist's biography, his work and this studio's history. This technology is intrinsic to the experience, certainly providing information but also compensating for the facts that we are not allowed in and that this is not Bacon's studio at all but a simulacrum. It is used to provide a 'total visitor experience' for what effectively cannot be experienced.

In the case of Brancusi, more or less the whole studio reconstruction has been provided with glass walls, so that visitors can walk around the site in its entirety and look in at the works on display.[4] In the earlier 1977 version visitors were able to walk into the studio and experience the work close up. Now worth millions of euros, the sculptures can no longer be put out on display in this way – it is simply too risky. Renzo Piano's reconstruction is thus an elegant compromise to a difficult curatorial problem, but for some the new reconstruction does have something of the 'fish tank' about it.[5] By not letting visitors inside, it gives them an unreal experience. Brancusi himself, of course, would never have seen his studio from the outside in. This is important, since we are dealing here with a sculptor for whom metaphors of enclosure, interiority and essence were central to his work, quietly echoing his studio environment.

This reconstruction would also have us believe that all the rooms of the original studio functioned as display spaces. This was, of course, not the case. The last was the artist's junk room where materials and all kinds of bits and pieces were stored and sculptures were assembled. This was not a part of the studio that Brancusi's visitors would normally be shown – it was too much of a mess – but it is nevertheless here on display through glass, as visitors come to the last part of the reconstruction. It has to be said, however, that the contents of this room have been arranged in close accordance with the way they were left by the sculptor when he died in 1957, his studio having been closely documented photographically during his lifetime. Thus, despite some creative curating, the Brancusi studio, like the Bacon studio in Dublin, is treated as an 'archaeological' subject, painstakingly reconstructed piece by piece to recreate the look and arrangement of the final studio. Despite their inherent impossibilities, these installations do provide some sense of the scale, materials, atmosphere and overall style of things as they appear to have been.

If this is what happens after the death of the artist, might this (we can be forgiven for asking) be taking art's *things* too seriously? The journey from working studio to studio reconstruction is, as I have noted, a problematic and uneven one; is this in fact a journey too far? Is it a way of making the studio 'travel' posthumously beyond its limits? Does it merely turn 'live site' into 'tourist trap', with a misplaced nostalgia for the irretrievable, sited conditions of art's making? And what in the end can we really learn from these reconstructions? Whatever their educational play, it seems important to be clear-headed about their limitations and the fictions that these reconstructions contain. Visitors in years to come may increasingly need to be reminded that these places are fabrications. Location, location, location, one might say. If we want to know more about why Bacon's studio was packed full of empty champagne cases (which he often used as palettes) we would look to Kensington and Soho for answers. And if we want to know why Brancusi lived in his studio for 41 years in the countrified impasse Ronsin, perhaps we should take the walk (as hundreds did in his lifetime) from the busy metropolitan centre of Paris down this city's longest street to get there. You didn't drop in at Brancusi's on the way somewhere else, you made a dedicated trip, a pilgrimage even, to this semi-rural retreat that was prefaced by Paris itself.

Studio Installations: Nelson and Venlet

It is interesting to note that the concept of the 'journey' figures in a number of contemporary artists' discussions of the studio. Despite the fact that with the studio we are dealing primarily with stasis – the physical space of a single room or building – the image of travelling is often cast as central to its status and function, central to the way it operates both metaphorically and literally, in the imagination or in the marketplace. This is neatly articulated in Jason Rhoades' studio-installation *My Brother/Brancusi* (1995), in which he surrounded a room full of doughnut-making equipment with framed photographs of Brancusi's studio and of a contemporary North American home. Rhoades thus playfully compared this modernist studio with a fast-food factory, the production of unique, directly carved and finished sculptures with doughnut production. It is telling that an installation piece of that time included specific reference to Brancusi's studio: Rhoades was sardonically tapping into an overlap of concerns – such as the status of distinctions between 'high' and 'low' – explored in different ways equally in curatorial reconstruction projects and in much installation-based art of the 1990s.

The journey metaphor is used also by a number of British artists when asked about what the studio means to them. Phyllida Barlow, Graham Gussin, Simon Starling, Keith Tyson and Keith Wilson, for example, have all quietly evoked the idea of the journey when discussing their love-hate relationship with their studios: they can't, it seems, live either with or without them.[6] All are alert to the historical baggage of the studio and to its problematic mythic status as the place of genius and creative endeavour. The studio is a place to escape to and escape from; a place to twiddle one's thumbs and have brainwaves in; a place to stop off at, like a layby, and a place of discipline and routine; a place to hide in and a place to be on display in. It can be a place of tremendous triumph and achievement, and as dull as ditchwater. In keeping with this sensibility, Bruce Nauman's *Mapping the Studio (Fat Chance John Cage)* is a wonderful example not only of taking the studio into the gallery but also of the casting of the studio as a place at once magical and utterly banal, overwhelming and underwhelming. First shown in 2001 at the Dia Center in New York, this installation comprises wall-to-wall screens displaying an infra-red camera's recording of Nauman's studio at night when mice take over the space, with the occasional appearance of the artist's cat.[7]

The issue of the studio in the gallery is explored particularly in the work of the artists Mike Nelson and Richard Venlet. For an exhibition at Camden Arts Centre, London, in 1998 Nelson created the installation *Studio Apparatus for Camden Arts Centre: An Introductory Structure or Temporary Monument.*[8] Its main room was titled 'The Mysterious Island'. The installation created a kind of smoke and mirrors effect, playing with an audience's desire to witness art-making and gain access to the 'real' studio work. This 'studio apparatus' is, in effect, the 'behind the scenes' of Nelson's art – the jumbled structures, images and iconographies of his practice, and what was going on in his head and in the studio at the time. We spot objects from earlier shows stuck in new places and next to new and recycled paraphernalia, evocative of multiple times, places and people. What you see is what you get, but it is also of course a good deal more, and the title 'The Mysterious Island' links the nomadic artistic imagination in process with the idea of a Jules Verne-like journey. Perhaps Nelson himself is offering something that is still a mystery to himself, or a bundle of secrets and narratives that he is presently keeping from himself but has put on display anyway, because he's got a show to do.

Nelson's work always plays hide and seek with visitors' perceptions, with what is real and what is make-believe, and toys with the poetry of ambiguity, disguise and the impostorous. In this way it shares some of the tactics of engagement characteristic of studio reconstructions but in a deliberately mischievous, obfuscating and self-conscious way. One of the strategies he employs to make his installations so compelling for the visitor is to take himself out of the picture, making directed installations that privilege the experience of the visitor with the stuff at hand, rather than with him, the artist. Nelson's absence thus encourages the visitor to think less about the the 'artistic persona' of the artist and more about the material environment presented and how it has been constructed, reconstructed and treated. He uses every trick possible to harness the visitor's imaginative and self-conscious attention and thus attempts to implicate the visitor in his works. Exploring one of his works one becomes a kind of imaginary participant, witnessing the aftermath of a mysterious event, like a tourist on a film set after the film has been made but with the camera still rolling. In the installation *To the Memory of H.P. Lovecraft*, staged at the Collective Gallery, Edinburgh, in 1999, the gallery was fitted up and destroyed in such a way that we would wonder what kind of gothic monster had been there before us.[9] The walls were slashed with an axe, yet the presence of a dog bowl and a large gnawed bone suggested a hound rather than a human being. What, we wonder, was the cause of the fury? The longer we look the more it becomes apparent that it might indeed be the white cube gallery itself that is motivating this rage, as if the agent responsible felt caged and imprisoned by it, and so vandalized it, when attempts to escape it became futile. Creative space is here destructive space and Nelson's piece is a strangely beautiful response to a now traditional white cube condition of display.

Richard Venlet's contribution to the 2002 São Paulo Bienal offered a more well-mannered and minimal form of theatre and subversion.[10] In this untitled installation Venlet constructed a room, read as his studio, at the centre of a gallery. Its external walls were mirror-panelled, reflecting the walls, floors, ceiling and windows of the surrounding exhibition space. Visitors could enter the studio room and have a look around. On the floor inside and around the edge of the room Venlet placed a number of cardboard boxes containing A4 photocopies of his own (largely photographic) work. Visitors could take away what they wanted, choosing any option between taking one of each – thus gaining a set replicating the whole of Venlet's recent oeuvre in photocopied form – and going away empty handed. By staging his studio as a gallery with free reproductions on offer Venlet thus subverted any connotations of creative authenticity.

The studio, like the gallery mirrored on its external walls, was presented as being neither here nor there – a mirage-like place that was secondary to the ideas that were on offer inside it. So what was it in the end, if it was not really a studio and not really a gallery? Venlet's master touch was invisible, or rather only visible at the end of the day, when the visitors had left and the lights had been turned off. Hanging down (about a metre from the ceiling and in the middle of this box room) was a large light bulb. Producing a very bright light, it cast on the walls shadows of the visitors in motion so striking and remarkable that they could clearly be read as an important part of the work. It thus animated the room in 'collaboration' with the visitors' presence. When the light was turned off, however, you could see that Venlet had written in felt-tip pen the dimensions of the room around the bulb. It was a witty, minimal conceit – at once marvellous and banal – articulating much of what the studio in the gallery might mean for contemporary artists.

If for Venlet the studio is partly about reconstruction, documentation and the transposition of space, it is also equally about the mere interaction between art, the artist, a visitor and a room. It is a cipher, a device and a conceit: on one hand, the piece at São Paulo punctures the myth of the studio; on the other, it attempts to seduce the viewer (thus the mirrors). The studio is thus a way of harnessing a more heightened, engaged and imaginative kind of visitor attention: studios, after all, make the audience captive. If the light source – the timeworn symbol of conception, illumination and the imagination – connotes the creative and intellectual energy that can charge the artist, it is also an energy that closely interacts with the architecture that frames the work and houses the visitor. Like moths to a flame, visitors to Venlet's studio/gallery space seeking privileged and revelatory insight into artistic inspiration might well get it: if you want to know more about the work, turn the light on.

1   [footnote 5 in source] See accompanying exhibition catalogue and essay, Jon Wood, 'Close Encounters: The Sculptor's Studio in the Age of the Camera', in *Close Encounters* (Leeds: Henry Moore Institute, 2001) 8–27.

2   [6] These were Brancusi's *Danaïde* (c. 1918), Despui's *Bust of Mme Jean Arthur Fontane* (1933), Giacometti's *Spoon Woman* (1926–27), Laurens' *Océanide* (1933), Lipchitz's *Figure* (1926–30) and Maillol's *Ile de France* (1925).

3   [7] For recent publications on the Bacon studio in both Dublin and London, see *Francis Bacon's Studio at the Hugh Lane* (Dublin: Hugh Lane Municipal Art Gallery, 2001), and its useful essays by Barbara Dawson and Margarita Cappock; and J. Edwards, Foreword, *7 Reece Mews: Francis Bacon's Studio* (photographs by Perry Ogden) (London: Thames & Hudson, 2001) 10–13.

4   [8] For a useful and well illustrated book on the new studio see M. Tabart, *L'Atelier Brancusi Album* (Paris: Éditions du Centre Georges Pompidou, 1997). For a recent reading of the history of the Brancusi studio and its reconstruction see Jon Wood, 'Brancusi's White Studio', *The Sculpture Journal*, vol. 7 (2002) 108–20.

5   [9] A point made by Eric Shanes in 'Brancusi's Studio Flattened', *Apollo* (December 1997) 61.

6   [10] These artists gave talks about their studios in October 2001 at the Henry Moore Institute, Leeds, as part of a programme accompanying the 'Close Encounters' exhibition.

7   [11] Bruce Nauman, *Mapping the Studio I (Fat Chance John Cage)*, Dia Center for the Arts, New York, 10 January – 27 July 2002.

8   [12] See also *Mike Nelson: Extinction Beckons* (texts by Jaki Irvine) (London: Matts Gallery, 2000) 86–95.

9   [13] Ibid.

10   [14] For further documentation of this display, curated by Moritz Küng, see *Richard Venlet/00* (Antwerp: MuHKA, 2002).

Jon Wood, extract (revised for this volume) from 'The Studio in the Gallery?', in *Reshaping Museum Space: Architecture, Design, Exhibitions*, ed. Suzanne MacLeod (London and New York: Routledge, 2005) 158–69.

Lynne Cooke
Gerhard Richter: *Atlas*//1995

In 1964 Gerhard Richter began amassing onto panels photographs he had collected over the previous few years – sometimes as potential sources for his paintings and sometimes on their own account. Eight years later these and subsequent related panels were exhibited in Utrecht under the title *Atlas van de foto's en schetsen* (*Atlas of photos and sketches*). Since then Richter has continued, albeit intermittently, to supplement his 'picture album'.[1] And periodically it has been returned to public view: it was shown at Krefeld in 1976, Munich in 1989, and Cologne in 1990.[2] Recently updated, it now comprises almost six hundred panels and some five thousand photographs.

Atlas is not quite as homogeneous as its first panels seemed to predict. While they contain mostly amateur snapshots together with reproductions from newspapers and popular magazines, these categories were rapidly expanded to include portraits, pornographic imagery, and pictures of famous historical figures and events – Hitler and concentration camp survivors among them. In addition, the artist's own photographs, working sketches and seemingly casual views and vistas soon infiltrated the increasingly heterogenous array. That *Atlas* would serve other functions than simply those of a repository for storing memorable images became evident when sketches for installations, plans for public commissions, technical drawings for domestic furnishings, and collages of hypothetical settings on a truly monumental scale were added.[3] More recently, large sequences of almost serially produced landscapes, travel vistas and still lifes have been incorporated, suggesting that once the piece grew, the artist began to orchestrate it in terms of an overall composition, establishing larger rhythms, conjunctions and references among the parts, and instituting a more strictly gridded layout. That is, what initially had a contingent, improvisational, cumulative character has taken on, with time and with repeated public presentation, a certain internal logic and dynamic peculiar to itself. In this way an album has metamorphosed into a potentially encyclopaedic project, notwithstanding the personal, provisional and incremental impulses continuing to generate it.

It is apposite that photography is the pivot of this, the most extensive work in Richter's oeuvre. A constant in his art of the past three decades, for him it has always had a dialectical relationship with painting. Given that questions of representation lie at the heart of Richter's enterprise, this relationship has inevitably proven a shifting, mutating one – from the early 1960s when photography provided motifs for paintings to the past decade when the artist has both overpainted photographs and exhibited as prints photographs of certain paintings originally generated by rephotographed photographs. Dave Hickey has persuasively argued against the canonical historical rationale for the changes that took place in the practice of painting after the advent of photography: namely, that painting changed because photography appropriated its descriptive and representational functions. 'Richter's photo-paintings infer', Hickey argues, '[that] painting changed after the advent of photography not because photography usurped its descriptive function, but because photography *prioritized* it, thus valorizing the referent over what it signified.'[4]

If photography provided the painter, faced with the question of *what* to paint, with certain basics, abstraction offered another set of possibilities that were, for Richter, equally but not necessarily more plausible; abstraction and figuration, he believes, have parallel status as pictures. Through recourse to mirrors, panes of glass and small reflective aluminium spheres, Richter then further permutated this preoccupation with representation by wedding these works to their contexts.

Incorporating the surroundings – in effect, an idiosyncratic mode of working *in situ* – allowed him to extend in more encompassing ways the dialectic between what is seen and what is represented, as well as the media of that representation.

Richter has frequently asserted that he has no programme and no ideology, and that he proceeds according to no preconceived plan. For all its compendious nature, *Atlas* is governed by no overriding logic and no polemic. Unlike, for example, Bernd and Hilla Bechers' projects, *Atlas* is not an archive: there is neither a coherent and systematic compilation of an identifiable body of material nor an archaeological exhaustion of a specific subject. In retaining a hybrid identity, *Atlas* loosely adheres to some of the preoccupations informing Richter's paintings without being exclusively governed by them. Most of its recent components are photographs taken by the artist himself rather than images culled from published sources, corresponding to the fact that since 1975 Richter has seldom depended on found motifs for subject matter. Not only are the initial images now his own, but they are often made in closely related series or sequences. Nonetheless, those that have been retrospectively included in *Atlas* do not necessarily constitute all that the artist took of any particular motif, nor are they always the very ones that provided the models for individual paintings. Images only exceptionally stand alone, independent and iconic; on such occasions they are framed within pencil borders as with presentation drawings, contextualized in hypothetical installations, or masked and glued to sheets onto which colour studies can be developed in preparation for painting. The relational character of the groupings within most of the panels is fully in accord with the contingency underpinning the presentation of the work as a whole. For the arrangement of the panels follows a loose rather than strict chronology, with placement determined in part by the character of the venues – wall dimensions, heights and proportions – in which *Atlas* is to be exhibited. Sequencing and grouping is thus employed to establish a mode of reading that is differential and contextual.

Faced with the mass of imagery available today, Richter asserts that all one can do is try to order it. He makes no attempt to offer an overriding interpretation, there is no promise of comprehensibility and definitiveness of the kind vouchsafe in an archive or by archaeology. As Benjamin Buchloh astutely notes, the relati ships between the images 'generate meanings and disintegrate readings. Hence, something provisional and resistant to precise meaning emerges in *Atlas*, something which Buchloh eloquently characterizes as a check both against the impulse to generate understanding and the ever-present desire for It. *Atlas* hovers, therefore, between the promise of taxonomic order as divulged in the archive and the total devastation of that promise, which is implicit, for example, in the morcellated, anti-relational potential of photomontage. The images, fragments or details are commonplace, almost stereotypical. In their sheer ordinariness, conventionality and ubiquity, many of these photographs seem almost interchangeable or generic, and hence serve to underplay those staples of photographic discourse: the photo as icon and the photo as index. They approach the condition Richter seeks for his paintings, which as pictures are located always between the concrete and the abstract. Buchloh argues persuasively that 'we can no longer speak of "photography" in terms of a homogeneous formation of practices, discourses and institutions (no more than we could speak of "politics"). Photography can be discussed as a private phenomenology and as a partial semiotics, but not as a coherent, comprehensive history.'[6] At a moment when the digital is replacing the analogue and the dominant paradigms of photography are undergoing a sea-change, *Atlas* returns the question of the referent to centre stage.

1   Gerhard Richter and Jan Thorn-Prikker, 'Ruminations on the *18. Oktober 1977* Cycle', *Parkett*, no. 19 (Spring 1989) 143.

2   Small sections of *Atlas* have been shown on occasion, for example, in the retrospective, 'Gerhard Richter', Kunst-und-Austellungshalle der Bundesrepublik Deutschland, Bonn, 1993.

3   In a recent interview, Richter spoke of the 'dream of mine – that the pictures will become an environment or become architecture, that would be even more effective'. Quoted in Dorothea Dietrich, 'Gerhard Richter: An Interview', *The Print Collector's Newsletter*, vol. 16, no. 4 (September/ October 1985) 130. In effect *Atlas* does this when fully on view.

4   Dave Hickey, 'Richter in Tahiti', *Parkett*, no. 35 (Spring 1993) 86.

5   Benjamin H.D. Buchloh, 'Gerhard Richters Atlas: Das Archiv der Anomie', in *Gerhard Richter*, vol. 2 (Bonn: Kunst-und-Austellungshalle der Bundesrepublik Deutschland, 1993); trans. Benjamin H.D. Buchloh.

6   Ibid.

Lynne Cooke, 'Gerhard Richter: Atlas', in *Gerhard Richter: Atlas 1964–1995* (New York: Dia Center for the Arts, 1995); reprinted in *Gerhard Richter: Atlas. The Reader* (London: Whitechapel Gallery, 2003) 117–19.

Alexander Alberro
The Catalogue of Robert Smithson's Library//2004

Once you have approached the mountains of cases in order to mine the books from them and bring them to the light of day ... what memories crowd in upon you!
– Walter Benjamin, 'Unpacking My Library'[1]

In an archive, the possibility of meaning is 'liberated' from the actual contingencies of use. But this liberation is also a loss, an *abstraction* from the complexity and richness of use, a loss of context. ... New meanings come to supplant old ones, with the archive serving as a kind of 'clearing house' of meaning.
– Allan Sekula, 'Reading an Archive'[2]

Over a sustained shot of a rocky embankment close to the beginning of Robert Smithson's thirty-five-minute 16mm film *The Spiral Jetty* (1970), the voice of the artist matter-of-factly observes that 'The earth's history seems at times like a story recorded in a book, each page of which is torn into small pieces. Many of the pages and some of the pieces of each page are missing.' Shreds of at-first indistinguishable debris flitter in the air, buoyantly descending along the slope in a manner evocative of a slow-motion landslide. Suddenly there is a cut, followed by a close-up shot that reveals the featherweight flakes, whirling down the promontory, to be sheets of white paper. The ground on which they settle is barren and parched, the sun-baked mud cracking into a multitude of small tectonic surfaces that curl at their edges. The manufactured leaves of paper add one more stratum to the earth. The next shot focuses on the sheets of paper and reveals that some remain whole while others have been torn into halves and quarters. Here and there we get glimpses of text, maps, tables and graphs of different sorts printed on the paper. Yet the knowledge promised by the fragments of information is necessarily incomplete. Amid the earth and the book lies a vast expanse of meaning, filled with narratives but punctuated with gaps and holes.

The parallels that the sequence described above establish between the printed page (culture) and the earth's skin (nature) point to the enormous significance of books for Smithson. The catalogue of Smithson's library,[3] a posthumously compiled list of the contents of the artist's personal library, reveals that he was an avid collector of books. By the time of his premature death he had amassed well over a thousand volumes. The collection concentrates on a broad array of disciplines ranging from literature and philosophy to mathematics and science. In addition, the fringes of his library harboured issues of more than fifty different magazines and journals; in some cases only one volume of a periodical is included, while for other titles we find a more complete run (e.g. twenty-six issues of *The Partisan Review* published between 1964 and 1972). Many of the journals in the collection, including *Contemporary Literature, Daedalus, The Southern Review* and *Yale French Studies*, are literary reviews. There are also the seeds of a set of science-fiction magazines, with titles such as *Fantasy* and *Science Fiction, Flying Saucers, Galaxy* and *Worlds of Tomorrow*. Surprisingly, with but a few exceptions, contemporary art journals are lacking from the library. Those that are present – for instance several crumpled issues of *Art and Literature* and the swan-white box volume of *Aspen*, no. 5 and 6, edited by Brian O'Doherty (1967) – focus as much on literature and drama as they do on art. Even periodicals such as *Artforum, Art Voices, Arts Magazine* and *Harper's Bazaar*, in which Smithson's writings were featured, are missing. Also conspicuously absent are books the artist often cited, such as Anton Ehrenzweig's *The Hidden Order of Art* (1967), and that he obviously owned, such as J.G. Ballard's *The Crystal World* (1966), from which the title of Smithson's essay 'The Crystal Land' (1966) is derived. Furthermore, Brian W. Aldiss' *Earthworks* (1965), which Smithson took with him on the travels captured in 'A Tour of the Monuments of Passaic, New Jersey' (1967), is nowhere to be found. As with the spectral suburbs often evoked in the artist's early writings, the catalogue of Smithson's library is full of holes.

Like the suburbs, too, Smithson's library is entropic, with the multifarious variety of books, journals and records intermingling and coalescing to form a homogenous mass. The significance of each of the parts shifts in favour of the meaning they acquire in their relationship to each other and to their owner. Alone as a monad, each item in the catalogue has its own life and meaning, Yet, as part of a larger collection, the books, journals and records form constellations; this alters their meanings considerably. For instance, the hallucinatory novels of William S. Burroughs – when brought together with historical studies of ancient civilizations, a coterie of psychedelic and glam-rock records, and anthropological texts by Georges Bataille and Claude Lévi-Strauss – assume meanings considerably different from those they would take on in other configurations. In a similar manner, when the Marquis de Sade is paralleled with Elizabeth Bowen, and Lewis Carroll with Anthony Burgess, a new relation of equivalence is established between classical literary texts and the most contemporary. Likewise, unfathomable nuances are lost as canonical philosophical texts and authoritative mathematical treatises are placed in the context of the popular history of Hugh Trevor-Roper's *The Last Days of Hitler* (1947) or brush up against the new religion advanced by L. Ron Hubbard's *Dianetics* (1950). Thus the personal library at once erases and constructs meaning through a process of decontextualization and reconfiguration. It functions as what Allan Sekula refers to as a 'clearing house' of meaning.[4]

Nowhere is this collision of widely disparate elements in Smithson's library more striking than in its extensive and eclectic accumulation of long-play records. Organized alphabetically, Joan Baez's *Blessed Are* (1971) is squeezed between Glenn Gould's recording of Johann Sebastian Bach's *Partita no. 5* and an album of Balinese Gamelan (1967); *Music from Mathematics* (1962) and *Music of Southern India* (1965) follow several discs by Muddy Waters; and records by New York-rock bands such as Vanilla Fudge and the Velvet Underground are juxtaposed with the atonal and serial music of Steve Reich, Arnold Schönberg and La Monte Young. The large number of movie soundtracks attest to Smithson's great interest in film, and there are also many spoken word recordings in the collection: from stories of American adventure told by Senator Everett McKinley Dirksen (*Gallant Men*, 1967) and no less than three volumes of burlesque humor by the Firesign Theater to James Joyce's Ulysses, T.S. Eliot's *The Waste Land* and four recordings of Samuel Beckett's plays on vinyl. A Berlitz *Basic Spanish* disc reveals Smithson's attempt to learn the language in preparation for his trip to Mexico in 1969.

That Smithson ultimately did not learn Spanish does not indicate that he did not listen to the Berlitz record. Indeed, whether or not he actually read all of the books or listened to all of the records in his possession is of little importance. For, as Walter Benjamin affirmed in 'Unpacking My Library,' an essay anthologized in a volume that Smithson had in his own collection (Benjamin, *Illuminations*, 1968), 'Experts will bear me out when I say that [the non-reading of books in one's library] is the oldest thing in the world.'[5] Discerning the idiosyncratic structure of Smithson's collection is presently more relevant than determining which texts the artist carefully read (or read at all!) and which records he regularly listened to, since the particular items that he chose to gather together provide a glimpse of his cultural landscape. It also enables us to gain a better understanding of the intellectual milieu of New York artists during the 1960s as they read their way through the studied coolness of the French *nouveau roman*, the hyper-sensual psychedelia of Aldous Huxley, the eventless dramas of Beckett, the delirious optimism of Marshall McLuhan, and many other modes of writing that characterized the period. Mining Smithson's library is like biting into a madeleine, each book and record triggering what Benjamin referred to as a crowd of memories, providing a whiff of a previous time, while the volumes dovetail into a complex intertextual dialogue between themselves.

Yet it is not enough simply to list the contents in Smithson's library, for its essential substance is what it contains in addition to the sum total of the parts – the 'make-up', the character, the personality. This is much more difficult to understand. There are two forms of diachronic order that can be ascertained: the sequence in which Smithson accumulated the items and the chronology of the dates in which each individual item was published or released. While both are informative, each order is also highly limiting in significant ways. The catalogue of dates in which the items were collected reveals little of their subsequent use value, and the date of production tells us even less about what they came to mean to the artist. More fruitful in this case might be an analysis of the taxonomic orders discernable in the library. These could be based on categories of authorship, genre, subject matter, medium, and so on, each of which endows the inventory with a particular logic. [...]

Thus the most apt way to order Smithson's library is with the conjunction *and*: science *and* religion; modernism *and* mass culture; what is present *and* what is missing. That this conjunction also structured much of Smithson's artwork – with the parallels it establishes between the past *and* the future, the site *and* the non-site, the earth's skin *and* the printed page – might be the greatest insight that the library provides about the artist's working method. But in the end it is the view that it offers of an artistic methodology that effectively bridged the conventional separation between an array of media and disciplines that makes Smithson's library such a valuable time capsule today.[6] [...]

1   Walter Benjamin, 'Unpacking My Library' (1931), in *Walter Benjamin. Illuminations: Essays and Reflections*, ed. Hannah Arendt, trans. Harry Zohn (New York: Schocken books, 1969) 66.

2   Allan Sekula, 'Reading an Archive' (1983), in Brian Wallis, ed., *Blasted Allegories: An Anthology of Writings by Contemporary Artists* (New York: New Museum of Contemporary Art/Cambridge, Massachusetts: The MIT Press, 1989) 117.

3   A catalogue of Smithson's library, compiled by Valentin Tatransky, appears elsewhere in this volume [*Robert Smithson* (Los Angeles: The Museum of Contemporary Art, 2004)]

4   Allan Sekula, op cit.

5   Walter Benjamin, 'Unpacking My Library', op. cit., 62

6   Nancy Holt offered the following recollections regarding Smithson's relationship with books. Around 1958 Smithson worked at the Eighth Street Bookshop [in Greenwich Village, New York], where he browsed and read many more books than are evident in the library. Even after he stopped working there, the bookshop continued to be the destination of his daily walks for many years. Four or five books on the art and archaeology of Mexico were loaned to a friend and not returned. In the library were a collection of 'Great Books of the Western World', fifty-four books in all. These were overlooked at the time of the inventory of books because they were stored in a closet.

Alexander Alberro, extracts from 'The Catalogue of Robert Smithson's Library', in *Robert Smithson*, ed. Eugenie Tsai and Cornelia Butler (Los Angeles: The Museum of Contemporary Art, 2004) 245–8.

Henri Lefebvre
Social Space//1974

[...] The object produced often bears traces of the *matériel* and time that have gone into its production – clues to the operations that have modified the raw material used. This makes it possible for us to reconstruct those operations. The fact remains, however, that productive operations tend in the main to cover their tracks; some even have this as their prime goal: polishing, staining, facing, plastering, and so on. When construction is completed, the scaffolding is taken down; likewise, the fate of an author's rough draft is to be torn up and tossed away, while for a painter the distinction between a study and a painting is a very clear one. It is for reasons such as these that products, and even works, are further characterized by their tendency to detach themselves from productive labour. So much so, in fact, that productive labour is sometimes forgotten altogether, and it is this 'forgetfulness' – or, as a philosopher might say, this mystification – that makes possible the fetishism of commodities: the fact that commodities imply certain social relationships whose misapprehension they also ensure.

It is never easy to get back from the object (product or work) to the activity that produced and/or created it. It is the only way, however, to illuminate the object's nature, or, if you will, the object's relationship to nature, and reconstitute the process of its genesis and the development of its meaning. All other ways of proceeding can succeed only in constructing an abstract object – a model. It is not sufficient, in any case, merely to bring out an object's structure and to understand that structure: we need to generate an object in its entirety – that is, to reproduce, by and in thought, that object's forms, structures and functions.

How does one (where 'one' designates any 'subject') perceive a picture, a landscape or a monument? Perception naturally depends on the 'subject': a peasant does not perceive 'his' landscape in the same way as a town-dweller strolling through it. Take the case of a cultured art-lover looking at a painting. His eye is neither that of a professional nor that of an uncultivated person. He considers first one and then another of the objects depicted in the painting; he starts out by apprehending the relationships between these objects, and allows himself to experience the effect or effects intended by the painter. From this he derives a certain pleasure – assuming that the painting in question is of the type supposed to give pleasure to eye or mind. But our amateur is also aware that the picture is framed, and that the internal relations between colours and forms are governed by the work as a whole. He thus moves from consideration of the objects in the painting to consideration of the picture as an object, from what he has perceived in the pictural space to what he can comprehend about that space. He thus comes to sense or understand various 'effects', including some which have not been intentionally sought by the painter. He deciphers the picture and finds surprises in it, but always within the limits of its formal framework, and in the ratios or proportions dictated by that framework. His discoveries occur on the plane of (pictural) *space*. At this point in his aesthetic inquiry, the 'subject' asks a number of questions: he seeks to solve one problem in particular, that of the relationship between effects of meaning that have been sought by means of technique and those which have come about independently of the artist's intentions (some of which depend on him, the 'looker'). In this way he begins to trace a path back from the effects he has experienced to the meaning-producing activity that gave rise to them; his aim is to rediscover that activity and to try and identify (perhaps illusorily) with it. His 'aesthetic' perception thus operates, as one would expect, on several levels.

It is not hard to see that this paradigm case is paralleled by a trend in the history of philosophy that was taken up and advanced by Marx and by Marxist thought. The post-Socratic Greek philosophers analysed knowledge as social practice; reflecting the state of understanding itself, they inventoried the ways in which known *objects* were apprehended. The high-point of this theoretical work was Aristotelian teaching on *discourse* (*Logos*), and on the *categories* as at once elements of discourse and means for apprehending (or classifying) objects. Much later, in Europe, Cartesian philosophy refined and modified the definition of 'Logos'. Philosophers were now supposed to question the Logos – and put it into question: to demand its credentials, its pedigree, its certificate of origin, its citizenship papers. With Descartes, therefore, philosophy shifted the position of both questions and answers. It changed its focus, moving from 'thought thought' to 'thinking thought', from the objects of thought to the act of thinking, from a discourse upon the known to the operation of knowing. The result was a new 'problematic' – and new difficulties.

Marx recommenced this Cartesian revolution, perfecting and broadening it in the process. His concern was no longer merely with works generated by knowledge, but now also with *things* in industrial practice. Following Hegel and the British economists, he worked his way back from the results of productive activity to productive activity itself. Marx concluded that any reality presenting itself in space can be expounded and explained in terms of its genesis in time. But any activity developed over (historical) time engenders (produces) a space, and can only attain practical 'reality' or concrete existence within that space. This view of matters emerged in Marx's thinking only in an ill-defined form; it was in fact inherited by him in that form from Hegel. It applies to any landscape, to any monument, and to any spatial ensemble (so long as it is not 'given' in nature), as it does to any picture, work or product. Once deciphered, a landscape or a monument refers us back to a creative capacity and to a signifying process. This capacity may in principle be dated, for it is a historical fact. Not, however, in the sense that an event can be dated: we are not referring to the exact date of a monument's inauguration, for example, or to the day that the *command* that it be erected was issued by some notability. Nor is it a matter of a date in the institutional sense of the word: the moment when a particular social organization acceded to a pressing *demand* that it embody itself in a particular edifice – the judiciary in a court house, for instance, or the Church in a cathedral. Rather, the creative capacity in question here is invariably that of a community or collectivity, of a group, of a fraction of a class in action, or of an 'agent' (i.e. 'one who acts'). Even though 'commanding' and 'demanding' may be the functions of distinct groups, no individual or entity may be considered ultimately responsible for production itself: such responsibility may be attributed only to a social reality capable of investing a space – capable, given the resources (productive forces, technology and knowledge, means of labour, etc.), of producing that space. Manifestly, if a countryside exists, there must have been peasants to give it form, and hence too communities (villages), whether autonomous or subject to a higher (political) power. Similarly, the existence of a monument implies its construction by an urban group which may also be either free or subordinate to a (political) authority. It is certainly necessary to describe such states of affairs, but it is hardly sufficient. It would be utterly inadequate from the standpoint of an understanding of space merely to describe first rural landscapes, then industrial landscapes, and finally urban spatiality, for this would simply leave all transitions out of the picture. In as much as the quest for the relevant productive capacity or creative process leads us in many cases to political power, there arises the question of how such power is exercised. Does it merely command, or does it 'demand' also? What is the nature of its relationship to the groups subordinate to it, which are themselves 'demanders', sometimes also 'commanders', and invariably 'participants'? This is a historical problem – that of all cities, all monuments, all landscapes. The analysis of any space brings us up against the dialectical relationship between demand and command, along with its attendant questions: 'Who?', 'For whom?', 'By whose agency?', 'Why and how?' If and when this dialectical (and hence conflictual) relationship ceases to obtain – if demand were to outlive command, or vice versa – the history of space must come to an end. The same goes for the capacity to create, without a doubt. The production of space might proceed, but solely according to the dictates of Power: production without creation – mere reproduction. But is it really possible for us to envision an end to demand? Suffice it to say that silence is not the same thing as quietus.

What we are concerned with, then, is the long *history of space*, even though space is neither a 'subject' nor an 'object' but rather a social reality – that is to say, a set of relations and forms. This history is to be distinguished from an inventory of things *in space* (or what has recently been called material culture or civilization), as also from ideas and discourse *about space*. It must account for both representational spaces and representations of space, but above all for their interrelationships and their links with social practice. The history of space thus has its place between anthropology and political economy. The nomenclature, description and classification of objects certainly has a contribution to make to traditional history, especially when the historian is concerned with the ordinary objects of daily life, with types of food, kitchen utensils and the preparation and presentation of meals, with clothing, or with the building of houses and the materials and *matériel* it calls for. But everyday life also figures in representational spaces – or perhaps it would be more accurate to say that it forms such spaces. As for representations of space (and of time), they are part of the history of ideologies, provided that the concept of ideology is not restricted, as it too often is, to the ideologies of the philosophers and of the ruling classes – or, in other words, to the 'noble' ideas of philosophy, religion and ethics. A history of space would explain the development, and hence the temporal conditions, of those realities which some geographers call 'networks' and which are subordinated to the frameworks of politics.

The history of space does not have to choose between 'processes' and 'structures', change and invariability, events and institutions. Its periodizations, moreover, will differ from generally accepted ones. Naturally, the history of space should not be distanced in any way from the history of time (a history clearly distinct from all philosophical theories of time in general). The departure point for this history of space is not to be found in geographical descriptions of natural space, but rather in the study of natural rhythms, and of the modification of those rhythms and their inscription in space by means of human actions, especially work-related actions. It begins, then, with the spatio-temporal rhythms of nature as transformed by a social practice. [...]

Henri Lefebvre, extract from *La Production de l'espace* (Paris: Éditions Anthropos, 1974); trans. Donald Nicholson-Smith, *The Production of Space* (Oxford: Blackwell, 1991) 113–17.

Carles Guerra
The Last Possessions: A Dialogical Restoration
of Art & Language//1999

[...] If in the last twenty years Art & Language has addressed the problem of political form and social content largely through images and painting, for the ten years before that they posed the problem primarily within the space of dialogue. In the 1970s, as they would say themselves, Art & Language worked to establish the conditions in which it would be possible to speak non-trivially of a social or socialist art. In a circumstance characterized by the international distribution of art, in which Art & Language was implicated, such intentions had to be formulated in confrontation with the contradictions and paradoxes entailed. Not only were there episodes that confirmed conversation as a social tool, but also moments when socializing implied disorder. For it is evident that dialogical socialization can have disruptive political implications, and that the concept of conversation as a solution to social conflicts is an idealization. What is not clear is the exact dimension we allocate to the social. Political art takes advantage of that imprecision about the coordinates of the social – mostly so as to leave reality intact.

If, in order to simplify matters, we have to focus the dialogical characterization of Art & Language on a period, we would choose the one between 1972 and 1976. This was a moment powerfully characterized by the activity of conversation and by the problems of its representation. By this time the arguments about ontology and de-ontology had ceased to be central to the continuance of the work. These had in a sense been preliminary questions. By 1972 Art & Language had exhausted all the clichés peculiar to the purist agenda of conceptual art. Whereas conceptual art never went beyond a task of identifying and representing ideas (idea art, concept art, analytical art, etc.), Art & Language now embarked on an investigation into the circulation of those ideas. In the *Grundrisse* Marx suggested that systems of social relations based on money and capital were forms of production characteristic of advanced capitalism. Similarly, Art & Language examined the distribution of ideas as a form of production that would bring about an increase in cultural and cognitive capital. The system of circulation itself would be the object to be produced – a condition of learning and thus of value added to work with ideas. Paradoxically, as genuinely capitalist as that form of production seems, far from integrating Art & Language, it distanced them still more from the dominant economic structure and the forms of distribution of the art market.

AL and me ... What I know, care about ... Going-on as Grammar. No money, no prospects ... Fear ... Starvation. ('Handbook[s] to Going-On', *Art–Language*, vol. 2, no. 4 [1974] 26)

The conversations of this period can be more or less reconstructed from publications such as *Handbook(s) to Going-On* (1974), *Draft for an Anti-Textbook* (1974) and the next three or four numbers of *Art–Language* (vol. 3, nos. 2, 3 and 4). The transcribed discourses are grouped according to subject. The moment around which the activity revolved was an implosion which sucked the effort of revision into the mass of text accumulated so far. So there was conversation, and there were two main forms of presentation: on the one hand, the Index as an expositive form of that conversation, and on the other the *Art–Language* journal that had been distributing the work of the group since 1969.

... and there is no clear demarcation when our socializing becomes work. (*Art–Language*, vol. 3, no. 1 [1974] 98)

The Index unfolds in the transformation of the links that can be found between the sequences of text. The accumulation of vectors which represent connections between speakers, subdivisions of expressions, or segments of text, is distributed on a map. With no dominant theory, informal arguments systematically confront one another on centre stage. The accumulation of fragments of discourse, the lack of distinction between theories incorporated into the conversation, the ideologies themselves in constant transformation, and even inarticulate exclamations, make up a heterodox mass of discourse.

In the end, quantity was no less a problem than questions of methodology. The processes of those years, marked simultaneously by conversation and the production of different versions of the Index, resulted in a dialectical explosion. There was a superficial growth of conversation. But 'the more "index" you write-in, the more difficult it is to go on ...' (*Art–Language*, vol. 3, no. 1 [1984] 83). That combination of growth with difficulty suggests the unfinalizability that Bakhtin and his commentators attribute to dialogical processes. In reference to *Art & Language*, we have to translate unfinalizability by incompleteness, which could be considered an explicit virtue, a positive feature that determined the use the spectator would make of the Index or any fragment of it: 'It denies completeness, and it might be useful.' (*Art–Language*, vol. 3, no. 1 [1984] 7). As Philip Pilkington has said, such incompleteness prevents anyone from being able to exercise a psychological privilege over the contents. 'Because indexing was an *actualizing* process, the Indexes were not a metalanguage and not a metapractice. They were not an explanation or guide to what Art & Language thought; they *were* Art & Language thought.' (*Art–Language*, new series, no. 2 [1997] 10). The rest was mere furniture, about which Art & Language felt some continuing anxiety. Curiously, the growth of information technology, the quintessential instrument of administered societies, might have saved Art & Language this anxiety over the aesthetic gestalt of its Indexes.

Ideology is just a failure to conform to the conditions of rationality. (Art & Language, 'Dialectical Materialism' [1974])

Even if the quantitative and cognitive problems of the Index proved capable of solution, the whole effort at organization that had characterized the period was threatened by the impossibility of containing the ideological implications of the conversational activity. The machine for dealing with problems of that kind has still to be invented. Dialogical reflectiveness displaced the monological reflectiveness of modernity (which still invested Minimalism, conceptualism, etc. …). This transformation marked the beginning of an effectively boundless ideological critique. '*Pace* Lukács, the icy finality of criticism in the dialectic is only the margin of (our) index (soul) contents' (from *Proceedings 0012 Child's Play* [1973–74]). '… dialogue is the context in which learning occurs' (*Art-Language*, vol. 2, no. 4 [1974] 52)

Art & Language's sense of a public, as viewer or as spectator, becomes in this process an objective to be worked for – something to be produced by the work and inseparable from any conception of it. […]

Carles Guerra, extract from 'The Last Possessions: A Dialogical Restoration of Art & Language', in *Art & Language in Practice/Volume II: Critical Symposium*, ed. Charles Harrison (Barcelona: Fundació Antoni Tàpies, 1999) 187–9.

Elena Filipovic
If You Read Here ... Martha Rosler's Library//2007

[...] [Between 15 November 2005 and 15 April 2006, Martha Rosler's] books – nearly eight thousand of them – were temporarily removed from the artist's home and shelved in impressive row after row in a cramped storefront space in New York's Lower East Side run by e-flux. There they stood, free and open to the public for months. The books were then packed and relocated to other venues, occupying reorganized rows in the Frankfurter Kunstverein and, later, in a walk-up space in Antwerp as part of MuHKA's 'Academy. Learning from Art' exhibition. [...]

The library is the first of Rosler's projects in which reading isn't the contextual background or component to something larger, but is the project. And for this, organization is paramount. The displaced library originally followed the logic of the shelves in Rosler's own Greenpoint, New York, home. For instance, books lining the individual stairs of her home were gathered and placed on corresponding shelves in the e-flux space, as were books from the hallway, the bathroom, the office, etc. Thus their organization was one of use and practicality, a homespun logic that nevertheless reveals Rosler's ideas and positions on publications that make sense together. This shifted when the library was moved to Frankfurt and Antwerp, because in each case new spatial conditions (and new interpretations of Rosler's organizational universe by herself or others) helped determine its form.

MuHKA curator Dieter Roelstraete calls it a library that follows a 'domino theory of history'.[1] And indeed a look at its offerings shows, as he suggests, that the section with literature by women leads to books on feminism leads to gender studies leads to family studies leads to psychoanalysis leads to Jewish studies leads to books on the Holocaust which leads to German history, and so on. And in its shelving and re-shelving, the 'Martha Rosler Library' reorganizes the history of the world and makes us sensitive to the way the presentation of that thing we call 'history' matters. Libraries, after all (and this library reminds us of it), not only store but also participate in the production of history. They beg the question of the ideologies they promote and the roles they fulfil in the process of truth-production. While the library isn't Borges' Chinese encyclopaedia, it employs a taxonomy that doesn't quite follow the Dewey decimal system either. And just as Foucault claimed of Borges' fictive encyclopaedia's incomprehensively wild taxonomy that it allowed one to apprehend 'the exotic charm of another system of thought' as well as 'the limitation of our own', so does Rosler's personal system of order and classification beg us to attend to the rules that govern our own positions.[2] Her library is a world picture – one in which women are prolific science-fiction writers, the political Left has a voice, 'marginal' cultures have a place, colonial history is not forgotten and feminism didn't begin and end in the 1970s.

Rosler might just tell you that it is another one of her 'decoys', and that her work is a series of them – one thing camouflaged as another so that 'the more you look at it, the more you see that it's asking you to think about something else'.[3] About this Roelstraete recounted an anecdote that speaks volumes: after arranging the library for its Antwerp presentation Rosler lamented that a section of writings about black history found itself tucked on a shelf in a corner. It would have to be moved, she insisted; black history could not be marginalized further. Rosler's attention to the position and placement of the books is a key to understanding the library. Like Foucault's concern with the mechanisms by which power 'reaches into the very grain of individuals, touches their bodies and inserts itself into their actions and attitudes, their discourses, learning processes and everyday lives', Rosler offers readers off the street the free use of a library that refuses to reproduce the hegemonic positions of our present and indeed begs us to think about how they function in our everyday.[4] And therein lies one of the library's most critical roles and its conceptual connection to so much of the artist's larger oeuvre.

The gaps in the library (Rosler held back several thousand books that she was convinced she might need to consult) suggest something of its necessary incompleteness and fragile claim to anything like absolute authority, pointing at one of the important questions of the project: within this sanctuary to the author and to authorship itself (what more likely a piece to ask such a question than a library of books) – who is the author? Its very title heralds some of its expiation of authority and its wilful ambiguity as a library-cum-artwork. The project is, after all, the 'Martha Rosler Library'. Not '*The* Martha Rosler Library'. The difference is small but significant. And, as Rosler is quick to point out, the former is incorrect, grammatically speaking. So what happened? The artist did not give the project its title, and she didn't insist on a change when she was confronted with it. Had Rosler named the project, she might have given it another name (and perhaps not one with her name in it at all), she easily volunteers; or, at the very least, she would not have left off the definite article that its Mexican- and Russian-born *e-flux* initiators (Julieta Aranda and Anton Vidokle, respectively, both artists themselves) did. But the 'error' is perhaps no mistake, for in that lies a clue to the complexity of this project that sits between a functional space/service and an artwork in which Martha Rosler, the proper name, abandoned authority so that we could sit, read and make of her books what we will … […]

1   [footnote 5 in source] Conversation between the author, Dieter Roelstraete and Martha Rosler, January 2007.

2   [6] Michel Foucault, *Les Mots et les choses* (1966), trans. The Order of Things (New York: Vintage Books, 1973) xv.

3   [7] Cynthia Carr, 'Rethinking Everyday Life', *Village Voice* (16–22 August 2000)

4   [8] Michel Foucault, *Power/Knowledge: Selected Interviews and Other Writings 1972–1977*, ed. Colin Gordon (New York: Pantheon Books, 1980) 30.

Elena Filipovic, extracts from 'If You Read Here … Martha Rosler's Library', *Afterall*, no. 15 (Spring/ Summer 2007) 91–2; 93–5.

Joanna Mytkowska and Andrzej Przywara
Edward Krasinski's Studio//2004

During the dozen or so years he spent in his studio/flat, Edward Krasinski created a changing yet precisely thought-out collection of works from various periods and objects he made specifically for the place. A version of this collection has been preserved in the studio. We found out about Edward Krasinski's death on 5 April 2004 while away in the Netherlands doing research for our participation in 'Who if not we …?' All new contacts and developments suddenly lost their allure. Krasinski (born 1925) had been seriously ill for many months, his flat had been vacant for more than two years and we were taking care of the space. The flat was not a typical artist's studio, and we were always reluctant to call it a 'studio'. Krasinski never let anybody see him 'working' and was indignant whenever someone called what he was doing 'work'. If he invited anyone to the studio, it was to show the final effect rather than the process itself. The studio seemed a perfect setting for celebrating solitude and friends' visits. We knew that it would be up to us and the artist's daughter, Paulina Krasinska, to decide what to do with the place. We rejected outright the idea of turning it into a museum, firstly because of the nature of Krasinski's 'oeuvre', and secondly because of the deadness into which artists' studios fall if turned into memorial rooms. We were tempted to leave everything as it was, slightly coated with dust, and to show it rarely, to keep this unusual place semi-concealed, without subjecting it to any of the known procedures of memory recording. We realized, however, that if we did this, the fragile objects and subtle meanings would soon fade and vanish irretrievably. Besides, because of its location on the eleventh floor of an ordinary apartment block in downtown Warsaw, the place would soon gain the status of an oddity. Instead, we have decided to settle for a different solution: to leave the main part of the studio unchanged and undisturbed, but to surround it with a framework of contemporary architecture that would help extend its function and create various contemporary references to the historic studio.

We have decided to rebuild the corridor leading to the studio's two main rooms – Krasinski's private room and a 70 square-metre terrace – into a multifunctional space, suitable for organizing meetings or exhibitions, and serving as a studio for visiting artists. A small office space and a guest room would also be squeezed in. We have decided to commission this project to Rotterdam's BAR architecture studio, whose work we know from Utrecht, where they converted a historic tenement house into the contemporary art centre BAK (*basis voor actuele kunst*).

Edward Krasinski's studio has a lengthy history, and has in fact become a legendary place in the history of Polish art. In 1962 (when the building was erected) the government offered the studio to Henryk Stazewski who moved in with painter Mewa Lunkiewicz and her husband Jan Rogoyski. Stazewski was one of the founders of the avant-garde movement, a member of international art groups of the 1920s and 1930s such as *Cercle et Carré* or *Abstraction–Création*. In 1927, he was one of the organizers of Kasimir Malevich's first exhibition outside of Russia, which took place at the Institute for the Promotion of Art at Warsaw's Polonia Hotel. In 1931, he established (along with Wladyslaw Strzeminski and Katarzyna Kobro) and helped organize Muzeum Sztuki w Lodzi in Lodz, the world's first museum of modern art. The works donated to him by foreign artists, including Piet Mondrian and Theo van Doesburg, now form the core of its collection. Stazewski founded and wrote theoretical texts for the periodicals *Blok* and *Praesens*. He was particularly interested in the concept of neoplasticism, which he popularized in Poland and used to define creatively his own artistic position. In the 1960s, Stazewski returned to painting with his critically acclaimed series of white reliefs (1961). Stazewski's artistic attitude and vitality gained him the respect of many young artists, and in 1966 he co-founded Galeria Foksal in Warsaw. From the 1960s onwards Stazewski spent his mornings painting in an armchair that has been preserved to this day (and exhibited regularly), and entertained guests in the afternoons. His flat was a place of meetings and discussions, an enclave of freedom in communist Poland, and Stazewski himself was a link to the avant-garde tradition whose continuity had been broken after the war. Krasinski started visiting Stazewski and Mewa in the mid 1960s, staying on and off in the small room adjacent to the studio after Mewa's death in 1967, and moved in for good around 1970. After Stazewski died in 1988, the studio, once full of abstract paintings, gradually emptied, leaving Krasinski alone in an empty apartment.

The studio began taking its present shape in 1988 as Krasinski filled the place with works he had shown at exhibitions and objects created specifically for the studio. The new objects always turned up as if *en passant*; slight readjustments gradually changed the mood of the apartment, making it a true expression of Krasinski's personality. Living alone in the studio inspired him to produce a number of important works, which transformed the nature of his art. In 1989, Krasinski organized the 'Hommage à Henryk Stazewski' exhibition at Galeria Foksal. The exhibition included black-and-white photographs of the studio's furniture: bookshelves, cupboards, windows and doors, as well as several real objects, including a table topped by a shark's fin (as if a shark were swimming under the table), designed in collaboration with Stazewski. The illusion in the photographs is almost perfect, with only small details revealing which photo was made in the gallery and which in the studio. Lifesize black-and-white photographs of the studio transposed into exhibition spaces would become a natural background for the blue strip. Krasinski's means of communication. On at least two occasions the studio was the protagonist of exhibitions: in Münster (1993), where two photographed views of the studio were cut into strips and stuck to two sides of columns; and at the Zacheta Gallery in Warsaw (1998), where Krasinski showed a labyrinth ending in a wardrobe. As the studio gradually filled with these objects duplicating its features, it became a play of reflections and repetitions.

The objects now in the studio refer to Krasinski's earliest artistic activities. His early objects, made since the beginning of the 1960s, were gravity-defying sculptures that try to hang in space or imitate movement: wooden spikes suspended on thin wires, falling drops arrested a moment before falling, bent and twisted cables and wires. The studio contains either the original objects or copies Krasinski made in the 1980s. The logic of their functioning hints at a predilection for theatricality governing the structure of the studio, an almost childish delight in imitation, subtly subverting the laws of nature and transforming the studio into a visual trap set for the viewers. Numerous objects suspended in space, improbable combinations of objects, omnipresent puns and situational jokes give the place an air of the absurd. However, contrary to what has often been said, they have little to do with Surrealism. Suspending things on threads, leaning the heavy on the fragile, and a general inclination towards the peripheries, are more in keeping with Alfred Jarry's pataphysics.[1] Things halted in mid-drop, frozen movement, repetitions and tricks all testify to the artist's search for the impossible. The logic of absurdity reigns supreme in Krasinski's studio, though it avoids being pushy. An egg in an open bird cage, a tree branch growing out of the floor. A clasp fastened to the light switch, suggesting it has been hung on the wall like a painting; swelled floorboards rising several inches above the floor. A faucet in the middle of the living room wall. A stick growing out of the floor throwing a painted shadow. Photographs of friends stuck to wooden cubes suspended in the centre of the room. Furry mice fastened to various objects are embodiments of hallucination. All these imperfect instruments of illusion have something childish about them, and childishness is something Krasinski embraced, as when he insisted that others call him by the diminutive name of Edzio.

Running around the whole studio is a strip of the blue Scotch tape Krasinski would become perhaps most famous for, stuck at a height of 130 cm. Its first appearance in his work dates back to 1968, when he stuck it to tree trunks in Zalesie near Warsaw. In 1970, Daniel Buren helped Krasinski stick the tape onto the front wall of the Musée d'art moderne de la Ville de Paris. From that moment on, the blue tape became his trademark. Buren visited the studio in 1974 and stuck his own tape on the windows of Stazewski's room. During his next visit, in 1993, to attend a seminar organized in the studio, Buren glued strips of tape on the windows of the apartment's central room. The blue strip can be perceived as a continuation of Krasinski's earlier sculptures, a natural consequence of their gravitation towards the linear, but also as a manifestation of the quest for dematerialization, the desire to replace the theatre of cheap illusion with a total figurative gesture. The strip could potentially appear everywhere, run without end: its possibilities were inexhaustible. It was by accident that Krasinski came across a 19 mm-wide strip of blue Scotch tape, but it was an accident that Krasinski had been waiting for. Towards the end of the 1960s, the magical causative power of linear objects, in spite of their illusionistic nature, was starting to become exhausted. Krasinski was searching for a way out of the dilemma, as reflected in photographic records of his performances showing him entangled in the line (*J'ai perdu la fin*, 1969), standing next to coils of wire, photographed with moving objects: a folding and unfolding wooden zigzag. Photographs from the late 1960s show Krasinski at work; by the early 1990s, they would celebrate only his presence. One such portrait hung on the apartment's front door. Another, fixed to the frame of the bed in which Henryk Stazewski died, traced the course of spiritual heritage. Yet another shows Krasinski playing table tennis with a gallery owner; a red ball hangs in the air between them. Krasinski's most radical conceptual gesture preceding the blue ribbon was to send a message with the word 'blue' repeated 5,000 times as his contribution to the Tokyo Biennale (1970). When the ship carrying the works was stopped in transit, Krasinski, knowing the works would not get there in time, sent a telegram. The telegram and the exhibition plans have been preserved at the studio.

The strip was a means of self-definition often applied in external, urban space, and above all inside, in enclosed spaces. The ribbon could cut through everything in its way. It was particularly good for defining all kinds of back rooms, recesses and other margins of official spaces. In museums, it was a useful device to determine scale. In the early 1970s, Krasinski introduced objects that were something of an obstacle for the strip. At first, these would resemble fragments of rooms: a section of wall with piping and a toilet chain (now in the studio), part of a door, or a wallpapered surface. Then, around 1975, the objects gave way to abstract diagrams of spaces, their axonometric projections. This gave birth to a series Krasinski would work on and modify for the rest of his life.

Other objects returning from exhibitions to the studio include the black-and-white reproductions of historical paintings Krasinski hung in the place of the originals at various museums (Lodz, Münster and Göteborg). Another object reflecting his struggle with the act of painting is a black ladder used when mounting exhibitions, to which a slaughterhouse hook, complete with a blood-red point, has been fastened.

The only thing hanging from the sturdy hook, however, is a thin string. The frailty of painting is also implied by several randomly arranged shot-glasses, each containing a drop of dried red paint and signed with a printed 'E'. Krasinski gave these small tributes to the death of painting to guests attending his seventy-fifth birthday party. Krasinski described his situation as follows:

I inherited a large, empty studio from Henio [Henryk Stazewski]. I had put up at other people's places for all my life, and here I was with this studio all of a sudden: 120 square metres, and to top it all off, a terrace. Traces of his paintings were on the walls, the ghosts of Henio's paintings, these whitish rectangles on the walls. And wires. And now the place is too full again. But I haven't been arranging anything, it has been mounting, accruing by itself. Is accruing by itself. Building up, like dust on the floor. From time to time I made some decision, hang something, Henio's shelves were photographed for an exhibition and got back here; paintings, still packed, stand in the corridor because there is no place for them anywhere else. But I have the situation in hand, and I'm very careful for the place not to get cluttered. At the same time, it's neither an exhibition nor a collection. I only live here, though I'm still staying in the small room, just as it was when Mewa and Henio were here. The studio is there to sit in, have a drink; sometimes someone will show up. I rarely go to the other room. There are only all kinds of remnants here. There is a large painting by Henio, which is a remnant. Hang something on the wall today, a painting for instance, and the next day it will have become a remnant, that's why there are only remnants here'.[2]

Edward Krasinski was an important figure in the art world when we met him in the late 1980s, and for us he became a friend and a reference point in art. His strategy of abstaining from action and distancing himself jocularly from the paradigms of modernism enabled us to understand the changing principles of art. Krasinski was always in tune with the times, liking to show his work with that of young artists, as he did with Pawel Althamer at Manifesta 3 in Ljubljana (2000), an exhibition that was very important for us. The gesture of sticking on the tape, marking one's territory, belongs to the unsurpassed romantic utopias of the past. Transforming one's life into a work of art is one of the few forms of asceticism available today. His studio was a microcosm, a world he arranged his own way. We would like this world to survive.

1   Pataphysics was introduced to the critical work on Edward Krasinski by Marek Gozdziewski in his text 'The Blue Tape Stripe Line', in *Edward Krasinski* (Warsaw: Fundaja Galerii Foksal, 1997).

2   Krasinski, interview with Wieslaw Borowski, *Edward Krasinski* (Warsaw: Galeria Zacheta, 1998).

Joanna Mytkowska and Andrzej Przywara, 'Edward Krasinski's Studio', trans. Marcin Wawrzynczak, in *Who if not we should at least try to imagine the future of all this?: 7 episodes on (ex)changing Europe*, ed. Maria Hlavajova, Jill Winder (Amsterdam: Artimo, 2004) 128–45.

Bernadette Walter
Dieter Roth's Mats//2003

Beginning in the early 1980s, Dieter Roth placed grey cardboard mats measuring about 39 x 31 inches on all his tables: in his apartment at Hammerstrasse, his studios in St Johanns-Vorstadt and on Hegenheimerstrasse in Basel, and in his houses in Mols and Mosfellssveit. He used them as writing mats or repositories for the 'traces of my domestic activities'. They functioned as underlays in two of his 'household departments, cooking & eating and painting & pasting.'[1] From the dining room table they made their way to the 'painting and pasting department', where Roth and his family continued to process them. The mats incorporate several elements of Roth's art in a single work: drawing, painting and the use of objects and photographs.

Although the mats are reminiscent of Daniel Spoerri's *tableaux pièges*, or 'snare pictures', these work complexes differ substantially in two respects. Spoerri had been making his 'snare pictures' since the 1960s, by glueing a random arrangement of objects found on a work or dining table to the surface underneath. He interfered in scenes that he himself had staged – for example, dinner with guests – at a specific moment of his choosing in order to preserve a record of that moment by attaching the objects to their underlying surface. By contrast, Roth's mats render progression through time, in as much as they often remained in place for several years, and the arrangement of objects and drawings on them was not left to chance.

For Roth, the most important element in the design of the mats was the 'ornamental = symmetrical' treatment of drips and stains. The spots intercepted in the kitchen department were complemented with a drafted counterpart on an imaginary pictorial axis in the office department. Roth undermined this 'clumsy symmetry', however, by reworking the surface many times. The axis also assisted in the representation of various concepts of abstract or real mirror images. In the Holderbank [exhibition hall near Zurich] catalogue of 1987 Roth explained that a painted air space on one side might be juxtaposed with a colourless paintbrush on the other, or a 'sinking boat' paired with a 'lifesaving ring'. He also juxtaposed colours. Optical regimentation was countered by the use of objects glued to the surface: 'When symmetry has been clearly established in the picture, duplication – the same thing appearing twice – can offer this impression somewhere: the same thing twice, e.g. two curlicues, two cigarette butts, two any old things – even three (or even more)'.[2]

On most of the mats one can distinguish the extent of Roth's radius of action. When you sit at a desk, the most convenient place to draw and paint is the area directly in front of you. Roth composed still lifes out of left-over food, ashtrays, office utensils, painting tools and photographs, which he then glued to the surface. He either left the mats as is, which meant that the top part presented a relatively empty, grey surface, or he rotated them 180 degrees in order to continue working on them. In some cases he would work at mats placed on a table accessible from both sides. After finishing work on both ends, he would cut the mats in half and adjoin them again in a mirror image, resulting in a compact pictorial centre that becomes looser towards the edges.

Roth himself considered the mats important for the development of his painting in the late 1980s. In the course of exploring their mirror imagery, he discovered that he was moving increasingly in the direction of ornamental 'flower painting': 'The axis looks like a stem, the spots like leaves, the objects like blossoms.' The 'bouquet' was to play a central role in the subject matter of his prints and paintings in the early 1980s.

1   *Dieter Roth* (Glaris, Switzerland: Holderbank, 1987) 1.

2   Ibid., 3.

Bernadette Walter, 'Mats', trans. Catherine Schelbert, in *Roth Time: A Dieter Roth Retrospective*, ed. Theodora Vischer, Bernadette Walter (New York: The Museum of Modern Art/Baden: Lars Müller, 2003) 222.

Jan Verwoert
Bernd Krauß//2006

The Bauhaus taught that, if form was to follow function, the first rule was to observe the principle of *Materialgerechtigkeit*: the need to do justice to the material you work with. This ideal of a transparent materialist aesthetic based on a strict economy of means still remains compelling. In practice we know what an object, building or sculpture will look like when it is designed to reflect the properties of industrial materials such as steel, glass or concrete. But what would it mean to do justice to materials that are neither plain nor pure but mixed and messy, like most of the stuff that makes up the reality of our surroundings?

Bernd Krauß's works address just this question. With a no-nonsense, pragmatic approach to making art, he finds systematic solutions to the problem of what to do with the stuff that accumulates around him every day – waste paper, lumps of wood, cardboard boxes, Sellotape, linoleum flooring, oil paint or mouldy fruit. He may tear every page out of a magazine, then fold each one to form a strip an inch wide and then stick all the strips together with Sellotape to form a cylinder, or make tiny alterations to a cardboard box and then re-box it in a Perspex case. Just as he will squeeze tube after tube of oil paint onto pieces of chipboard and consider the resulting abstractions, so Krauß will carve compositions into the lino on the floor of his studio or scrape the bark off a pile of logs and treat it as a sculpture. These wood pieces echo the rare beauty of work made by art enthusiasts in evening classes who, in the process of discovering the joys of abstract sculpture, create infinite and surprising variations on the phallic form.

All Krauß's works are produced in series, with each one forming an independent strand in his overall practice, which has developed consistently over the years. He establishes a range of basic methods and then applies them to various tasks. He used the paper-folding technique, for instance, to tape a tutu together from strips of paper which he then did ballet exercises in. The scraped logs in turn feature in Krauß's 1999 home-video remake of Rainer Werner Fassbinder's *Der Müll, Die Stadt und der Tod* (The Garbage, the City and Death, 1975–84). Each log had its own name tag and objects attached to it, identifying it as a particular character: two balls of string for a girl's breasts, for example, or a baseball cap for a playboy. Krauß then animated the pieces with basic stop-frame editing and dubbed in the dialogue from behind the camera.

Through the formalized treatment of his materials Krauß displaces meaning in unpredictable ways. Still, content seeps inexorably into his work, in the same way you involuntarily pick up bits of gossip. Another of Krauß's ongoing projects is *Der Riecher* (The Sniffer, first published 1997), a photocopied A4 magazine with handwritten articles and hand-drawn illustrations. Based on the idea that any material is suitable for publication, *Der Riecher* mixes articles on food, sport, sexual fantasies and other everyday concerns with comments on other people's private lives that are funny, insidious and, as likely as not, true. Krauß interprets things in a style that, like gossip, is both cursory and pointed. *Mutti (Pressel)* (which can mean Mama, Old Lady or Cow) and *Vati* (Daddy, Old Man, Twit; both 2004) are two sculptures made from cardboard boxes hung on the wall. The former is a box dented in the middle on both sides to form a waistline, with its front flaps folded to resemble something like a vagina. The latter is a brown box with six vertical slits cut in the front, through which a light blue belt is drawn to hold the flaps together like a zip over the beginnings of a paunch.

Managing to be both spontaneous and conceptually strict, Krauß deals with each cardboard box he finds in the same way: one box, one material problem, one sculptural solution. So, unlike many of his contemporaries, he neither reifies sloppiness as a virtue nor cultivates a crypto-individualist mythology to back up his work with a narrative. Instead he voids artistic parameters of quality and meaning by methodically reducing his art to a day-to-day practice of working on materials. If there is beauty, it comes as a surprise. *Avokado* (2005), for instance, is a shrivelled avocado cast in bronze and placed on top of a boulder. The piece immortalizes the avocado's state of decay in an utterly inconspicuous monument. What better way to do justice to a dead fruit?

Jan Verwoert, 'Bernd Krauß', *frieze*, no. 97 (March 2006). www.frieze.com

Herzog & de Meuron
Just Waste//2002

In this exhibition ['Herzog & de Meuron: Archaeology of the Mind', Canadian Centre for Contemporary Art, Toronto, 2002], all of our models and experiments with materials have been carefully numbered, labelled and displayed on tables: we are exhibiting an archive, that is, a physical accumulation of the documents that we have produced in order to initiate and accelerate mental processes or, on the contrary, to arrest and propel them in another direction. They bear mute and lifeless witness to the considerable energy that we as a group, in varying combinations, have invested over the years in order to set such intellectual processes in motion. In some cases buildings have actually emerged as a result.

These archived objects are therefore nothing but waste products, since the immaterial, mental processes of understanding, learning and developing always have priority. We have never been interested in producing objects invested with an aura, in the nature of an artwork. These objects are not works of art; they are an accumulation of waste. In this respect, but only in this respect, they have something in common with natural history, as explicitly foregrounded by the curators of this exhibition: accumulated archival documents or accumulated bones and fossils – whatever the case, it would all be lifeless waste were it not for the special gaze, the creative, attentive, sometimes even loving gaze of the interested beholder who is able to interpret and interrelate the moulded shapes, grooves, indentations and discolouration.

In and among all the waste products, the curators have cleverly smuggled a few real works of art, such as a genuine object by Joseph Beuys, an original Yves Klein Blue, and a hand-sculpted figure by Giacometti. Are these simply more waste products or does the panoply of archived waste seek to enhance its status by basking in the radiance of a familiar, brand-name aesthetic? Or conversely, are the works of art, as victims of name-recognition, trying for once to escape the tyranny of the White Cube, so that they may be seen and appreciated in the new light cast on them by this unusual context? [...]

We have opened our archive to the interested viewer like a *Wunderkammer* and transferred its contents to the space of the gallery. Since architecture itself cannot be exhibited, we are forever compelled to find substitutes for it.

Herzog & de Meuron, extract from 'Just Waste' (2002), in *Herzog & de Meuron: Natural History*, ed. Philip Ursprung (Baden: Lars Müller, 2005) 74–5.

Ian Wallace
Corner of the Studio and *El Taller*: A Reflection on Two Works from 1993//2005

When I began to make photographic documentation of my workspace in the late 1960s, I came to realize that this documentation could be considered as a part of the work process, and even as a finished work in itself. It also became apparent that the space or place of production, the studio as an actual as well as a symbolic environment, would be a necessary element in the imagery of this process, as the actual *mise-en-scène* for the materialization of the conceptual, non-objective nature of art. As a self-consciously modernist strategy that still informs my work, this approach combined the intellectual aspects of conceptual art with the material production of the art object in the space of its making. In my attempt to link references to literary and conceptual practice, represented by books and papers, with the technical processes associated with the actual construction of a work, I was creating a dramatized form of intellectual montage.

This coincided with new developments of photographic and language-based practice in conceptual art that freed modernist pictorial art from both the studio and the darkroom. Although I participated in the discussions about 'post-studio' practice that were current in the 1970s, my simultaneous and somewhat contradictory commitment to a modernist and even 'constructivist' practice, as well as to the postmodern critique of craft implicit in aspects of conceptual art, led me to resist the abandonment of either the one or the other approach and to search for a synthesis. I came eventually to stress the importance of the studio as a symbolic space of production, aware also that during the Renaissance there was a similar shift in the space of production of art from the craft workshop to the more literary *studium*, a shift that was essential to the intellectual liberation of the artist and the eventual repositioning of the visual arts as a branch of the humanities. As an artist also educated as an art historian and active in promoting the introduction of visual arts studio practice within a university curriculum, I had a vested interest in legitimizing and rationalizing this development. This I attempted to do within the thematic framework of my artistic practice.

As the space of production, as the specific location of the construction of artwork in both the material and intellectual sense, as the place where the aesthetic 'idea' is produced as an object for contemplation and distribution, the studio functions as a *mise-en-scène* and pictorial grounding of the more conceptual aspects in my work. As my work developed through various stages over the next few decades, the *Studio Series* (1969–) not only continued to play an important role in my conscious attempt to bridge the gap between the sensory and the intellectual, but it also provided a means for self-reflection on the work process itself in relation to the objective or social space of the other two recurring thematic 'locations' that appear in my work: the 'museum' and the 'street'.

The studio as a space showing the production of work appears in my photographs as early as 1969. A self-reflexive reference to a text that produces a work is a significant element in *The Summer Script* (1974), a large-scaled photographic work that was, in its early stages, a collaborative cinematic project with Jeff Wall and Rodney Graham. But it was in *Image/Text* (1979) that the studio appeared for the first time as a primary framing space for the construction of a major work. *Image/Text* can be considered an architectural self-portrait, in which I am shown in the act of composing the final work, and visible on the work table in front of me, which is a dominant motif in the image, are scattered various drawings and sketches, including a sketch of the final composition. This work is a meditation on the studio primarily as a place for thinking and organizing intellectual material, and images of the space for thinking are interwoven with images of writing that self-reflexively refers back to the space itself. Following *Image/Text* was a quasi-performance piece titled *At Work* (1983), in which I transformed the exhibition space of the OR Gallery in Vancouver into a studio space that could be viewed from the public space of the street. As in the earlier work, the emphasis in *At Work* was also on intellectual practice, since in the gallery/studio space I presented myself as a reader and intellectual worker rather than as a craft worker.

However, during the mid 1980s when I reintroduced painting as a support for my photographic enlargements, the emphasis gradually turned from an image of intellectual work to the technical practice and materials of a more conventional conception of the artist's studio – that of the painter. Nevertheless, in such a work as *Studio/Museum/Street* (1986), which was a triptych consisting of photographic enlargements mounted on canvas, I drew attention to the fact that my interest in developing the theme of the studio was balanced with a wider variety of thematic locations that were equally important in my overall practice. Subsequently, the theme of the studio has branched out to include work in both a very personal, intimate and transitory space, such as in the *Hotel Series* (1988–), and in a commentary on workplaces in general, as in the architectural and constructivist references that appear in an ongoing series of works about construction sites, such as the *Barcelona Series* (1992–93). There are other continuing series of related works that document the workspaces of other artists: for instance, in the *Fontana Series* (1988), the *Doberemer Series* (1988–89), *Messes on the Floor of the Studio of Elspeth Pratt* (1988), and *Constellations* (1992).

The two works featured in this discussion, *Corner of the Studio* and *El Taller*, both made in 1993, were an important step in signalling a return to the image of my studio, to the metaphor of painting as a support and to a reflection on both the intellectual and the technical aspects of my way of working. In these works and the ongoing series that have followed, I have expanded this theme to include images of the production of the artworks themselves, with an emphasis on the materials of painting, the texture of canvas, the stretcher bars that form the support, and the studio space with its tools and accessories. In doing so, I am fully aware that there is a well-established genre in the history of modernist art of photographic documentation of artist's studios; often by the artists themselves, as in the photography of Constantin Brancusi or Pablo Picasso, and more recently by Bruce Nauman; but also by established documentary photographers such as Brassaï, Arnold Newman, Ugo Mulas, Hans Namuth and many others. Although these precedents are of interest to me in my own work, I focus only on the distribution of materials, random or otherwise, that is specific to my immediate observation. The photographs are more than documentation of the work process; they are an integral part of the final product of the finished work.

Corner of the Studio and El Taller are related to each other in more than theme alone. Both works are of identical dimensions, formats and techniques. They both consist of an arrangement of four canvases, each 200 by 122 centimetres, and which combine photographs of my studio with rectangular sections of inked monoprint impressions of plywood on acrylic and canvas.

The first work, Corner of the Studio, was completed in March 1993. In this particular view of my studio there is no visible evidence of the production of any artwork and nothing in any of the photographs has been arranged for the sake of the photograph. Although, in 1987, at the time that I photographed Corner of the Studio, I was producing several large canvases (for instance. My Heroes in the Street, 1986–); what is represented in this work is more a 'space for thinking' than production. On the other hand, the series that immediately followed, El Taller, which was photographed in the same studio space (to the right of the windows visible in Corner of the Studio) after the completion of the first series is, in effect, a reprise, a 'correction' of the intellectual ambience of the first work, in so far as it emphasizes the physical fabrication of the work as a 'working space' ('working space' is el taller in Spanish – this work was first exhibited in Spain and therefore acquired the Spanish title).

To return to a discussion of the earlier work, Corner of the Studio, the image represents the studio as a place for intellectual production only in an indirect way. Unlike other works of this type (for example, the Hotel Series), there is not any paperwork in evidence, only boxed musical and recording equipment, and a single open book on the couch. Yet the various objects and furniture in the image do indicate potential activity: the book, musical equipment, an ashtray and a case of beer. Industrial buildings can be seen through the window. The open book, on the edge of the couch next to the chair (largely obscured) where I had been sitting, is, although indecipherable as such in the photograph, *Un Coup de Dès*, the poem by Stéphane Mallarmé, which over the past thirty years has functioned for me as a cipher for the 'unreadable' at those moments when there seemed to be 'nothing to say' (it appears in the foreground of the table in the earlier work related to the theme of the studio, *Image/Text*, 1979). The actual making of the photograph involved an interruption in the act of reading the poem. This interruption stimulated me out of a passive act of reading and daydreaming, into an active state of production, of photographing the space of my reverie, much the same way as *Image/Text* or *At Work* functioned some years earlier. The photographic image intersected my 'absent-mindedness' with another kind of purposive activity: the positioning of the camera, taking light readings, and so on. The technical operation of photography functioned as a self-conscious witness to my private act of reading, as well as providing a concrete spatial reference for an abstract conceptual activity, a document of a specific, narrative autobiographical moment, an 'objective' preservation of an abstract instance of time, that instance being the spring of 1987. The photograph was then put into the archives until resurrected five years later.

When I retrieved this photograph of the corner of my studio, which initially referenced a conceptual space and a specific moment, to be the basis for a large canvas assembly, I reconstructed the space of the original photograph by cutting it into four distinct parts. The photograph was first cut in half, then a rectangular section was cut from the inside centre of each half, thus providing four segments in all, each of which was assigned to be laminated onto a separate canvas, all of which were then arranged to approximate the spatial logic of the original photograph. The specificity of each segment (identified by its photographic information) is also determined by the distinct and dynamic spatial contrasts, textures and colours of the 'abstract' sections of the canvas area that replace the areas of the 'cut-away' section of each part of the original photograph. The cutting away of photographic space has provided a catalyst for what is latent as painterly practice. These 'abstract' sections are the dynamic, 'hot', shifting part of the canvas, as contrasted to the 'cool', more inert quality of the monochromatic, black and white photographic elements, and thus they make a figurative effect against the pictorial ground. Other than the fact that they are all rectangular segments 'cut from the whole', they are limited in number and are clustered together so that they replace the approximate area of the canvas in which the photographic segment is missing.

Yet despite the limits that this almost systematic procedure might seem to place on spontaneity, the accidental textural effects created by these imprinted elements do, in fact, create a sensuous and pictorially expressive reciprocity with the work as a whole. The contrasts of colour and tone between the painted ground and the woodblock impression, between the chromatic and textural contrasts of the abstract segments themselves, and in the interplay between their rectangularity and rectangular forms within the photographic portion of the images, contribute to what I would identify as the 'painterly' in the classic sense; that is, as pictorial representations formed primarily through particularized manipulations of textural material.

However, I also realize in retrospect that by giving the painted sections a more active part than its previous metaphorical function as the 'ground' to the 'figurative' photograph, which carried the signifying function (as in *My Heroes in the Streets*), I have repositioned the painted segments to now function as the figure, and the photograph as the ground. Some implications of this inversion will be elaborated upon later in the discussion of the subsequent work, *El Taller*. This raises some theoretical questions that have yet to be fully answered. What, for example, are the implications of this for the relative hierarchical relationships between painting and photography as it has evolved historically? Is this a repositioning of painting as a signifying gesture? (Until this point 'gesture' has always been repressed in my work and is, in my opinion, the most problematic aspect of painterly technique.) In more general terms, does this constitute a fundamental 'break'?

In any case, the 'hermeneutic substance', the aspect of the subject matter available for interpretation given by the photographic element in these works, is considerably tamed and relatively neutral. I say only 'relatively neutral' because the genre of the studio as a subject for painting has a considerable historical tradition. It carries implications of material production that offer a precise sociological index of the production of the work, especially in view of the fact that this is the space where the work originated. Nevertheless the absence in these works of the human figure, the artist as 'actor', protagonist, producer, sublimates the 'figurative' function of the photograph as a signifying representation to the relatively more dynamic painterly performance of the abstract segments. The 'author as producer' here is present not as a self-legitimizing 'hero', but as an 'absence' looking back through the 'space of production', reflecting on work in the process of its self-definition. This incessant self-reflexivity is perhaps a form of modernist pathology.

Self-reflection on the process of production is even more accentuated in the second work of the series, *El Taller*. Although it is a reprise of the first series (it consists of four canvases of the same dimensions and of the same studio photographed six years later) there are some fundamental differences: the photographs are in colour and the abstract segments in black and white – a reversal of the system in *Corner of the Studio*; there are four distinct photographs, while in the first series a single photograph was cut into four parts. The imagery shows the actual process, materials and production of the canvases themselves, while the first showed only the space of future production.

The four photographs of *El Taller*, taken in the summer of 1993, document the space of the studio in a precisely determined structure, with distinct angle shots that combine to represent a unified space, specifically work tables and a wall against which stretched canvases are propped (these canvases are the same ones upon which their own photographic images are laminated). The four distinct photographs, each laminated onto a canvas of identical dimensions, were shot from two different, adjacent positions a short distance apart and in the same direction. From each position of the camera, two shots were taken; one straight ahead and the other at an oblique angle, giving a total of four photographs of the same scene, but of slightly altered perspectives.

This structure is not necessarily significant from an interpretive point of view, but does involve the attentive spectator in a comprehension of the unity of the work through close observation of the photographic information. The self-referencing of the photographic 'ground' is also effected by the referencing of the tools of production and their relative position in the image. Even though there is an apparent arbitrariness in the positioning of the objects themselves (nothing in the image was arranged for the benefit of the photographic composition), it is not difficult for a spectator to recognize that the table coming into the right-hand side of the first canvas on the left is the same table that almost touches the left-hand side of the canvas adjacent to it, and that the ladder in the third canvas is the same as that in the first, and so on. The 'topography' of the photographic space can thus assume great complexity if studied in detail. The tools of production (ladder, tables, stretcher bars, canvas, ruler and tape, canvas pliers and stapler, etc.) stand out in the image as figurative emblems that refer to a particular stage in the production process; that is, in the preparation of the canvas ground only, for neither the photographic nor the painting process in itself are represented. There is an emphasis on the 'ground' then, that draws attention to the problematic of 'figure-ground' relations that are central to this series and all works on canvas related to it.

There is an ironic effect produced by the fact that this emphatic reference to the canvas support as pictorial ground is conveyed specifically by the photographic element that covers most of the surface of each canvas. The photographic reference becomes the 'ground' that establishes the visual field for 'painterly' figuration – the abstract sections of woodblock impressions. The field of photographic practice that has historically provided a competitive, and often opposing force to the traditional dominance of painting and the materiality of the canvas support, now ironically acts as a reifying and 'affirmative' reference. Just as text subscribes image, here photography subscribes painting – it confirms its existence through mechanical representation. However, it would not be entirely accurate to say that this reifying and affirmative effect ceases to be critical of these relations. Rather, through the 'displacement' of the 'ideal' ground (the white, virginal space of the primed canvas) of painting by the 'vulgar' specificity of photographic representation, this ironic reversal has critical effect, especially in so far as it provides the opportunity for reflection upon the relative status of the pictorial arts and what we might call the 'idea of the picture', the discursive logos of modern thought as represented in the pictorial image.

The point that must be acknowledged here is that painting, even in its most idealized and essentialist sense, is not 'immaculately conceived'. It is a technical invention, historically evolved to function as the dominant form of pictorial representation throughout most of the history that established its privileged position as the horizon of meaning in western high culture; that is, as 'the idea of the picture'. Photographic representation continues this logic as a mechanized mode of production. Compromised and displaced at the onset of modernism by the industrialization of pictorial representation through mechanical reproduction, primarily photography and cinema, painting fell back on its historically evolved status as an ideal essentialist space for meaning: that of modernist abstraction and the rhetoric of gesture associated with recuperated subjectivity. The referencing power of photography returns to the 'deconstructed' materiality of painting and its canvas support the possibility of representation, but now as the field rather than the figure.

The theme of displacement that shadows this series of works on the theme of the studio serves as a critical reference for the legitimacy of painting (and photography) and to my particular position on it, which is as follows: that the ideal space of painting as a historically produced space of potential meaning, as the 'ground of signification', can be itself also a 'material effect'; that the 'poetics' of painting, rendered apparently (only 'apparently') obsolete by the specificity of the mechanical representation of the 'real', can be recuperated, needs to be recuperated, as a functional element in the construction of significant (historically compelling) meaning. This recuperation of the conversion of the ideality of painting into a material effect, is carried out through the dialectical and critical (and ironic, for what is given away is also taken back) contestation of representational function of both painting and photography in the field of the picture.

Yet – to continue questioning the logic of this displacement (if photography now assumes the position of the 'ground' of representation in the horizon of the pictorial field) – what becomes of painting when it is pushed into the foreground as 'figuration', but still stripped of its representational capability? A description of how this functions in the 'abstract' segments of the canvases of *El Taller* follows. In each canvas of *El Taller*, the abstract, painterly elements are composed of an arrangement of only two rectangular sections, or elongated bars, one of which is imprinted with a plywood texture in white ink on a white acrylic field, and the other of a plywood imprint in black ink on a white acrylic field. These textural sections are monoprints made by rubbing the canvas directly onto inked plywood. These rectangles are not, in fact (although they might at first appear to be), superimposed over the photographic ground, but instead the photograph has been physically cut away at this point, revealing the canvas texture, and allowing the abstract sections to make an intrusion into the photographic field. The binary relations between the abstract rectangles also follows (like the formal structure for the camera positions) a specific structure: in the two outside canvases (when arranged as a series of four) the rectangles are connected to each other, and the white vertical bar is secured to the edge of the canvas, with the black horizontal bar cantilevered from the white bar so that it projects aggressively into the space of the image. The rectangles in the two central canvases are 'synaptic'; that is, although they do not actually touch, they move in the direction of each other, the white from the top and the black from the bottom, so that the space that separated them is charged with a dynamic potentiality.

There is, in this movement, a residual rhetorical element that flows from the relations between these figurations. It is possible that this stems from the sublimation of painterly gesture to dominantly mechanical processes in the photographic (printed and laminated in a laboratory) and wood monoprint elements directly transferred without any intentional expressivity. Because there is almost never any painterly gesture as such in my work, rhetorical figuration emerges indirectly and at the extremes of the pictorial vocabulary, both in the general organization of theme and form and often in apparently incidental details of the photographs. Even the texture of the natural grain of the wood impression is produced by pressure of the feet. But for the most part the rhetorical drama of what is latent as painterly figuration is contained in a dynamic but controlled equilibrium between the abstract sections and the spatial unity of the photographic ground, which, since it is the more potent representational field, already has a superfluity of expressivity on its own. The visual thrusts and parries, the luminous textures, the contrasts of tone and chroma all contribute to a painterly vocabulary latent in both the abstract and photograph elements. But overriding all those movements that carry a figurative function, there is the 'opticality' of the work: the illusions of virtual space carried by the material difference between the photographic imagery and the woodblock monoprint, both of which articulate space in a forceful but distinct way. This 'opticality' is reinforced by various contrapuntal spatializing devices in both the photographic and abstract sections.

In the photographic element of both series there is a visual interplay between flat, closed space and open, recessive space, such as can be seen in the perspective in the tilt of the plane of the floor, a distant view through an open window, the flatness of a canvas leaning against a wall, a dark space under a table, and so on. Since these images were shot on large-format negatives, the precision of the details and the modelling of light contribute to a particularly photographic feeling for space. Space is 'carved-out' optically, so to speak, and the eye is 'trapped' into plotting the logic of virtual space, the mirror simulation of actual space that is inherent to photography.

Further suggestions of pictorial depth are enhanced by the technical differences that distinguish the abstract wood impressions from the photographic sections. This difference makes the abstract rectangles appear to float in space in front of the photograph, as well as in front of each other when they are layered. Furthermore, the chromatic and tonal contrasts that exist between the rectangles reinforces the spatial dramatization that gives each canvas a baroque complexity that is intensified when they are considered as a group. What is important to me in these works, as the outcome of a formal experiment, in effect, is that this optical complexity derives from a few direct, opaque, almost 'granular' (in the sense that the illusion of deep space is, upon close inspection, confounded by the clearly visible grain of the canvas surface) technical devices. The result is a self-reflexive, theoretically problematic visuality produced by an economy of means.

This interactive drama plays out what is essential to all radical pictorial art; not the formulation of frozen iconic emblems that 'illustrate' ideas, but the active recognition (I stress the dynamic aspect here – 'seeing it new') in the 'minds' eye' during the contemplation of pictorial art of our own comparative experiences of the visual complexity of everyday life. New pictorial art provides the 'codes' for experience. It tunes the eye. This fundamental function is the 'grounding' of experiential rationality. As such, it is truly classical, but also modern in its experimental self-consciousness, so that the process of seeing itself comes again under examination as a subject for pictorial art – as it did during the experiment with linear perspective systems of representation as formulated by Leon Battista Alberti in the fifteenth century, and the dissolution of these perspective systems in the evolution of modernist abstraction, in particular, during the early years of Cubism.

Corner of the Studio and El Taller, and other works related to them, apart from their connection to the subject of the studio as a place of production, are part of a digression in my work as a whole, a digression from thematic models of subject matter that still dominates most of my work, towards an experimental reflection on technical problems and a theorization of means essential to modernist art of all kinds. Yet there still remains an unresolved problematic in this work, which can only be answered in time and through the development of new work; that of the limits of the aesthetic as well as the technical models that inform these pieces. That is to say, the models of vision provided by both painting and photography (the 'static' visual arts) have been substantially superseded by new technology: cinema, video, television and computer-generated imagery. Nevertheless, the presence of the aesthetic dimension, the grounding of the medium, whatever the medium may be, in an 'idealist' or 'essentialist' signification that transcends its spectacular or representational power remains, in my view, an indispensable factor for the future legitimacy of contemporary art.

Ian Wallace, 'Corner of the Studio and El Taller: A Reflection on Two Works from 1993', in Ian Wallace: The Idea of the University (Vancouver: Charles H. Scott Gallery, 2005) 27–36.

1   First, listen to the news on the radio.

2   Prepare a cup of tea and drink it standing at the window. You see people walking in the street, cars, shops, it's fascinating.

3   Wash the cup because you hate starting to work while there's something dirty in the sink.

4   Make one or two phone calls.

5   Clean your table.

6   Go to the post office to get a registered letter. Wait half an hour.

7   Take cash from an automat.

8   Buy a magazine.

9   When you're back home, have a quick look at it. Read the main articles.

10   Drink a glass of water, eat a plum.

11   The phone rings, answer and talk.

12   You suddenly remember that you need to make a call.

13   The mobile rings. It's a friend: chat.

14   Check your emails again, in case you received any new ones.

15   It's almost lunchtime: you start feeling hungry. You need strength before you start working, so go to the market and shop.

Valérie Mréjen, *Start Working*, instructional piece for 'Do It', curated by Hans Ulrich Obrist, 2004

Steven Watson
Factory Made//2003

Billy Linich [later Billy Name] first saw Andy Warhol's new space at 231 East 47th Street in early December 1963. He rode up the freight elevator, opened the gated doors at the fourth floor, and stepped into the front corner of an industrial loft about 50 feet deep and 100 feet long. One of the walls was brick, and the ceiling had three arches. A bank of windows to the south offered the only available light for seeing the raw space: the previous tenant, a hat manufacturer, had removed all his electrical fixtures. Wires hung down from holes in the ceiling, and the floor was dirty grey concrete. It possessed none of the trademarks of the era's artists' studios: it wasn't white, it wasn't light-shot, and it wasn't downtown. Whoever heard of an artist's studio down the street from the United Nations building?

Billy Linich began working on this unpromising space in January 1964. For the first weeks working time was restricted to winter's meagre daylight hours. Then Billy installed wiring and 300-watt General Electric indoor-outdoor floodlights and spotlights, bright enough for making art or for making movies. He soon tired of the subway ride downtown and the long walk from the Astor Place subway stop over to 272 East Seventh Street, where he still kept his silver apartment. Once the lighting was installed, Billy asked Andy for the key to the loft so he could work whatever hours he wanted. In late January 1964 Billy moved into the back northwest corner of the space. His home for the next four years consisted of his found-on-the-street couch, a sink, and two Factory bathrooms, where he screwed a bare bulb and posted a hand-lettered sign that read *Please Flush GENTLY!!!*

Around the same time Gerard Malanga also moved into the new space. He was perennially without an apartment and couldn't travel back to his mother's house in the Bronx because of a subway strike. Billy and Gerard were entirely different kinds of residents. Billy was neat, spare and ascetic; less was more, and he could sleep on the couch or on the floor. Gerard introduced boxes of his poetry books to the loft, and when they were set in the middle of the space, Andy drew the line. He could abide the clutter involved with art making, and he welcomed the stray objects that Billy would find in the street to embellish the raw loft, but he didn't want books in a place where art projects filled the space. After a few weeks Gerard moved into a spare room in Allen Ginsberg's apartment on East Fifth Street.

Drawing on his theatre experience building sets, Billy ordered wholesale four-by-eight-foot sheets of three eighth-inch plywood and hinged them together. They were simple, flexible and cheap. 'They were like flats on the stage, and they were all painted silver', Billy said. 'If you put them together, they were very large. They became backgrounds for movies and area dividers. So if I was going to sleep, I was just invisible behind them on my couch.'

Billy started the monumental task of silvering the former hat factory. The simple way would have been to paint the walls silver with an industrial sprayer. But Billy opted for the more painstaking job of attaching long rolls of Reynolds aluminium wrap to walls and columns, using glue and an industrial staple gun; he climbed high ladders and covered hot-water pipes, covering even the windows. Billy was drawn not only to aluminium foil's shiny reflectivity but also to its used, lived-in-look surface. Even when the shinier Mylar became cheaply available, Billy preferred the crumpled aesthetic. He sprayed the floor and sections of the brick wall, using DuPont Krylon paint. Each day Billy sniffed amphetamine, a drug that was ideal for the task of meticulously transforming the dingy loft. Its influence, combined with Billy's diligence, allowed him to focus intently on each silver inch of its surface, right down to the toilet bowl, which was newly silvered down to the water line. In the process Billy bonded with the physical space, and before the winter was over, he became its custodian and protector.

Billy not only created the outlines, he also filled in the space with objects. He began with mirrors, some of them whole, some shards, which he installed in the bathroom, over sinks, next to film cabinets. The mirrors seemed to extend the space, and Billy sometimes checked himself out in them as he worked; the teenager with acne had grown into a graceful, lithe man with a coolly handsome face. Warhol recalled, 'He had a dancer's strut that he liked to check in motion.'

Billy furnished the space, and the biggest cache was found right down in the basement, where a previous tenant had left old furniture. Billy hauled pieces up in the freight elevator – a work table for Andy, a desk, wooden chairs on wheels. 'I would just bring them up piece by piece, and Andy would spray them silver', Billy said. 'And they would be absolutely glowing and brilliant.' In addition to borrowing from the basement cache, Billy brought things from home, from theatrical supply stores, and especially from the street. 'I would just walk everywhere, and I would find things scavenging', Billy said. On a roof he found a white plastic sign for Vic Tanny's gym with blue plastic letters, and in front of a Second Avenue club he found Sammy Davis placards, and on a mid-town sidewalk he picked up the bottom half of a mannequin. He bought carpet at a steep discount because a section was badly bleached. He picked up a Lucite and glass china cabinet, added a heart-shaped sign that Ivan Karp had found in a former firehouse, and installed a mannequin's hand that so intrigued Jack Smith that he stole it. In the middle of the floor sat a used mirrored ball that came from a theatrical supply house.

'It was like constructing this environment – for me, the whole place was a sculpture', said Billy. 'And each time I added a piece to it was like adding another gem to the collection. I never did a specifically articulated thing, I always did a maximal job. But it was the same art thing, it was the same signature, or my tag: the whole silver thing.'

'One of my finds became a movie star', he said. He spied a large old maroon couch on Forty-seventh Street, with Art Deco lines and grey piping along the edge. Since the couch was already mounted on casters, he just wheeled it down the block, onto the freight elevator, and up to the fourth floor. Six months later it would become the title star of Warhol's film *Couch*.

Billy also provided the soundtrack for the space. He borrowed Andy's Harmon Kardon hi-fi and brought in his collection of opera records. He had been schooled by Ondine, who loved not only to play opera but to sing along during his favourite passages and to give impromptu talks. 'Ondine would play records and explain what we should listen for', said his friend Dale Joe. 'He could really get you involved.' When Ondine was around, Maria Callas was usually the centrepiece, singing *Aïda*, *Iphigenia in Tauris* or *Lucia de Lammermoor*. Billy and Ondine listened to a wide range from bel canto to the expressionism of Richard Strauss' *Die Frau ohne Schatten*.

Andy and Gerard played rock music in the front, and for the first few months Dionne Warwick's voice dominated the work area. The artificial light bouncing off surfaces of wrinkled silver gave the Factory an eerie atmosphere. 'It looked like a horror show', said Ondine. 'It was the Big Rocky Horror Show.' To catch a bit of natural sunlight, one had to go up to the roof or step out onto the fire escape. Chatting there one afternoon, Andy, Billy and Ondine named the new space. Andy knew he didn't want it to be the Studio, which was too much of a cliché. The Lodge? They settled on the Factory, referring to its previous state and to a new industrial style of art production. 'Factory is as good a name as any', said Andy. 'A factory is where you build things. This is where I make or *build* my work. In my artwork hand painting would take much too long, and anyway that's not the age we live in. Mechanical means are today, and using them I can get more art to more people. Art should be for everyone.'

Silver became the trademark of that era of the Factory, and it provided the perfectly ambiguous symbol of the activities that took place at 231 West 47th Street over the next few years. Silver meant different things to all those who participated. Warhol speculated that Billy loved silver because it was 'an amphetamine thing – everything always went back to that.' Warhol associated it with the shiny space suits of astronauts and the past – the silver screen – Hollywood actresses photographed in silver sets.

Billy's description of his silvering job reflected his philosophical outlook, which was both completely concrete and utterly abstract. 'Conceptually chrome is all colours', he said. 'It isn't minimalism, it's maximalism.' And since he thought in terms of light rather than colour, a combination of everything came together in bright white rather than dense black. 'It's electric. It's synthetic, it's fusion. It's out of the ordinary, and it's tense and it's hip and it's cool and it's spacey. It's a knock-out Wonderland.'

Henry Geldzahler saw reflected in the Factory installation everything from the silver screen to Andy's frosted silver wig. He also recalled Warhol's brainstorm one afternoon in the summer of 1963 while silk-screening an Elvis with Gerard Malanga: 'He realized it was possible to double the size – and therefore the price – of his paintings by twinning them with a silver blank, a canvas of the same dimensions as his full-sized Elvis silk-screened black on a silver-painted ground ... There, I think, we can pinpoint the birthplace of the silvered factory.'

'Silver was perfect too because it was a mirror', wrote critic Stephen Koch. 'It was everything turned inward and imploding and at the same time light, the pallor of Warhol's face as if it never saw daylight. It was the space of a mirror. Warhol's responsibilities were the mirror's responsibilities, his replies the mirror's replies'. [...]

Steven Watson, extract from '1964', *Factory Made: Warhol and the Sixties* (New York: Pantheon Books, 2003) 121–7.

Lawrence Weschler
Seeing is Forgetting the Name of the Thing One Sees//2009

[...] 'A prisoner in solitary confinement': with this phrase, Kierkegaard seems to anticipate the lifestyle Robert Irwin was presently imposing on himself [during the years 1962–64]. What he was attempting to accomplish was nothing less than a complete suspension of the world's aesthetic values, a bracketing of the usual standards for the 'aesthetically correct' in order better to gauge what he himself experienced. 'But to withdraw from the concepts of the world involved in a parallel way my withdrawing myself from the world.' Irwin explains. 'They were the same thing.'

'I embarked on two years of painting those paintings, two lines on each canvas, and at the end of two years there were ten of them. So I painted a total of twenty lines over a period of two years of very, very intense activity. I mean, I essentially spent twelve or fifteen hours a day in the studio, seven days a week. In fact I had no separation between my studio life and my outside life. There was no separation between me and those paintings. Everything else became subsumed to this: this became my whole life, and so the whole question as to whether I had a marriage or whether I had a social life just fell away.'

At first he continued seeing [his friends associated with the Ferus Gallery, Los Angeles] once in a while at the local bar, very late, for an hour or so of small talk. [...] But presently even this spindly connection began to fray.

His marriage, meanwhile, which was on its second try (Bob and Nancy had divorced in 1959 but remarried in 1961), entered a period of widening suspension. One afternoon I asked Bob where his studio had been during those years and he had no trouble describing it and its location in exacting detail, but when I asked him where he and Nancy were living during the period when he was painting the line paintings, he registered a blank; nor could he summon the memory at any time during the next several days.

The outside world progressively receded from his experience. As Irving Blum recalled for me: 'Whenever I was sitting at the front desk at Ferus in those days and a collector would come in who wanted to visit one of the artists' studios, well, I always had to call Billy Al Bengston to make sure he'd be there or call Ed Moses to make sure he could be found, but Robert Irwin was the one person I never had to call. I always knew that he would be in his studio, and he always was. He was never any place else but that studio.'

When you think about Irwin's activity during this period, you keep expecting Rod Serling's voice (that other epiphany of the early sixties) to intrude, amidst a falling spangle of percussion, confirming that, yes, this man has definitely strayed ... 'into the Twilight Zone'. The entire enterprise basks in irreality.

'In the beginning, all this was not very considered', Irwin recalls. 'It was done very intuitively. My concentration was not real good. It was mostly a question of just staying in the studio and simply not going out. Whether I did anything or didn't do anything, whether I was able to work or not. I simply would not let myself leave. But after a while, if you don't let yourself leave, then everything else begins to leave, that is, all your other reasons or ambitions in being there; and if you're very fortunate, you might then reach a point of being completely alone in an intimate dialogue with yourself as acted out in the realm of the painting.'

Irwin would sit in his closed studio, staring at a monotone, textured canvas of fairly bright colour, such as orange or yellow, with two thin lines in the same colour spread horizontally across the field. 'I would sit there and look at those two lines. Then I'd remove one of them and move it up an eighth of an inch – I had a way of doing this that I'd worked out ...' And to his astonishment, Irwin noticed one afternoon that just raising the line that one eighth of an inch *changed the entire perceptual field!*' [...]

[...] Irwin emerged from his studio after two years, eyes blinking at the daylight, and started trying to show these paintings in galleries, first at Ferus and then later, in New York, at the Sidney Janis Gallery (as part of a group show). He had spent months and months working out particular solutions within the context of the conditions in his studio – the light, the spatial proportions, the angles of the encompassing walls – one canvas against a bare plane receiving weeks and weeks of even attention. What sense did it make to have a show of four or five of them along one wall of a gallery or a museum, or even optimally, one on each wall, a space where, in all likelihood, the light and spatial relationships were entirely different from those in his studio, and the extent of the viewer's attention would likely be minutes at best? Even the ideal viewer would still have to go home when the gallery closed, and most viewers were far from ideal; they paced the gallery in much the same way they would had it been stocked with Van Eycks or Cézannes.

This growing divergence of intention between the artist and his audience was to plague Irwin for some time to come. In subsequent shows – of the lines, and then of the dots and especially of the discs – he concentrated on trying to control every physical circumstance of the work's presentation. Thus he repainted the gallery wall and floors, smoothed over cracks, spent hours turning the lights, even tried to 'paint out' the shadows cast by guard rails, all in an attempt to replicate the situation in his studio and especially to minimize the kinds of distractions to which he had become hypersensitive. [...]

With the late paintings, Irwin began to fall into a pattern that was to characterize his attitude towards public display of his works throughout the next decade. During the first few exhibitions of the work, as we have seen, he lavished maniacal attention upon every detail of the show's circumstances, spending days and sometimes weeks preparing the gallery space, and when pieces were sold, devoting similar attention to their installation. But at a certain moment, after maybe the third or fourth show, the third or fourth sale, he simply washed his hands of his involvement. [...]

Slowly, Irwin returned to the world. During the next several years he continued to focus his attentions in the studio – first on the dot paintings, then on the discs, eventually on the scrim experiments – but gradually his exclusive self-exile dissolved. This was partly because he no longer needed the discipline; he had developed an ability to retain his focus while still interacting socially. [...]

Furthermore, the more Irwin worked, the more the world itself seeped into his focus. Already by 1964 Irwin was spending much of his time *outside* the canvas, attending to cracks and windows and floorboards, because all of these things were impinging on the reality of the canvas. But those incidental circumstances were becoming interesting to Irwin in their own right. And as he now admits: 'Already then I was literally breaking out of the picture plane as the centre of my concern. I was becoming more interested in the room.' This interest would now expand over the next few years: by 1969 he would be making rooms without objects and by 1970 he would abandon his studio altogether.

[In 1970] he got rid of everything. The studio he sold to Doug Chrismas, who quickly turned it into the Ace Gallery. The supplies he threw out. The collection of other artists' work, which he had built up over the years through a series of trades, he returned piece by piece to the respective artists. Then he went out on the Venice boardwalk, and for a long time, he just sat there.

Did nothing. Didn't even think about what to do next. In fact, began having a hard time thinking at all.

'You know what the biggest loss was in giving up the studio?' Irwin asked me one afternoon. 'It wasn't the loss of my art world identity. It wasn't the scuttling of my economics. No, it was the loss of a way of thinking, it was the loss of the physical things themselves. For twenty years I'd thought in terms of making objects; I'd worked out my ideas by working on physical things. I'm a very tactile person. I think by feel, and not having anything tangible to handle really threw me for a while. I mean, I understood how I'd gotten myself into that predicament – the questions simply mandated it – I just didn't know how to deal with it. I had to train myself to think in a new way.'

He'd go to the races. He'd hang out at hamburger joints, idle about in his car. He'd leave town and head out into the desert ... and it was in the desert that he picked up the trail once again.

'For some reason I started heading out into the Mojave, early morning drives out of the city to the end of the road. At first just a day at a time, and then later, on out into Arizona or south towards Mexico. I began pursuing a line of inquiry, or anyway retrieved the one I was already on.

'The Southwest desert attracted me, I think, because it was the area with the least kinds of identifications or connotations. It's a place where you can go along for a long while and nothing seems to be happening. It's all just flat desert, no particular events, no mountains or trees or rivers. And then, all of a sudden, it can just take on this sort of ... I mean, it's hard to explain, but it takes on an almost magical quality. It just suddenly stands up and hums, it becomes so beautiful, incredibly, the presence is so strong. Then twenty minutes later, it will simply stop. And I began wondering why, what those events were really about, because they were so close to my interests, the quality of phenomena.'

It was not that Irwin had suddenly become some sort of nature fanatic, à la Edward Abbey. He never packed a sleeping bag ('Who, me? Are you kidding?'). Come evening, he'd usually stop at a seedy, roadside motel. He seldom hiked too far off the road. He did not become obsessed by the spare adaptations of plants and creatures, nor did he start reading up on geckos and iguanas, or collecting Indian blankets and pots. It was just this thing of presence. And Irwin's only resources in that regard were still his own perceptions.

'In the beginning I proceeded in a very awkward and obvious way. Say, for example, there are a lot of things that visually contradict your expectations; they will not fall into perspective: foreground becomes background, background becomes foreground, or the land seems to stand up on end rather than lie flat the way one logically knows it's supposed to be. So I began simply to mark those events, to put down sightlines, in a way. And I found that there were certain continuing situations: if I returned to them a year later, I could find the same place, and essentially the same energy would be there. I'm not talking about some sort of spiritual or mystical activity. I'm simply talking about my ability to perceive what was going on around me, that there was something very "tactiley", tangibly existent in this one particular area, say, which was not present two miles down the road.

'So originally I marked these places, quite literally. I laid a small concrete block flush to the ground at the place where I was standing and stretched a stainless steel piano wire out towards the horizon. It might go off a mile; it simply pointed in a direction. And that was the piece. All of which now seems really corny, and I don't do that any more (although I do still head out to the desert occasionally). I understand why I did that at first, but it soon became clear to me that the mark was a distraction; it was about me, about my identity, my discovery. Whereas all that really mattered in such a situation was the place's presence. In other words, if I'd taken you out there to a place like that, what you would have perceived was yourself perceiving. You would have been the one dealing with it, and my hand would have been a distraction. Furthermore, I suddenly had this terrible fantasy of thousands of artists coming out and graffitoing the landscape with their art world initials. So I stopped leaving traces.

'Still, I had the problem of how any of this could be brought to bear on what we call art. How was I going to deal with these situations? Was I going to take photos? Well, that didn't really make any sense. Make plans, draw maps? That wasn't critical. How about loading people onto buses and dragging them out there to show it to them?'

He couldn't do what, say, Michael Heizer was doing around that time, taking such situations and transformations back to New York in the form of giant photo-murals in elegant galleries with written accounts and so forth.

'Somehow, everything that was really important got lost in that kind of translation. And while I had a certain interest in some of the issues people like Robert Smithson, Michael Heizer and Walter De Maria were beginning to explore around that time, I had no interest in most of the resultant "Earth art", the big, ambitious projects in which they applied massive technologies to several desert sites and transformed them into art – spiral jetties and carved buttes, that sort of thing – huge drawings, in effect, made out of packed dirt. Somehow to me such art in nature is completely arbitrary. I mean, nature is overwhelmingly beautiful and overwhelmingly aesthetic, and the necessity to change it or alter it is simply not there, except when we start talking about our own identities and our need to dominate and control.'

What Irwin ended up doing with his desert situations was nothing. He didn't even take his friends out to see them. 'I don't even describe them to anyone.' He certainly did not try to transpose them to the galleries in the form of photo installations. Indeed, the comparison with some of Heizer's photo-murals is particularly apt, because Irwin, too, was interested in how he might recreate that uncanny sense of presence in a gallery. But rather than literally pasting the desert vista to the walls of such spaces, Irwin chose to absorb the *lessons* of the desert and apply them, on a site by site basis, to each new room whose presence he would be confronting and trying to modulate during the coming years.

Lawrence Weschler, extracts from *Seeing is Forgetting the Name of the Thing One Sees: Over Thirty Years of Conversation with Robert Irwin* (Berkeley and Los Angeles: University of California Press, 2009) 69–71; 77–8; 79–80; 159–62.

Caroline A. Jones
The Machine in the Studio//1996

[…] The post-studio diatribes Robert Smithson generated in his essays would be interesting, philosophically, without the *Spiral Jetty* or the numerous sites and non-sites he designated and produced. But we glean inklings of the historical source of that post-studio impulse, and sense some of its cultural context, when we read those diatribes through the physical gigantism of the sites and the peripheral emptiness of their locations (and when we go back still further to trace the early sources for the libido still evident in their forms). These peripheries present the visceral field in which the Beat impulse plays itself out, and where the sublime overwhelms. They are akin to the Indian burial mounds and howling wastelands that Abstract Expressionists such as Barnett Newman sought in their pronouncements about the sublime, but it is a kinship that had experienced a post-industrial torque in the peripheries Smithson prowled. These desolate industrial wastelands are bordered by highways and littered with rusting equipment, tumbled rocks and tumble-down shacks, abandoned derricks that are signs not of progress but of dereliction. These outlying, industrially disrupted sites are the continuous goal figured by Smithson's peripatetic narratives, from the imaginary wanderings of Cézanne to the locations for the film, photographs and essay that represent Smithson's part of the discourse that constitutes the *Spiral Jetty*. Having left the studio, the machine is seen as manifestly incapable of mastery in the vast and indifferent environment of the Utah desert; postmodernism appears here in the guise of an end to (human) history and a dwarfing of its effects.

The desires to preserve a last, apocalyptic and ahistorical sublimity from Smithson's rust-laden critique are still at play, as witnessed by the most recent reproductions of the recently re-emerged *Spiral Jetty*. Photographs taken by a local professional in 1994 showed the barely projecting salt-encrusted rocks of the Jetty strung like pearls out into the shimmering lake, a small private plane moving inquisitively overhead. When reproduced in the summer issue of *Artforum*, however, the photograph was cropped, no longer showing the airplane – returning the jetty to a timeless, oceanic frame. There is nothing inherent about Smithson's desublimating critique; it is as subject to mutation as any discursive product, as capable of recuperation as any destabilizing attempt.

History does make some interpretations less possible than others, however. The leitmotif of Tony Smith's odyssey onto the New Jersey freeway, and the epic journeys of the Beats which it mimicked in miniature, were encounters with a sublimity that was no longer tenable in its nineteenth-century form, or in the twentieth-century variant animated by Abstract Expressionism. Waterfalls and thunderstorms, canyons and jungles – these had been signs and wonders enough for the late nineteenth-century audience hungry for the frisson of danger remanent in the vanishing American frontier. Even when those landscapes could no longer support literal representation in the art of the New York School, their vastness and existential significance still resonated in the paintings of Pollock, Still, Rothko and Newman. But for Smith, Smithson and others like them in the post-war economic boom, sublimity was more forcefully experienced among the stinking smokestacks of Esso-Exxon than in the riparian valleys of the Hudson River. What they sought to record was not merely the look of the expanding post-war industrial landscape that was America, but their experience of it; not merely the iconic recollection of a technological sublime, but a performative re-enactment of the ways it had been produced. This was a new goal for American art, and it was fateful for American modernism that it was played out in, and against, the studio.

What interests me about Smithson, and what links him to Stella, Warhol and other American artists of the post-war period, are both practices and productions. When those practices and productions are viewed comparatively and diachronically, the issue of postmodernism becomes clear. Texts are a way into those practices, they provide a window onto cultural perceptions of the productions, and they can also be practices and productions in themselves (and rarely more so than for Smithson). But they contribute most to our understanding of art's history when they are read against and through the still-marketed objects they accompany, and scanned against the traces of production those objects can convey. [...]

I have argued that the studio was a particularly privileged kind of signifier in the contested discourse on authorship and the industrial aesthetic in the 1960s. Securely modernist in the immediate post-war period, the solitary space of the studio was guarantor of the Abstract Expressionist canvas's authenticity, its presence as an individuating object created (authorized) by an isolated, heroic artist-genius. The films and photographs that constructed such a view of the studio also sutured a particular subject: the viewer of these popularizations was structured as a privileged voyeur, witnessing a deeply private act of creation in the studio that would also be figured on the canvases that issued from it.

But as the cameras themselves whirred away in the 'solitary' studio, they became participants in the socialization and expansion of that space. And as the industrial aesthetic emerged in the work of painters such as Stella and Warhol, what happened in the studio became a central issue in the presentation of their art. Stella's rhetoric of executive artistry and Warhol's celebration of his Factory delegations had meaning only when referenced against this established trope of the authorizing studio, and when played out in the hardened discourse of their art. Similarly, Smithson's dispersals of the art object, and of the site of production, were staged against the already established backdrop of the machine in the studio. This, then, was where Smithson staged his critique, deconstructing the still-centralized studio and seeking to reorient art to the decaying peripheries of the post-industrial landscape. The union of the iconic and the performative in the place of the studio (and against it) was what gave the 1960s work of these artists its salience, and what has fascinated me here.

The romance of the studio had been predicated on the exclusion of others, and by extension, the critique of that romance might suggest the potential for their inclusion and the possible origin of a practical political result. That 'others' might be included only to be dominated is a possibility inherent in any hierarchical productive system, particularly capitalist ones – as implied by Stella's 'dictatorial proletarianism', Warhol's management of 'the Business Art Business', and even Smithson's copyrighted ownership of the necessarily collaborative labour that went into the *Spiral Jetty* film. But even in such dominated forms, the presence of other authors always shadows the expanded studio's productions – explicitly in Warhol's provocative claim that 'Gerard does all my paintings', implicitly in Stella's praise of the executive artist, and visually through the final shot of the editing room that concludes the *Spiral Jetty* film. These shadowy possibilities – for collaboration, delegation and even appropriation of others' labour – became major themes for artists emerging after the 1970s, and reveal themselves forcefully as part of the ongoing critique of the studio in American art.

When Sol LeWitt wrote in 1967 that 'the idea becomes a machine that makes the art', the studio had already dropped out of his formulation, as his hand had dropped out of his art. The art would be made *outside the studio*, by other hands, the artists' authorship remanent only in an idea that would be performed (and appear) differently with each incarnation. From Cal Art's *Womanhouse* to Buren's simultaneous but very different critiques in 1971, the studio's vexed status became clear. After the polemical reconstruction of Warhol's Factory in 1984 by appropriation artist Mike Bidlo, the dispersed studio became, in postmodernism, the emptied point of origin for the much-celebrated 'death of the author'. The dispersal of the studio also figured in the dramatic, post-1970 appearance of collaborative 'team artists' (such as Gilbert and George, Anne and Patrick Poirier, Komar and Melamid, Clegg and Guttman, and the Starn Twins). The work of such artists implied a critique of the 'original hand of the artist' that was already implicit in Warhol's and Stella's depersonalizing techniques, and made it clear that there would always be more than one individual making the art. In many cases, such collaborations were tied to an 'anonymous' photographic technology or located in a literally expanded studio – such as 'Tim Rollins + K.O.S'., the symbiotic union of an artist-teacher and the learning-disabled Bronx students who made the art. More cynical 'appropriation art' objects, such as Sherrie Levine's photographs of reproductions of photographs by Walker Evans (1981), or Jeff Koons' presentations of machine-made objects produced from others' 'kitsch' images (1991), are also the beneficiaries of the dispersed studio and its de-authorizing presence in American art.

As is characteristic in the anti-totalizing discourse of postmodernism (which has hovered over this book like a ragged aegis), the re-emergence of previous forms in different guises and contexts produces different results. During the moment of the 1960s that I have chosen to place at the centre of my inquiry, the machines in the studios of Stella and Warhol ground out an industrial aesthetic of tremendous force and cultural resonance; in his dialectics and discursive *Spiral Jetty* Smithson later pushed that aesthetic to one logical, entropic conclusion. The dynamic expansion of capital in the early 1960s, and its conversion into signs and simulacra for the necessary exchanges of an increasingly global consumer culture, are figured in the early years of this industrial aesthetic. The subsequent electronic mobilization of capital and the exhaustion of heavy industry at the end of the decade are elements in the dispersal of that same industrial aesthetic. Dispersal does not mean demise, however. In the 1980s, the charms of cyberpunk, junk bonds, 'smart' bombs, patriotic missiles and other cultural fantasies attest to the continuing appeal of, and to, the technological sublime.

Where our libidinous attachments to technology will lead us – aesthetically, economically, biologically, militarily – is still very unclear; but art will continue to play a powerful role in charting that path. Chances are, artists won't be drawn back to the studio – but if they are, it will be a radically different place than it was in 1948. Machines are now so deep in our Imaginary that we are cultural, if not yet biological, cyborgs; we are soft-wired for technology in our desiring machines.

Caroline A. Jones, extract from 'Conclusion: The Machine in the Studio', *Machine in the Studio: Constructing the Postwar American Artist* (Chicago: University of Chicago Press, 1996) 369–73 [footnotes not included].

Laura Meyer
A Studio of Their Own//2009

The Fresno Feminist Art Program made a radical departure from traditional art classes. Instead of being oriented towards developing skills in a particular medium, such as oil painting or bronze sculpture, class projects had a conceptual basis, with no limitations on the media to be used. Program alumna Faith Wilding recalls that ideas for artworks arose during group discussions organized along the lines of feminist 'consciousness raising'.

The procedure was to 'go around the room' and hear each woman speak from her personal experience about a key topic such as work, money, ambition, sexuality, parents, power, clothing, body image or violence. As each woman spoke it became apparent that what had seemed to be purely 'personal' experiences were actually shared by all the other women; we were discovering a common oppression based on our gender, which was defining our roles and [sense of] identity as women.

Thus, in Wilding's words, the 'unspoken curriculum' of the Fresno feminist program was 'learning to contend with manifestations of power: female, male, political and social'.

Rejecting the modernist paradigm of the autonomous artist/genius creating his work in isolation from the rest of society, the Fresno Feminist Art Program emphasized the value of collaboration. Each participant brought her personal history, interests and desires to the group, and each contributed to the outcome of the experiment. Graduate students Faith Wilding and Suzanne Lacy, for example, had extensive backgrounds in political and community organizing. Even before joining the feminist art program, Wilding and Lacy initiated a feminist consciousness-raising group on the Fresno State campus, and in spring 1970 Wilding offered a course on feminist theory and practice, 'The Second Sex'. Lacy and Wilding's activist backgrounds informed the group's use of consciousness-raising as a learning tool and a political strategy. Entering the program with a background in theatrical make-up and costume design, Nancy Youdelman established a 'costume room' in the feminist studio. Youdelman's enthusiasm for self-transformation and role-play helped inspire the group's experiments with performance art. Dori Atlantis, who studied photography before joining the class, served as its unofficial photo-historian. Atlantis also served as photographer for many of the groups' collaborative performance projects, including the Costume series in which participants enacted culturally-scripted female roles or 'types', including the Bride, the Whore, the Entertainer and the Kewpie Doll.

The Fresno Feminist Art Program served as the model for many better-known feminist projects and programs, including *Womanhouse*, the collaborative feminist art exhibition that attracted national media coverage and introduced the broader public to feminist art. *Womanhouse* was the first project carried out by the relocated Feminist Art Program after it moved from Fresno State to the California Institute of the Arts in fall 1971. Like the creation of the feminist studio in Fresno, the production of *Womanhouse* began by laying claim to a separate space, apart from the main campus, and then repairing and refurbishing it to meet the needs of its new occupants. Many of the art-making strategies initially developed at Fresno State – including collaboration, the use of new 'female' media such as costume and performance, and an emphasis on gender issues – were deployed in public for the first time at *Womanhouse*.

The Feminist Studio Workshop, a fully-accredited, independent feminist art school established in conjunction with the Los Angeles Woman's Building in 1973, realized the goals of the Fresno Feminist Art Program on an even larger scale. [...]

Laura Meyer, extract from 'A Studio of Their Own: The Legacy of the Fresno Feminist Art Experiment' (September 2009) (www.astudiooftheirown.org)

Judy Chicago
In Conversation with Jane Collings//2003

Judy Chicago Mimi [Miriam Schapiro] and I organized probably one of the first – and it became very popular after that – the first sort of women artists' conference, where women came and showed their slides all weekend. Then Mimi, Dextra [Frankel] and I, particularly Dextra and I, visited all these women artists' studios from all over. There were a couple of women in San Francisco, Jay DeFeo and Joan Brown. They were a little older than me, and they were the only women artists who were visible at that time [1970–71]. I tried to get to know them. They weren't really receptive.

But everything changed in the early seventies. Then all of a sudden a different climate was developing. There were all these women who were just completely unknown, whose work was unknown. They were working in the kitchens of their boyfriends' studios, or they were working in the back, or they were not showing. At that point, I wasn't even looking at men's work anymore. I wasn't reading anything by men, either. I stopped. I just did a sort of remedial education and just confined myself to looking at women's art and reading women's writing. I didn't care anymore what men were doing, I wanted to know what women were doing. I just went 180 degrees ... 360 degrees [...]

Collings What was your role at the Woman's Building [in Los Angeles, initiated in 1973]?

Chicago I suppose in a way I had a leadership role, although I sort of didn't totally acknowledge it. Sheila [de Bretteville], Arlene [Raven] and I came together out of Cal Arts to form the Feminist Studio Workshop, but then I brought all these different groups together to create the Woman's Building.

Collings And part of your idea was that you needed to have a feminist exhibition space, you needed ...

Chicago We needed a context ... we needed a context. There was a young woman who was in the feminist art program at Cal Arts named Mira Schor, who's now a well-known painter and feminist theorist, she works out of New York. She wrote the really important essay titled 'Patrilineage' about how women artists are still put into a 'patrilineage' as opposed to in a 'matrilineage.' The Woman's Building idea was that you would see women's work in a feminist context. [...]

Collings People applied to come to the Feminist Studio Workshop at the Woman's Building.

Chicago Yeah. And also I was going around the country a lot, and I would solicit young women that I met.

Collings How did you select these people when they applied? Did you have a selection process?

Chicago I think so, but I don't quite remember that. I think it was pretty loose. After all, there's a lot of self-selection. Somebody picks up from Las Cruces and moves to Los Angeles to be in the program, pretty well they're like … It was a lot of self-selection. […]

Collings How did you incorporate the things that you had learned as a teacher at Fresno and CalArts into what you were doing at the Woman's Building?

Chicago First of all, we often team taught, Sheila and Arlene and I. I had expanded from teaching alone at Fresno to teaching with Mimi at CalArts, so I integrated collaborative teaching.

Collings Did that work for you better?

Chicago With Sheila and Arlene it was really easy. Also, Sheila was a designer and Arlene was an art historian, so it wasn't two artists. That was, I think, a better arrangement. And also, we had had an art historian [Paula Harper] at CalArts, too, who also did some team teaching with us, so that got integrated in. I used a lot of the same methods. But I was only there a year.

Collings What was different about working with this group?

Chicago Well, there was no contradiction. They didn't leave the Feminist Studio Workshop and walk into patriarchy. They left the Feminist Studio Workshop and there was the Grandview Gallery and the Women's Gallery and the Sisterhood Bookstore. There was an entire context, so the workshop was in a context that supported and reinforced the values of the workshop. So it was completely different than at CalArts where they'd leave the Feminist Art Program and re-enter patriarchal values in two seconds. It was confusing, particularly for the young women.

Collings Do you think that this created better work?

Chicago Well, it created more … Of course, they still went back to their 'real lives' out of the building, but the building was pretty powerful. I mean, a *whole building*? Even though there were differences of opinion, there was still some coherence of values. […]

Collings I was talking with one of the participants from the Studio Workshop, and she said that one of the things that you taught her that was so important for her was the idea – it's just a simple thing – of introducing herself using her first name and last name, shaking hands firmly, looking people in the eye. And I was just wondering if you could think of other, what we might call charm school techniques, or reverse charm school techniques.

Chicago Oh, yes. I started that in Fresno. It used to drive me crazy. [*very soft voice*] 'Hello, my name's Cheryl and I have trouble talking in groups.' [*firm voice*] 'Stand up. My name is Cheryl Zurilgen and I am …' blah, blah, blah. Oh, my God! Absolutely.

Collings So this was something that you had brought with you all the way along. Were there other ground rules along those lines that you can think of?

Chicago I don't know if they were ground rules, but they were definitely my …

Collings … or basic building blocks of …

Chicago Yeah, now I can talk about the building blocks. Now that I'm trying to teach it to other people, I'm clearer about the building blocks. So, yeah, there's the use of the circle, going around in the circle to build synergy, to build group bonding. It was interesting having the facilitators we're training now talk about their observations about why we sit in a circle [at the 'Envisioning the Future' project, Pomona Arts Colony, 2003]. They said, 'Well, because then you have to see each other.' You actually look at each other. Also listening, deep listening – deep listening which says, when you listen to each other, you inherently communicate that what the person has to say is valuable. This is very important, especially for women, who are always told that what they have to say is not valuable. […]

Judy Chicago and Jane Collings, extracts from 2003 interview transcripts in *Judy Chicago: An Oral History*, part of the Archives of American Art Oral History Program (Los Angeles: University of California at Los Angeles, 2004) 22; 31–2; 33–4; 35–6.

Rozsika Parker
Housework//1975

Bless my little kitchen, lord,
I love its every nook,
And bless me as I do my work,
Wash pots and pans and cook.
– *Rhyme printed on souvenir plate*

This verse was on a souvenir ceramic plate tacked onto the wall of the kitchen at 14 Radnor Terrace, Lambeth – a kitchen knee-high in garbage, old newspapers, half-drunk coffees, milk rotting in bottles, fag ends and grubby plastic cartons. The kitchen was part of a project undertaken by six women. For two weeks they worked together on the South London Women's Centre, painting it, renovating it and finally creating rooms which exposed the hidden side of the domestic dream.

> Rooms as images of mental states – from unconscious basements to hot tin rooftops.
> – Kate Walker

> A room as a chrysalis – using my appearance and the room as a projection of myself – positive and negative.
> – Sue Madden

The house was on view during April and May. An orange front door opened onto a hall carpeted with artificial grass where a black staircase, covered in chalked poems and quotations, led to Kate Walker's kitchen – a nightmare kitchen, oppressive and cluttered. Footsteps on the floor marked an endless, persistent circle from fridge to basin to stove and back again. Out of the stove floated an enormous wedding cake complete with silver bells, lace and blossoms, while below it, half submerged in a heap of garbage, lay a woman's body. Scattered on the floor nearby were traces of a female childhood – dolls and the story of Cinderella written out in coloured crayons. In contrast to the general sordid chaos, the cupboards were obsessively tidy with packets of food carefully balanced on top of each other and towels precisely piled and neatly folded.

If the basement represents the instinctual, nurturing aspect of the home in its darkest form, the ground floor rooms dealt with the social and emotional expectations bound up with marriage. On one side of two adjoining rooms there was a bride swathed in white gauze who stretched out her arms to welcome an unseen groom. She was placed in an all white environment with chocolate box landscapes and collages of Princess Anne's wedding decorating the walls. On the mantelpiece, along with a copy of the *Common Prayer Book* and Charles Dickens' *Great Expectations*, was a long line of silver beer bottles capped by baby-bottle teats. The other room was all black and contained a corpse wrapped in a grey blanket. Dust surrounded the body, a pair of scuffed slippers lay nearby and a man's carefully folded grey shirt was placed in the grate. On the mantelpiece a black piece of paper read 'died ... believed ... had failed ... half embalmed ... road of love and unselfishness'. And the room was presided over by a big, black leather chair. Kate Walker says that she purposely used the most trite, stale images associated with women in an effort to bring over their true implications.

She stopped painting and began to create environments because she wanted to find a more immediate way of working; a method which brings quick results and reactions. She couldn't integrate painting – for her a slow, intense, isolated process – into the rest of life with her children. 'I can't bear the idea of a one-sided existence totally dedicated to my art', she says. 'I'd rather think of myself as a housewife than an artist.' Looking back at the Radnor Terrace project she regrets that she stopped work while the house was on view – her rooms evolve as she works on them, and by presenting them as a finished product she thought the 'human, tatty immediacy was a bit lost'.

Upstairs was an all white, shaded, claustrophobic bedroom. Sue Madden called the room *Chrysalis* because she intended to use the room as a projection or a space in which 'to grow and transform'. She wanted to externalize and examine this process in a film using both the room and her appearance as an extension or reflection of her changing states of mind. She says that the following quotations were her starting points:

> A woman must continually watch herself ... From earliest childhood she has been taught and persuaded to survey herself continually. And so she comes to consider the surveyed and the surveyor within her as the two constituents yet always distinct elements of her identity as a woman.
> – John Berger

> Each sister wearing masks of Revlon, Clairol, Playtex, to survive. Each sister faking orgasm under the systems' very concrete bulk at night, to survive.
> – Robin Morgan

With these ideas in mind, Sue was going to start by filming removing rituals; plucking eyebrows, shaving armpits and legs, cutting toenails, applying face packs, astringents, etc. Working consciously through these activities 'which wipe away women's identity', and moving on from them, she hoped to bring together the surveyed and surveyor within herself. Yet when it came to filming herself she couldn't do it:

> As I started to wonder how I might explore these negative images I began to feel that performing these rituals yet again would be sacrificial and masochistic. For example, I recently stopped shaving my legs after ten years, and it was a genuinely significant experience – in a way it made me begin to experience my body as an integrated whole.

As a solution she made a 'second skin' on which to perform the rituals; a model other body complete even to embroidered moles, hairs and appendix scar. Making the model helped her to come to terms with her 'first skin' but the film was never made. 'The nature of my film', she says, 'was to communicate to women how I was feeling about myself, but this would have meant them being involved in the same kind of activity. I think for women to build up any significant working situation they must first commit themselves to developing close contact and communication between themselves' [...]

[Radnor Terrace] was criticized for being too depressing and too propagandist. Yet patriarchal society has always used art to propagandize particular limited and limiting images of women; mother, muse and sex object. Both Radnor Terrace and *Womanhouse* in Los Angeles are necessary steps towards breaking free of the stereotypes.

Rozsika Parker, extracts from 'Housework', *Spare Rib*, no. 26 (1975) 38.

Elizabeth Harney
The Laboratoire Agit-Art//2004

[...] Beginning with the first decade after Senegal's independence, the rules of the art world changed, as shifts in both local and global circumstances impacted on the efficacy of a singular, nationalist-driven patronage. By the late 1970s, the country had experienced one-party rule for over a decade and, despite relatively few major civil disturbances and a democratic reputation in the international arena, national cohesion and the African socialist dream of development were far from a reality. The autocracy of Senghorian rule manifested itself clearly in the relative stagnation of artistic practice among academy-trained artists, whose celebrations of African essence [informed by Senghor's concept of Negritude] produced a sour taste in the mouths of many younger artists. The attempts to reinvigorate artistic practice and to free it from its Senghorian straitjacket became most evident in the activities of two artistic groupings of the time: the Laboratoire Agit-Art and the Village des Arts. The former played the part of a classic avant-garde; the latter served as a crucible for expanding the use of indigenous materials and for reinventing the relationship between the artist, the state and the community. [...]

The debates held at the Café Terrasse [in the early 1970s between artists, performers, writers and others, on artistic freedom and production] led to the establishment in 1974 of an improvisational artistic laboratory, known as the Laboratoire Agit-Art. Youssouf John – comedian, thespian and teacher at the INAS [Institut National des Arts de Sénégal] – founded the Laboratoire, but he soon emigrated to Martinique and passed the grouping on to multimedia artist Issa Ramangelissa Samb. The main goal of the workshop, as the name would suggest, was to shake up or agitate the existing institutional framework, to question the tenets of Negritude, and to encourage artists to adopt a new approach towards their work. Its agenda, then, was based on a series of critiques of Negritude and its institutionalization in Senegal, which mirrored those of Wole Soyinka, Ousmane Sembene, Stanislaus Adotevi and others in the literary world whom Bennetta Jules-Rosette has labelled the Anti-Negritudinists.

According to the Laboratoire, institutionalization of the arts had resulted in a blockage of artistic creativity or, to use Soyinka's phrase, artists 'had tamed themselves into laudators of creative truncation'. Working under government patronage, they were divorced from their indigenous material, environment, domestic audience and cultural history, relying instead on 'a stock of particularisms' in a 'banal search for exoticism'. In addition, the structure created for the art world was largely an imported one, organized according to European criteria. [...]

This reliance on and/or preference for European institutions and criteria extended to the heart of the art world's structure – in the teachings at the Institut National des Arts du Sénégal, where students were instructed in the use of oil paints, paintbrushes and easel, and the Manufacture Sénégalaise des Arts Décoratifs, where the weavers' techniques, machinery and materials were all of foreign origin. As such, within the Senghorian field of cultural production, artists became inextricably dependent on imported materials and could not see the qualities and possibilities of indigenous ones. Despite the emphasis placed on African imagery and subject matter in the Section de Recherches en Arts Plastiques Nègres, the techniques of European easel painting – in oil, acrylic or gouache – in other words, beaux arts, became the symbols of 'fine art' in Senegal. […]

For members of the Laboratoire Agit-Art, the definition of the modern African artist advocated by the Senghorian art world was antithetical to Senegalese social life and history. Explaining the Laboratoire's objections, Samb insisted that 'people had confused the solitary nature of creation with the need for solitude of the creator' and that 'without collaboration and artistic exchange, the arts could not flourish'. […] The Laboratoire's critique of the Senghorian artist figure paralleled that made by Frantz Fanon of the native bourgeoisie. In *The Wretched of the Earth*, Fanon devoted many pages to exposing the artificiality of the populist rhetoric used by the native intellectuals to venerate the *Volk* (people). Like Fanon, Laboratoire Agit-Art members urged the Senegalese artist, who based his works on his people's culture, to recognize that he could not 'go forward resolutely unless he first realizes the extent of his estrangement from them'. […]

[T]he Laboratoire hoped to promote a new kind of art that could be provocative and critical, disturbing in imagery or political in content. The only means through which its members could demystify the reigning ideology supporting an École de Dakar was through reconfiguring the social roles for art in society. Therefore, Laboratoire Agit-Art's primary goal was to 'deblock' creative activities in Senegal at a political, social, technical and artistic level. It chose to focus on the medium of theatre, arguing that as one of the most [locally] favoured of the arts, it was also one most in need of their attention. Moreover, with its acceptance of improvisation, theatre provided a working environment in which artists could address a variety of media without it requiring a synthesis of all the arts. Its openness to innovation also ensured that the structure of Laboratoire Agit-Art could remain fluid enough to avoid institutionalization, a fate which would surely have led to its definition and destruction as a politically subversive body.

The Laboratoire claimed to operate under a traditional structure, with the guidance of a council or a group of *initiés* (initiates). Each workshop had a *maître d'atelier* (head of studio). When the *maître* was in control of a performance or studio, he ruled with the *autorité morale* (moral authority) conferred by the respect of his peers. The group put on one large annual production and held a series of rotating workshops throughout the year. As such, it was the first body to introduce the idea of artistic workshops into Senegal. The annual 'performances' were held in the open air and were, again, based on what the group defined as traditional models, which involved, on one level or another, all parts of the community. Thus there was no recognized division between actor and audience, and the audience, surrounding environment and objects all became part of the experience. This turn towards a different kind of traditionalism rarely produced formal solutions comparable to earlier École de Dakar artistic productions. Rather, in many works by participating artists, or in collaborative 'stage sets' used in the Laboratoire's performances, one could detect only schematic, subtle references to recognizable traditional forms.

A written script for performance was replaced by a *langage des gestes* (language of gestures). Issa Samb referred to this arrangement as *la technique du cercle* (circle technique) and *l'ensemble du corps* (whole body), insisting that the objects and individuals within this 'manifestation' had no existence except in relation to their environment. Moreover, he asserted that the process of creation was ultimately more important than the finished production. [...]

The practice of reusing, accumulating and layering diverse and often disparate materials is not new to either African or European aesthetic practices. The Laboratoire Agit-Art members' use of recycling [e.g. assemblages made with discarded everyday materials, or Samb's graffiti-like paintings that played on iconic images such as Che Guevara's portrait] is therefore both their own articulation of modernist debates about distinctions between high and low and elite and popular inherent in the Senghorian field of production and an intentional play on an international market that reads their works through a modernist lens. Thus the works of the Laboratoire represent not a simple mimicry of European forms but discrete appropriations of avant-gardist ideologies and practices and critical engagements with both local and global art discourses. [...]

Pierre Bourdieu points out that every avant-garde is a parody of the tradition it opposes and, as such, is also respectful of it, reiterating that which it attacks. Thus the Laboratoire was unable to transcend the Senghorian field of cultural production, but rather engaged in what Antonio Gramsci would call a 'war of manoeuvre' within it – or, to use Bourdieu's terminology, a process of 'position-taking'. [...]

Elizabeth Harney, extracts from *In Senghor's Shadow: Art, Politics and the Avant-Garde in Senegal, 1960–1995* (Durham, North Carolina: Duke University Press, 2004) 106; 107–8; 109; 112; 115 [footnotes not included].

Jeffrey Deitch
The Studio of the Street//2007

Downtown New York culture experienced an anti-golden age in the period between 1974 and 1981. It was perceived as a bleak chapter in the life of the city, beginning with the famous tabloid headline marking the president's disregard for New York's financial crisis: 'Ford to City: Drop Dead.' Much of the area between 14th Street and Wall Street was virtually abandoned. Tenement buildings in the East Village and the Lower East Side were lost to foreclosure by their owners because the rental income was less than the property taxes. Many of the trading businesses that had filled the loft buildings of SoHo and Tribeca had either shut down or had moved away. The subways exploded with wild-style graffiti. Entire blocks of Avenue B were open drug supermarkets. Chrystie Street below Delancey was an open prostitution market. The long hot summers brought events like the 1977 blackout and the terror of [the serial killer] Son of Sam.

The middle class was leaving. Corporate headquarters were moving to Connecticut or to the Sunbelt. Manufacturing jobs were going south or abroad. The economy was sinking and real estate prices hit bottom. Because of the new policy of 'de-institutionalization', mental hospitals had been shut down and many of their former patients were now living on the street.

In contrast to the decay that permeated the city, television and radio were selling a user-friendly, plasticized version of the late sixties/early seventies counterculture. Rock radio was dominated by groups like The Eagles, and it was almost impossible to hear real rock 'n' roll. Even the mainstream art world had gone soft after the radical innovations of anti-form and body art. [...]

This contradictory situation created a kind of artist's anti-paradise. The artists, musicians, writers and other creative people who were drawn to New York in the mid and late seventies could create their own community and not be bothered by the workaday world. They didn't have to interact with mainstream culture or even go above 14th Street, except maybe to see a movie in Times Square. The artists who arrived during this period had to settle for decrepit tenements or a warren of partitions in an abandoned warehouse, rather than the immense lofts homesteaded by the previous generation, but rent was cheap, or one figured out a way not to pay any rent at all. An entire community of artists was able to exist without regular jobs, keeping to their own schedule and living on their own terms.

By 1976, the creative energy had moved from the stagnating SoHo gallery and loft performance community to the punk and new wave music scene. The spontaneous combustion of the new music situation was generating a new band every week and attracting a new community of artists, photographers and writers who connected to the stripped down, radicalized spirit of the music. The music also energized the life of the streets in the area around the Bowery from the areas now known as Nolita and Noho to the nearby blocks of the East Village. The streets were animated with stark handmade posters for band performances, and spillover from clubs made the surrounding streets into a no-budget punk version of sidewalk cafes. Walking the blocks around the Bowery almost any time of day or night you were likely to run into an artist or musician of your acquaintance. Unlike the New York of today where people are running to their appointments, nobody on the scene was in a rush. A chance encounter would lead to an invitation to watch a band practice or a visit to someone's studio. You just had to walk the streets to become part of the community.

Something else was animating the streets around the Bowery in the late seventies and early eighties. Every time you went to a good loft party, visited the apartment of someone interesting, or attended the performance of a talked-about new band, it seemed that SAMO had been there first. His disconcerting but riveting haiku-like street poetry marked the walls of every building where artists and musicians congregated. His confounding lines, like 'Pay for soup, build a fort, set that on fire ©SAMO' were often incomprehensible from the point of view of conventional logic, but they stayed inside your consciousness. Repeated on doorways and walls all over the neighbourhood in his strong distinctive hand, SAMO's disjointed poetry permeated your mind. SAMO became an essential part of the downtown experience. His work was widely discussed and documented, and although some people on the scene claimed to know him, nobody I knew had actually met him or seen him working.

In the summer of 1980 several sectors of the downtown and uptown artist communities joined together to create the remarkable 'Times Square Show'. Filling two floors and the basement of an abandoned complex of massage parlours, the exhibition documented the convergence of punk/new wave, wild style, conceptual street work, radical feminism, gay liberation and the burgeoning neo-expressionism that would set the agenda for the dynamic New York art world of the early eighties. The exhibition was organized as a series of rooms put together by groups of like-minded artists. One of the strongest rooms was tied together by an energetic painting on all four walls, on top of which other paintings and drawings were hung. I praised the wall painting in my *Art in America* review of the 'Times Square Show' as a 'knockout combination of de Kooning and subway spray paint'. I was told that the artist was Jean-Michel Basquiat, a.k.a. SAMO. [...]

In the spring of 1981 Diego Cortez and I visited Jean-Michel in the tenement apartment that he was sharing with his girlfriend Suzanne Mallouk. Jean-Michel showed us the drawings that he was working on. There was no drawing table and no neat stack of finished work. The drawings were scattered all over the floor, walked on like they were part of the linoleum. Even the battered old refrigerator was covered with his images. He drew right onto the enamel. There did not seem to be any separation between life and art. Jean-Michel drew constantly, on the street and wherever he was staying. By the age of nineteen he already understood that he was an artist and projected a charismatic self-confidence. Without going to art school or having a mentor, he had the instinct to position himself at the centre of the most dynamic art community. From the beginning of his art career he was already the centre of attention. […]

Jeffrey Deitch, extract from *Jean-Michel Basquiat: 1981 – The Studio of the Street*, ed. Jeffrey Deitch et al. (New York: Deitch Projects/Milan: Charta, 2007) 8–9.

Brian Dillon
Street and Studio//2008

The title of Tate Modern's summer photography show, 'Street & Studio: An Urban History of Photography', seems to posit a somewhat too familiar schema: an overly neat equation that shows the spaces of intimate self-invention and ground-level glamour to have been usefully confused during the last century or so: from Jacques Henri Lartigue's Paris to Pieter Hugo's Lagos. The street, by this logic, is itself a studio – a workshop for cobbling a self together, or a screen on which multiple public selves may be projected – and the studio an artistic enclave increasingly invaded by unruly bodies expressing urban angst, ennui, eroticism and pop-cultural energy. Things are thankfully more complex than that superficial paradox allows: 'Street & Studio' may trade in a stock history of the spatial-cultural milieu of twentieth-century photography, but it allows for other, stranger stories to unfold about the 300 works on show. Among the more striking is the suspicion that the show's twin terms are not merely intertwined but constantly on the verge of evanescing.

If both street and studio are the places where a certain presence insists – as much a matter of self-assertion (or self-preservation) as of photographic apparition – then it is also obvious that that presence has been publicly threatened since the very invention of photography. The street is first of all a place where people vanish: the half-formed ghost who has stopped to have his boots cleaned in Daguerre's *Vue du boulevard du Temple* (1839), the entirely absent pedestrians who fail to populate Fox Talbot's *View of the Boulevards at Paris* four years later. Streetlife is eternally fleeting, and not only because of early technical limitations: in Charles Baudelaire's essay 'The Painter of Modern Life' (1863), the artist Constantin Guys may well be a mirror as vast as the crowd itself, his talent a kaleidoscope in which the fragmented city dissolves and resolves itself, but the street is always out of reach, the telling instant just past, life itself 'unstable and fugitive'. The street as such is already the subject of dreams and memories, even of nostalgia.

Hence the teenage Lartigue, *faux-innocent* voyeur at large in the Bois de Boulogne around 1912, photographing the *haute-bourgeoise* women of Paris as though they were the last exotic specimens of species destined for extinction. These women seem to have brought their own studios with them: their clothes and bearing are direct emanations of the opulent gloom of the belle-époque interior; they seem to move as if through the fronds of a Victorian aquarium. But they are also in danger of disappearing before the thrilled adolescent can fix their passing. In 1911, Lartigue wrote to his diary: 'Rue Cortambert. Before dinner, it was already getting quite dark and I didn't have my camera. … Suddenly, on the pavement, I saw the most beautiful woman I have ever seen coming towards me. … She had a large muff and such a pretty face under her large hat that regret for the missed photo is beginning to haunt me. Something different from regret even … like a kind of inconsolable sorrow?'

This doleful sense of belatedness is all over the photographs that Lartigue took a decade and a half later on the streets of London. In 1925, in *Mrs Dalloway*, Virginia Woolf had written of the city: 'In people's eyes, in the swing, tramp and trudge; in the bellow and the uproar; the carriages, motor cars, omnibuses, vans, sandwich men shuffling and swinging; brass bands; barrel organs; in the triumph and the jingle and the strange high singing of some aeroplane overhead was what she loved; life; London; this moment of June.' Lartigue, supposedly the photographer of pure happiness, appears to have missed his moment a year later. His wife, Bibi, steps off a pavement onto a manhole cover that looks like a trapdoor out of the unreal city: behind her, glum grey women hover like Eliotic typists whom life has passed by. On the upper deck of an open-topped bus, Bibi sits alone, wrapped in a fur coat, and is almost submerged in the profusion of dismal shopfronts, dawdling pedestrians and weakly glowing streetlamps. The street seems to exist behind a screen, its vaunted modern vividness a thing of the very recent past.

'Street & Studio' includes a photographer whom we habitually think of as among the most punctual of witnesses. The speed with which Weegee could arrive at the scene of a crime and photograph it was in part the result of his being well connected at the New York Police Department – quite literally: the photographer had his own police radio. But Weegee, of course, also arrives too late: what he captures is not the drama of the street per se, but its grisly aftermath.

In *Their First Murder* (1941), however, he turns around to photograph the eager crowd (in this case mostly children) that is usually peripheral to his images of bloodied gangsters. And what he sees is precisely an image of belatedness, or panic at the thought that the unseen corpse might be removed before the crowd can glimpse it. In fact, only one of the twelve people in the frame, a gawking young girl, seems actually to take in the scene.

Street photography in the middle of the twentieth century is almost wholly concerned with this dialectic of the seen and unseen, the way the city gives itself up visually on one level and hides in plain sight on another. It's the city, for example, that was recorded in prose by the Irish writer Maeve Brennan, whose delicate and often unnerving essays for *The New Yorker* (published as reports from 'the long-winded lady' from the late 1950s till the early 1980s) frequently consisted of localized tragedies in which citizens failed to notice, or really to see in any meaningful sense, what was happening before their eyes: a young woman collapsing on the street, a black man lost as he makes his way to a job interview, a down-at-heel middle-aged couple making the best of things in the sunshine. The brittle, neurasthenic Brennan spotted chaos, dereliction and dignity in details of city life that deserve by turns to have been photographed by Leon Levinstein or Norman Parkinson, Irving Penn or William Klein (all of whom are present in 'Street & Studio'). The proximity, in other words, of grime and glamour, modernity and nostalgia, was very much Brennan's métier; her writing was a kind of street photography, in which the city is almost a delusion: 'High in the fading sky, the big lights glimmered faintly, creating an architectural mirage that was like the reflection of another city – the New York no one has ever found, perhaps.'

This sense of the city beatified by light, of a stillness that expresses both the aspirations and the solitude of the individual, is one of the effects courted by a later street photographer such as Philip-Lorca diCorcia, whose subject is precisely the contemporary lack of a proper rapport between self and streetscape. In the 1960s, both Richard Avedon and Andy Warhol invited the energy of the street to disrupt the studio. In Avedon's collective portrait of the denizens of Warhol's Factory, and his similar study of the Chicago Seven (both from 1969), the blank white studio becomes a street on which his subjects disport themselves in a kind of downtown frieze. (Eventually, of course, Warhol would exclude such streetlife – that is, 'crazies' – from his life and work.) In diCorcia's *Streetwork* and *Heads*, by contrast, the street is lit like a studio: the subject is momentarily licked by the spotlight's tongue of cold flame, all other illumination sucked dramatically from the frame. In such images, the city looks to have fallen away, leaving the isolated individual lost in thought. The street is no longer the space of display but the arena of inferiority: the last place we allow ourselves to be importuned or even seduced.

How to counter, photographically, that retreat of the public persona from the screen of the street to the airless studio of one's own personal space? Superficially, Joel Sternfeld's street photographs share some of the stateliness of diCorcia's; indeed, his figures are on the face of it more isolated spatially, occupying the centre of an otherwise unpopulated frame. But Sternfeld consistently discerns a character in his subjects, even if that character, as in the case of his *Attorney with laundry, corner Bank and West 41 Street. NYC* (1988) is hostile and possibly faked (the lawyer's armful of striped shirts: as though en route to a studio portrait session). Like the prone, oblivious figures in Francis Alÿs' *Sleepers* – dead to the world on the streets of Mexico City – they have somehow found a way of inhabiting a real and unreal city at once, of living with, or through, or on the street and allowing for the distinct possibility that the street might drop out of consciousness at any moment.

Brian Dillon, 'Street and Studio', *Art Review*, no. 22 (May 2008) 82–5.

Jennifer Allen
Atelier Van Lieshout//2007

Welcome to the world of Atelier Van Lieshout (AVL). Founded in 1995 by Joep van Lieshout, the Rotterdam collective has produced a veritable cornucopia of works which straddle art, design and architecture. [...] The atelier makes its own designs and fabricates them, to boot, at its base on the Rotterdam harbour. [...]

AVL works fit into a set of circumstances. Of course, every design is consistent upon certain factors. Consider the architect who must take account of the client, budget and site, even natural light. However decisive, these factors often operate as an invisible frame around the final product, an autonomous 'object'.

While AVL values its own autonomy as an organization, many of its designs are manifestly adaptive and ad hoc. In contrast to architecture's realm of autonomous objects, AVL's works function as parasites that latch onto larger architectural hosts, often in an aggressive way that cannot be compared to the building extension. [...]

Clip-On (1997), a reading and relaxation unit installed on an exterior wall of Utrecht's Centraal Museum, provides an example of a parasitic cohabitation: the cube floated down from a crane and latched onto the third floor of the museum, like a tick floating from a tree and firmly lodging itself into a human head.

Beyond its parasitism, *Clip-On* shows how circumstances – including chance

– can determine the design and appearance of an AVL creation. *Clip-On*'s skylights take their curious shapes from automobile floor mats: the remains of Joep's crashed car, which happened to be sitting around the AVL studio when the unit was being built. By deciding to use the floor mats to shape the skylights, AVL made the fragment of a wreck into the crowning element of a new structure; part of a moving floor into part of a stable roof; protective coverage into translucent illumination. As this chance addition suggests, AVL parasites can become hosts for other parasites. While *Clip-On* housed spare auto parts, *Alfa Alfa with Chicken Run* (1999) fitted a chicken coop into the shell of Joep's old Alfa Romeo; its trunk doubled as a secure portal for the chickens to lay eggs and for the farmer to collect them with ease. AVL places the circumstances 'behind' every work – the invisible frame of determinant factors – firmly into the foreground. *Alfa Alfa* is visibly a sports car and a chicken coop, while *Clip-On*'s windows bear the traces of their automobile origin. To give rise to these new forms and functions, the car was not recycled – reduced to scrap metal, melted down and then reshaped into window frames or chickenwire – but rather maintains traces of its past, as skin holds wrinkles and scars. Parasite or host, an AVL work can preserve in a legible way the parts of other stories, from the personal memory of a car crash to the collective history of a car's design. Paradoxically, by making objects that fit into a given set of circumstances, AVL manages to make space for more history.

Far from a variation on 'form follows function', AVL's approach liberates design from a master plan: urban, architectural or even divine. By extension, this approach frees the temporality of design from duration, which imprisons one form and one function together forever. In AVL's world, form and function follow fate. A car could end up as a roof or as a nest without losing its original appearance; there is a visible process of adaptation, as an object follows its fate and catalyses the discovery of new uses that that were never anticipated in the original design. Again, the car must not be reduced to raw and reusable materials to serve different ends or to fulfil an unpredicted destiny. [...]

The distinction between the human body and its built surroundings dissolves in the AVL oeuvre. Humans are not just the ultimate users whose need determines a design; the human body is itself a design. This approach is exemplified by the watercolour *Self-Portrait* (2002), which depicts Joep van Lieshout, slumped over a table, from the classic perspective used in the architectural blueprint for a building. We see the artist from above, at various side angles and through a cross-section showing his interior structure of bones, organs and veins instead of support beams, air ducts and electrical wiring. For AVL, both the body's interior and its exterior can double as blueprints for a wide range of works, which get under the skin. [...]

Beyond basic needs and functions, the human body has a capacity for physical exertion. AVL's quest for total self-sufficiency – manifest in survivalist living units like *Autocrat* (1997) and the *Free State of AVL Ville* (2001) – puts the emphasis on manual labour and manual leisure. The realm of leisure includes the weightlifting and exercise area in *Sportopia* (2002), which also offers an antidte to the assembly line. While the factory alienates workers with specialized repetitive tasks, the AVL weights perform the same kind of specialized and repetitive tasks on the various muscles of the worker, who immediately enjoys – and gets to keep – the fruits of his or her efforts. Like a dynamic anatomical drawing, the weights make the muscles inside the body visible by stimulating them from the outside.

The realm of hard labour runs from the idyllic existence in *Pioneer Set* (with hoes, rakes and pitchforks for farming) to apocalyptic imprisonment in *The Disciplinator* (2003) (where inmates must use metal files to reduce logs to sawdust). Like AVL beds and toilets, these hand tools must stay close to the skin and involve the entire body; compare the rake with the tractor, or files with a shredder, activated by a button. *SlaveCity* (2005–6) breaks away from this intimate proximity with *CallCenter* (2005), where slaves outfitted with headsets are deprived of the possibility of even holding a telephone receiver.

While slavery is usually associated with hard physical labour, AVL finds slave labour in the socialized tasks of the service economy, which reduces the possibilities for physical exertion. *CallCenter*'s radical reduction of the body's forces – only to speaking and to listening – reflects the fate of the slaves, who are eventually killed off so their organs can be extracted for transplants to non-slaves. [...]

The atelier's most significant legacy is to build, occupy and operate in spaces that are created by the law and yet remain to a certain extent outside its jurisdiction. Like the state of emergency declared during a political crisis, wartime or in the wake of a natural disaster, the state of exception is filled with both danger and freedom. Since the norm of law and order is temporarily suspended, you could be shot as easily as you could construct a make-shift house around a public monument. AVL began to explore the state of exception by exploiting the relative autonomy of art in democratic states where artists enjoy a greater degree of freedom of expression.

The strategy is simple and ingenious: producing canons, guns or alcohol is illegal without the state's permission but artists may create these items as art, which is generally assumed to have more symbolic value than real use (although the police have not always been convinced by AVL's explosive approach to aesthetics). Beyond relying on the autonomy of aesthetics, AVL takes advantage of every exception to the rule, especially in the realm of state and municipal regulations. In relation to architecture, AVL's works constitute a negative reading of the law because these installations are often the result of what has not been included in the building code. While AVL occasionally breaks the law (for example, by building without a proper permit), the atelier is more likely to produce constructions that are simply not explicitly prohibited. [...]

AVL, responding to the state of exception and to bare life in all of its forms – both positive and negative – may operate at the edges of the law, yet its creations are instructive for an era caught between terrorism and globalization. On one hand, nation states fighting terrorism have increasingly declared a state of exception, where citizens might be killed accidentally when mistaken for terrorist suspects or might be imprisoned without trial.. On the other, the liberalization of markets, with the rise of free trade, has forced nation states to give up not only their monopolies on public services but also their ability to use legislation as a buffer against pure economy. Indeed, communal life cannot always be profitable. As AVL's oeuvre suggests, our exceptional states bring great dangers and great freedoms. Bare life may be imprisoned and subject to the market or be determined by the twin desires of sexuality and ecology. Everything is possible, from harvesting organs to recycling shit for biogas. AVL has already built the facilities; it's up to us to inhabit them.

Jennifer Allen, extracts from 'AVL for Dummies', in *Atelier van Lieshout* (Rotterdam: Eelco van Welie/ NAi Publishers, 2007) 5; 8–9; 20.

Lynne Cooke, Friedrich Meschede, Sune Nordgren
Artists at Work: Discussion//2001

Sune Nordgren Today we have a public discussion about providing artists with working possibilities, to make it possible for artists to work and to create new works. It's amazing, the change on the art scene, where even established or more traditional institutions for housing and showing art are now talking about residencies and commissions. The question is, is this a new way forward? Is it a way of revitalizing the traditional institutions? Of course, the other question in relation to BALTIC [Centre for Contemporary Art, Gateshead] is: is this a way for us to work? This is exactly what we've been talking about, creating BALTIC as an art factory, not only a place where contemporary art is shown, but where it is also created. [...]

To start, can I ask if you think it would have been possible to create a place like BALTIC, on the periphery, ten years ago? Has the art scene changed that much? Is it possible to create an institution which at the same time is not an institution?

Lynne Cooke It's a good question. I think the art scene has changed enormously in ten years. I used to live in London and coming back to visit periodically there is no question that the British art scene has changed dramatically. It's grown enormously; its visibility in terms of the general culture is much higher. But at the same time, looking outside Britain, contemporary art has changed radically too, and I think there are a number of reasons for this. There's been much discussion about multiculturalism and its pros and cons, but one of the consequences is that the art world has expanded geographically. I'm not sure that it has opened up in every dimension, but at least in terms of where one's looking to find out where artists are practising and contributing and being part of an international discourse or scene. It's far wider than it was fifteen or more years back and one thinks of artists like Tracey Moffatt from Australia, William Kentridge from South Africa or Ernesto Neto from South America, who are very visible, working and showing around the world. This was not the case in the 1970s and 1980s, although it was the case in the late 1960s.

There has been a lot of discussion about the difference between the internationalism of the 1960s and the 'globalism' of the late 1990s and the current moment. In some ways there's not much difference, except for terminology, I think. But perhaps there's one crucial difference, at least in my mind: in the 1960s, for all that artists were coming from Uruguay, Japan and Eastern Europe, the art centres were still very specifically identified. It was primarily New York, and then one or two other major cities. That simply isn't the case now. There's no one dominant art centre. For all that London is a key centre in the international art circuit, most of us find that we need to travel to Malmö, Milan or Vancouver – it could be virtually any city – to see the key shows now. There are no longer just one or two institutions that are systematically making the defining shows. They are happening all over the place and they are happening very unpredictably, although, as previously, they result from a synergy between an institution, the personnel of the institution, and the artists involved. I think that's a positive development. [...]

Friedrich Meschede I think it's really important that there's a prominent exchange between artists. Amongst the artists' community, artists meet other artists, and I think that is one purpose of a residency [such as the DAAD residencies in Berlin]. You know, Berlin is now a free city and we don't need this Berlin in-residence programme any more for political reasons, and many artists come to Berlin because they want to live there, or they may have shows at Kunst-Werke, the Neue Nationalgalerie, or the city's other institutions. There is always this question: what is the main reason for DAAD? First of all, from my point of view [as Director of the arts section], it's important that there's strong, permanent dialogue within the art scene and that artists meet others and are informed of what's going on, in the way this happens in the metropolis – London, Berlin, Amsterdam, Brussels, and so on.

But I feel that art was never about a centre, it was always about decentralization, so that it can be everywhere, although, Lynne, you are the curator at the Dia Center for the Arts and there is something in the name that conveys a belief in the idea of the centre. But again, it's this dialogue that is the most important thing. Also maybe another key idea is that one should not have a monopoly. Art is never about monopolizing; it is about different ideas and about seeing what the difference is from something that was articulated before. As soon as something becomes a monopoly it's boring. DAAD [*Deutscher Akademischer Austausch Dienst*] translates into German Academic Exchange Service, and I have learned during the past eight years of running this programme that this idea of exchange, which we do with students, professors and so on, is the most important thing for any field.

Just to provoke another question: although we have all these exchanges, there is not necessarily any better understanding of art. What I see in Germany right now is how people react to contemporary art after all these exhibitions that we've had. The last ten years were incredible: we had shows that you could never have imagined in the 1960s or 1970s. But I don't think that the understanding of art has grown. I think it's still a small community of people who understand what's going on in art. For this reason, I think it's not just about education. We really have to give much more support to what art is, what the meaning of art is, and what it can mean to others. [...]

Especially for the Berlin in-residence programme, it's the artist community and colleagues in Berlin who come to see the shows. I think that this Berlin in-residence programme has moved towards what Artangel does in London. We don't have as much funding as Artangel and we can't commission exhibitions like the Dia that continue over a long period, because we don't have that kind of exhibition space. But this combination of an artist coming to Berlin and thinking about an artwork that he or she wants to make is important, and I believe this is made generally for a special audience. The exhibitions or artists I can show in the Neue Nationalgalerie have a wider audience, of course. But the visitors coming to the daadgalerie, which is a tiny gallery in a domestic space ... I can't give you any figures but it's not a big audience. [...]

Nordgren You have several examples of artists who have had DAAD residencies, such as Jane and Louise Wilson, who produced their work *Stasi City* in the context of Berlin. Then other artists, such as Rachel Whiteread, whose experience of being in Berlin only comes to the surface several years after the DAAD residency.

Meschede Yes, but in both cases it was important to the artist to understand the whole political history of the past and to be in Berlin to see that. [...]

Audience questions

Piers Masterson The artist Richard Wentworth made an interesting point in an interview: that one of the watersheds for the development of art over the last few decades was the point when air travel became so affordable that it was cheaper to send the artist to make a project wherever it might be, rather than transporting a work. With residency schemes there tends to be a predominance of certain kinds of artist and practice. Is the residency circuit biased against more traditional studio-based practices such as painting and sculpture? Is there a prejudice because of the way the residency systems are set out?

Meschede Firstly, I don't think it's true anymore that it's cheaper to bring an artist than the artwork. When I think of some artists' names, just considering what they would need as facilities to make their work – especially video artists – I could have a breakdown! Secondly, we discuss within the jury whether it's interesting for the artist to come to Berlin, or whether it's interesting for the city to have these artists for a couple of months. But one idea of the DAAD – maybe it sounds a bit funny – is also to create a crisis. I mean, we invite people to allow themselves a crisis, to think about what they have done up to now. Nobody has to come to Berlin – it's an invitation still. The artist can decide to stay at home. For me it is always important that everything in the art world is an offer. The viewer can go to an exhibition, decide to see a show and everything there is on offer that one can participate in, or not, whether as an artist or a visitor.

Masterson My interest is more in the curatorial aspects of your relationship with the artists. You noted earlier that the art world has expanded; many institutions have also expanded physically. Tate Modern is a huge space, BALTIC will be a very large space, and the DAAD is the first of those super-accommodating spaces, in terms of the scope that it provides for the artist. Doesn't the necessity to fill these huge voids also limit some of the types of work that can be supported, or dictate, again, which kinds of artist get chosen?

Cooke Yes, I think it's true that spaces determine, to some extent, what it's possible to do inside them. The building that I work in is a fairly raw, industrial space. It's not an ideal space to show painting in and it's not a space for which it is easy to borrow extremely valuable works that require high levels of maintenance, of temperature and humidity control. We can't offer that and it would be irresponsible to try to fudge those boundaries in order to make it possible. There's only one floor where we can meet standard museum requirements, so we don't focus on that type of work: other institutions in the city can do that very well and easily. The amount of space available on each floor is large at Dia and therefore it seems to me counter-productive to approach an artist like Tom Friedman, for example, who deliberately works in miniature. It's simply neither to his benefit nor ours. So there are definite limitations. There are certain artists that I would, in another context or in a different job, very much like to work with but don't feel are appropriate for Dia's programme. I belive that's being practical and realistic. It's helped by the fact that there are other institutions nearby with different kinds of spaces who are better suited to make those invitations. But I think the art world is not so monolithic at the moment that interesting practice only takes one form. There is innovative work that is installation-based, there's challenging work that is video-based, and so on. There's such a spectrum that one isn't unnaturally constrained to look in certain areas and leave others aside.

Eivor Mydland We heard [in a previous seminar] that artists need to have a certain background or experience in order to be able to benefit from a commission. Do you think it's the same system with a residency, that it requires certain experiences of an artist before he or she can benefit from it? Or do you not really look at what kind of practice the artist has had?

Nordgren I could start with an answer based on my experience of building IASPIS [International Artists' Studio Programme in Stockholm], which was built up as an exchange programme between Swedish and international artists. There were eleven studios, three or four of which were for international – both established and emerging – artists. The other studios were for the Swedish artists, who could apply for them, and six times a year we invited artists who had just graduated from the eight different colleges of art and design in Sweden. So they had had virtually no studio practice or any experience of working as a professional. Of course, they shouldn't because they were students, but then suddenly they were professionals, and out of the whole context of the school. I think that this mixture is very important. It is important that an artist in residence programme not only invites famous artists to build up its prestige but has all kinds of artists working together. It's like Friedrich said: create the meeting place. I mean, sometimes it's even more important to have breakfast together than to go to seminars. [...]

Lynne Cooke, Friedrich Meschede, Sune Nordgren, extracts from 'Closing Discussion: Lynne Cooke and Friedrich Meschede in conversation, chaired by Sune Nordgren', *Artists at Work: Second BALTIC International Seminar* (Gateshead: BALTIC, 2001) 85–109.

Lane Relyea
Studio Unbound//2010

Nearly lost within the sprawling five-hundred-page catalogue for the similarly sprawling 1999 exhibition 'Laboratorium' (which 'declared the whole city of Antwerp a lab')[1] are a few pages devoted to a reprint of Daniel Buren's 1971 essay 'The Function of the Studio'. It would stand to reason that curators Hans Ulrich Obrist and Barbara Vanderlinden included it for historical contrast, to differentiate between art-world attitudes towards the studio then and now, except that contrasts, oppositions, distinctions, and any other means by which to order and determine thought were precisely what was annihilated by Laboratorium's inclusive onslaught of information and programming. Whereas Buren helped shape the premises of institutional critique by speaking of artists' studios and exhibition sites as belonging to a system of 'frames, envelopes and limits', Obrist and Vanderlinden talked about 'establishing … networks, fluctuating between highly specialized work by scientists, artists, dancers and writers'; about 'the laboratory within the museum, but also the question of the museum as a laboratory'; about the museum having 'multiple identities'; and ultimately about 'a creative blur between the making and the exhibiting of work'.[2]

Buren's essay has continued on something like a revival tour up to the present, although more often than not it's cited precisely for the sense of historical irony it now provides. For example, in a recent issue of *Modern Painters* devoted to the studio, Judith Rodenbeck pitted Buren's characterization against the updated studio Corin Hewitt advanced in his Whitney Museum of American Art installation *Seed Stage* (2009).[3] In the museum's lobby gallery Hewitt constructed a fully functioning workspace, in which he spent his days not only crafting art but also cooking food, sometimes making sculptural replicas of his food, and photographing both food and art before sorting the two into containers to which were affixed the printed-out photos, even maintaining a compost bin in which worms and microbes digested both left-over meals and discarded print-outs. Built as a room within a room, *Seed Stage* left a thin corridor for visitors to circumnavigate its perimeter, from which they could either peer inward through narrow vertical openings at Hewitt busying himself or turn their gaze instead towards the few photographs he had selected to mat and frame and have hung on the outer gallery walls. Studio and museum, inside and outside, public and private, organic and inorganic, original and reproduction, production and consumption, art and life – all these former oppositions were eroded, made continuous, as if so many conjoined and provisional states travelled through in a process of relentless conversion and transcription, one stop after another on a directionless procedural itinerary, an endless circuitry within which any sense of ultimate reference, of a final relay or destination – like an answer to the question 'What's the point?' – remained obscure at best. Like Jasper Johns' famous dictum – 'Take an object. Do something to it. Do something else to it' – looped to infinity.

Claire Bishop has recently remarked on the channelling of resources into new project spaces and kunsthallen so as to accommodate just this kind of work, projects that are time-based, open-ended and interactive, which Bishop claims 'is essentially institutionalized studio activity' – the studio made into a showroom display, a *tableau vivant*.[4] Gone are the days of antagonism and stalemate between the artist's studio, with its presumed autonomy, and the recuperating museum, with its permanent collection representing 'official' or canonical culture. Today studio and museum are superceded by more temporal, transient events, spaces of fluid interchange between objects, activities and people. Exhibition venues increasingly rely on residencies and commissions, on more flexible approaches to display (Obrist, for example, has advanced the notion of the 'evolutionary exhibition') and place greater emphasis on information, discussion and gatherings (from the audio tours, interactive data kiosks and lounge-like reading rooms that have become standard museum fare to the more elaborately arrayed assortments of publications and symposia that accompany the larger biennials and fairs). Commercial galleries are also known to host recreated artists' workspaces; think of Rirkrit Tiravanija's projects with 303 Gallery and Gavin Brown. In the March 2003 issue of *Texte zur Kunst*, another theme issue about the studio, Bennett Simpson reviewed Gareth James' 1999 show at MWMWM Gallery in Williamsburg, in which the artist erected a makeshift bar out of some drywall and lumber and ornamented the results with beer bottles, art magazines and unfinished or crumpled-up ink-on-paper drawings. Visitors drank, socialized and made graffiti on the walls. This half-pub, half-studio was 'like a threshold between private and public, actuality and potentiality, the individual and the social', Simpson writes, 'a place where meanings, properties and behaviours fluctuate radically'.[5]

So what is the function of this new kind of space? Much like when Buren penned his essay, interest today focuses not only on the studio but on the art school and the international exhibition, all looked at in terms of their roles within a larger array of interlocking functions, each with its own scale and modality for activity and production and with its own capacities for input and output (some larger and more formal, some more intimate and everyday, all with different placement possibilities within the city). But this art world map or itinerary to which the studio belongs, braided within channels of connection, distribution and circulation, now seems purely practical or technological, as if without political content. No longer does the studio appear as an ideological frame that mystifies production, a space where the realities of social or mass production are supposedly held at bay in favour of an antiquated craft model that showcases the individual artist's creative genius. And no longer is the studio seen as belonging to a 'system' such as Buren described, as a space characterized by box-like enclosures, of 'frames and limits', each assigned a discreet place in some rigid, stable and all-determining structure or order. What system or structure does exist today is more properly described as a *network*.

In contrast to enclosures, networks are characterized by what Gilles Deleuze has called 'modulation, like a self-deforming cast that will continuously change from one moment to the other, or like a sieve whose mesh will transmute from point to point'.[6] Along with the rise of networks comes a new ideology, one that advertises agency, practice and everyday life. Networks are said to be inherently democratic and egalitarian, this because of their horizontal, multidirectional and reciprocal capacity, the fact that, compared to more hierarchical forms of organization, in the network it's relatively easy for any one node to communicate with any other. This means that the forces governing networks appear more quotidian, immanent and dispersed, rather than concentrated in transcendent executive positions. By the same token, the characteristic flexibility and informality of network structures, the way they depend on the constant, relatively independent movement of their participating actors, is taken as evidence of diminished structure and greater agency. Thus networks are often championed for how they accommodate self-styled independent actors who, because their movements and decision-making are supposedly less embedded in and dictated by governing structure and context, are more loosely affiliated within a dispersed field. It's because of this kind of cosmopolitan character or effect of the network that people today can boast of being both insiders and do-it-yourselfers at the same time.

As with the larger network itself, what is thought to fill the studio today is technical or pragmatic, simply an artist's everyday practice. Hence the popularity of practical design, or folksy sculptural craft, or painting reconceived as a daily studio practice. This turn to practice can be considered part of an ongoing repudiation of 'theory' since the late 1980s, when art and criticism were supposedly preoccupied with consumer culture or spectacle or ideology – that is, with rigid, all-encompassing structure. Employed as theory's opposite term, practice is said to emphasize individual, concrete acts, their specific materiality and temporality, all of which are said to defy the sweeping, abstract and static totalizations of dominant structures. A good example of this shift can be found in a recent string of sculpture surveys that shared several of the same artists – artists like Isa Genzken, Rachel Harrison and Lara Schnitger. In her catalogue essay for one of these shows, 'The Uncertainty of Objects and Ideas', mounted by the Hirshhorn Museum in 2006, curator Anne Ellegood writes that the reason such sculpture appears so attractive today is that it features 'a mode of production rooted in the material and the physical'; it 'give[s] us something tangible rather than streams of data'. Such works 'embody physical exertion and dirty hands; they are the evidence of actions – composing, building, constructing, stacking, bending, connecting and adorning.'[7] The very title of a similar show mounted by the Hammer Museum a year earlier – 'Thing' – makes obvious this preference for indexicality over lexicality. The catalogue for 'Thing' also included photographs of the participating artists' studios, as well as references to critic Libby Lumpkin's 1997 essay 'The Redemption of Practice'. And in the catalogue for 'Unmonumental', yet another look-alike exhibition, which the New Museum opened in 2007, co-curator Massimiliano Gioni refers to the last few years of art-making as inaugurating a 'headless century' – another metaphor for today's sense of increasingly decentralized activity in the wake of ebbing dominant structure.[8] The Hirshhorn's Ellegood nodded in agreement: 'These artists have found sculpture to be the most meaningful medium in which to explore and represent the complexity, rapidity and ultimately the confusion of contemporary life ... the feeling that beliefs and meanings are continuously unmoored and in flux.'

And yet what was put forward by these sculpture shows, despite their emphasis on the studio and on the individual fabrication of physical things, were not autonomous objects. The bricolaged everyday materials that constitute the work of Genzken, Harrison, et al., though personalized through hands-on artistic intervention, still remain opened out and available to larger communities and cultures, continuous and interwoven with larger systems of exchange. Their constituent parts are never so transformed as to lose their prior, independent identities; the results are conglomerations of heterogeneous, loosely related items – in short, object networks. But such work also never goes so far as to suggest installation. Instead each sculpture remains enough of an independent, mobile unit to dissociate itself from the fetters of contextualizing site and circumstance. The work is too internally diverse and intersected to be characterized as unified and consistent, and in its heterogeneity and flexibility it refuses to commit to just one identity. Nor, in its mobility, will it commit to staying in only one place.

In this way the new bricolaged sculpture demonstrates a striking continuity between studio and post-studio approaches, as both increasingly manifest themselves as 'practices' that repurpose already existing objects, sites and discourses, the aim being to access and link various databases and platforms – maybe immaterial social acquaintances or information, maybe more material pop-culture inventories like old record collections or the intimately biographied yet anonymous cast-offs accumulated in thrift stores. Just as no single TV show or pop song is as hot today as the TiVo boxes and iPods that manage their organization, so too with art it is the ease and agility of access and navigation through and across data fields, sites and projects that takes precedence over any singular, lone *objet*. And the new sculpture celebrated in shows like 'Thing', 'Unmonumental' and 'The Uncertainty of Objects and Ideas' doesn't contradict this. It doesn't stand in defiance of network forces but rather proves their further extension by measuring how these forces have subsumed and changed the way we think about objects, have subsumed the very opposition between the single and multiple, the enclosed and interpenetrated.

Similarly changed are our notions of the solitary studio and the lone artist. Being part of a network that privileges itinerancy and circulation over fixity, that diminishes hierarchies and boundaries in favour of mobility and flexibility across a more open, extensive environment, also subordinates the studio and the individual practitioner to a general communicational demand, a decentralizing and integrative logic of interface and commensurability. Networks are both integrative and decentralizing, in that they privilege casual or weak ties over formal commitments, so as to heighten the possibility of chanced-upon links that lead outward from any one communicational nexus or group. Under such conditions both subjects and objects are obliged to shed not only pretences to autonomy but also long-term loyalties and identifications, and instead to become more mobile, promiscuous operators that mesh seamlessly with the system's mobile, promiscuous operations. Deleuze calls the new mobile creator who emerges in this transition from an industrial to information-based society a 'dividual', someone who is not a 'discontinuous producer' (making discreet objects one at a time) but is 'undulatory, in orbit, in a continuous network'.[9] Artists who are more 'dividualistic' discover themselves not by securing a role within the historical narrative of a chosen medium but by integrating into a more diffuse ecology that involves not only making art but also putting on shows, publishing, organizing events, teaching, networking, maybe belonging to one or more semi-collectives, even adopting one or more pseudonyms. As the late Jason Rhoades, an early public exhibitor of the private studio, remarked in 1998, 'Museum director, curator, collector, artist – none of that means anything anymore.'[10]

Much the same goes for the studio. It no longer offers retreat. It's no longer, as in Buren's earlier analysis, 'an ivory tower', no longer 'unique', or 'private'. The studio now integrates. It no longer defers or resists instrumentalization, no longer distances the artist from society, no longer holds out that kind of separate identity to the artist, one supposedly distilled from the privacy and depth of the sovereign individual who occupies it, just as the studio no longer identifies as separate and resistant or self-determining the artist's materials or medium or labour. Rather the studio is all exterior. It offers a purely negative difference premised on sameness, places the artist as a like item within an integrative inventory or database, gives the artist a mailing address and a doorstep, thus providing the means for one to show up within the network. The studio is now that place where we know we can always find the artist when we need to, where she or he is always plugged in and online, always accessible to and by an ever more integrated and ever more dispersed art world.

1   'A Rule of the Game: A Talk with Hans Ulrich Obrist', *Edge* (5 June 2008), http://www.edge.org/3rd_culture/obrist08/obrist08_index.html; extract reprinted in this volume, 113–16.

2   Hans Ulrich Obrist and Barbara Vanderlinden, eds, *Laboratorium* (Antwerp: DuMont, 2001), 17–21. This catalogue contains a new translation of Buren's essay.

3   Judith Rodenbeck, 'Studio Visit', *Modern Painters*, vol. 21, no. 2 (March 2009) 52.

4   Claire Bishop, 'Antagonism and Relational Aesthetics', *October*, no. 110 (Fall 2004).

5   Bennett Simpson, 'Can You Work as Fast as You Like to Think?' *Texte zur Kunst*, no. 49 (March 2003).

6   Gilles Deleuze, 'Postscript on the Societies of Control', *October*, no. 59 (Winter 1992) 4.

7   Anne Ellegood, *The Uncertainty of Objects and Ideas* (Washington, DC: Hirshhorn Museum and Sculpture Garden, 2006) 19.

8   Massimiliano Gioni, 'Ask the Dust', in *Unmonumental: The Object in the 21st Century*, ed. Richard Flood, Laura Hoptman and Massimiliano Gioni (London and New York: Phaidon Press, 2007) 65.

9   Deleuze, 'Postscript', op. cit., 5–6.

10 'A Thousand Words: Jason Rhoades Talks about His Impala Project', *Artforum*, vol. 37, no. 1 (September 1998) 135.

Lane Relyea, 'Studio Unbound', in *The Studio Reader*, ed. Mary Jane Jacob and Michelle Grabner (Chicago: University of Chicago Press, 2010) 341–9.

Biographical Notes

Alexander Alberro is Virginia Bloedel Wright '51 Associate Professor of Art History at Barnard College, Columbia University, New York.

Jennifer Allen is a writer on art and culture based in Berlin. She was awarded the 2009 prize for art criticism by the ADKV (German Kunstverein Association).

Albrecht Barthel is an architect and conservator who works in the Schleswig-Holstein State Department of Conservation.

Mary Bergstein is a Professor in the department of History of Art and Visual Culture at Rhode Island School of Design.

Iwona Blazwick OBE is Director of the Whitechapel Gallery and Series Editor of Documents of Contemporary Art.

Louise Bourgeois (1911–2010) was a French-born artist based in New York since the late 1940s.

Daniel Buren is a French artist based in Paris.

Sarah Burns is Ruth N. Halls Professor of Fine Arts at Indiana University.

Aimee Chang is an American artist and art professional who has worked in San Francisco, Berkely and New York.

Judy Chicago is an American artist, writer and educator, based in Los Angeles since 1957.

Lynne Cooke is chief curator of the Museo Centro de Arte Reina Sofía, Madrid, and curator at large of the Dia Foundation, New York.

Barbara Dawson is Director of Dublin City Gallery The Hugh Lane.

Jeffrey Deitch is Director of The Museum of Contemporary Art, Los Angeles.

Manthia Diawara is Professor of Comparative Literature and Africana Studies at New York University.

Brian Dillon is a writer and critic and a research fellow at the University of Kent, Canterbury.

Briony Fer is Professor of Modern and Contemporary Art at University College, London

Elena Filipovic is an independent curator and art critic based in Brussels.

Jori Finkel is arts reporter for the Los Angeles Times.

Jack Goldstein (1945–2003) was a Canadian-born artist who worked in New York and California.

Ulrike Groos is Director of the Kunstmuseum Stuttgart.

Carles Guerra is a curator and critic based in Barcelona.

Elizabeth Harney is Associate Professor of Art History at the University of Toronto.

Herzog & de Meuron is a Swiss architecture practice based in Basel.

Carsten Höller is a Belgian-born German artist who works in Sweden and Ghana.

Amelia Jones is Professor and Pilkington Chair in the History of Art and Visual Studies at the University of Manchester.

Caitlin Jones is a curator and critic and Executive Director of the Western Front Society, Vancouver.

Caroline A. Jones is director of the History, Theory and Criticism Program at Massachusetts Institute of Technology.

Sanford Kwinter is a Canadian-born, New York-based writer, architectural theorist and publisher.

Henri Lefebvre (1901–91) was a French sociologist and philosopher.

Alexander Liberman (1912–99) was a Russian-born American magazine editor and photographer.

Paul McCarthy is an American artist based in Los Angeles.

Friedrich Meschede is Director of the Kunsthalle Bielefeld, Germany.

Laura Meyer is Associate Professor in the department of Art and Design at California State University, Fresno.

Herbert Molderings is Professor of Art History at the Ruhr-University, Bochum, Germany

Valérie Mréjen is a French artist and filmmaker based in Paris.

Joanna Mytkowska is Director of the Warsaw Museum of Modern Art.

Bruce Nauman is an American artist based in New Mexico.

Sune Nordgren is a Swedish-born curator, critic, designer and broadcaster.

Hans Ulrich Obrist is Co-director of Exhibitions and Programmes and Director of International Projects at the Serpentine Gallery, London.

Francis V. O'Connor is an American art historian and poet.

Brian O'Doherty is an Irish-born artist and writer on art who lives and works in the United States.

Gabriel Orozco is a Mexican-born artist based in New York, Paris and Mexico City.

Rozsika Parker (1945–2010) was a British feminist writer, art historian and psychoanalyst.

Andrzej Przywara is a curator, critic and art historian based in Warsaw.

Lane Relyea is Chair of Art Theory and Practice at Northwestern University, Illinois.

Frances Richard is an art critic, poet, editor and educator based in Brooklyn.

Carolee Scheemann is an American artist based in New Paltz, New York.

Robert Smithson (1938–73) was an American artist who worked in New York, Nevada, Utah and New Mexico.

Ann Temkin is Chief Curator of Painting and Sculpture at The Museum of Modern Art, New York.

Sarah Thornton is a Canadian born, London-based writer on art and the sociology of culture.

Coosje van Bruggen (1942–2009) was an art historian, artist and critic, based in New York.

Jan Verwoert is an art critic, curator and editor based in Berlin.

Ian Wallace ia a British-born Canadian artist who lives and works in Vancouver.

Bernadette Walter is an art historian and curator who lives and works in Bern.

Steven Watson is a writer on twentieth-century American art and popular culture.

Lawrence Weiner is an American artist who lives and works in New York and Amsterdam.

Lawrence Weschler is a writer on art and culture, and director of the New York Institute for the Humanities at New York University.

Jon Wood is an art historian and curator at the Henry Moore Institute, Leeds.

Linda Yablonsky is the US art critic for Bloomberg News and a contributor to numerous art journals.

Phillip B. Zarrilli is an international director, performer and trainer in psychophysical process based in Llanarth, Wales.

Bibliography

Alberro, Alexander, 'The Catalogue of Robert Smithson's Library', in *Robert Smithson*, ed. Eugenie Tsai and Cornelia Butler (Los Angeles: The Museum of Contemporary Art, 2004).

Allen, Jennifer, 'AVL for Dummies', in *Atelier van Lieshout* (Rotterdam: Eelco van Welie/NAi Publishers, 2007).

Alpers, Svetlana, *Rembrandt's Enterprise: The Studio and the Market* (Chicago: University of Chicago Press, 1988).

Alpers, Svetlana, *The Vexations of Art: Velázquez and Others* (New Haven and London: Yale University Press, 2005).

Baldessari, John, 'In Conversation', in *The Studio Reader* (see Jacob, Mary Jane).

Barthel, Albrecht, 'The Paris Studio of Constantin Brancusi: A Critique of the Modern Period Room', *Future Anterior*, vol. III, no. 2 (Winter 2006).

Bergstein, Mary, '"The Artist in His Studio": Photography, Art and the Masculine Mystique', *Oxford Art Journal*, vol. 18, no. 2 (1995).

Beshty, Walead, 'Studio Narratives', in *The Studio Reader* (see Jacob, Mary Jane).

Brassaï, *Les Artistes de ma vie* (Paris: Denoël, 1982); trans. Richard Miller, *The Artists of My Life* (New York: Viking/London: Thames & Hudson, 1982).

Brockington, Horace, 'Gustave Courbet: The Studio of the Painter', *NY Arts* (July/August 2008).

Buren, Daniel, 'The Function of the Studio' (1971); trans. Thomas Repensek, *October*, no. 10 (Fall 1979).

Buren, Daniel, 'The Function of the Studio Revisited', conversation between Daniel Buren and the curators/editors in Jens Hoffmann, Christina Kennedy and Georgina Jackson, eds, *The Studio* (Dublin: Dublin City Gallery, 2007).

Burns, Sarah, *Inventing the Modern Artist: Art and Culture in Gilded Age America* (New Haven and London: Yale University Press, 1996).

Butler, Sharon, 'Lost in Space: Art Post-Studio', *Brooklyn Rail* (June 2008).

Certeau, Michel de, *L'Invention du quotidien, I. Arts de faire* (Paris: Gallimard, 1974); trans. Stephen Rendall, *The Practice of Everyday Life* (Berkeley and Los Angeles: University of California Press, 1984).

Chang, Aimee, exhibition text for *Edgar Arcenaux: Drawings of Removal* (Los Angeles: UCLA Hammer Museum, 25 November 2003 – 29 February 2004).

Chicago, Judy, and Jane Collings, interview transcripts in *Judy Chicago: An Oral History*, part of the Archives of American Art Oral History Program (Los Angeles: University of California at Los Angeles, 2004).

Cooke, Lynne, 'Gerhard Richter: Atlas', in *Gerhard Richter: Atlas 1964–1995* (New York: Dia Center for the Arts, 1995); reprinted in *Gerhard Richter: Atlas. The Reader* (London: Whitechapel Gallery, 2003).

Dawson, Barbara, 'Francis Bacon's Studio: A Stimulating Solitude', in *7 Reece Mews: Francis Bacon's Studio* (Dublin: Hugh Lane Gallery, 1998).

Deitch, Jeffrey, et al., eds, *Jean-Michel Basquiat: 1981 – The Studio of the Street* (New York: Deitch Projects/Milan: Charta, 2007).

Diawara, Manthia, 'The 1960s in Bamako: Malick Sidibé and James Brown' (2001), in *Arts Culture and Society* (The Andy Warhol Foundation for the Visual Arts) www.warholfoundation.org

Dillon, Brian, 'Street and Studio', *Art Review*, no. 22 (May 2008).

Dziewior, Yilmaz, ed., *Paul McCarthy: Videos 1970–1997* (Hamburg: Kunstverein in Hamburg/Cologne: Verlag der Buchhandlung Walther König, 2003).

Fer, Briony, *The Infinite Line: Remaking Art after Modernism* (New Haven and London: Yale University Press, 2004).

Fer, Briony, *Eva Hesse: Studiowork* (Edinburgh: Fruitmarket Gallery, 2009).

Filipovic, Elena, 'If You Read Here … Martha Rosler's Library', *Afterall*, no. 15 (Spring/Summer 2007).

Finkel, Jori, 'In the Studio: Wolfgang Tillmans', *Art+Auction* (May 2006).

Guerra, Carles, 'The Last Possessions: A Dialogical Restoration of Art & Language', in *Art & Language in Practice/Volume II: Critical Symposium*, ed. Charles Harrison (Barcelona: Fundació Antoni Tàpies, 1999).

Harney, Elizabeth, *In Senghor's Shadow: Art, Politics and the Avant-Garde in Senegal, 1960–1995* (Durham, North Carolina: Duke University Press, 2004).

Hertz, Richard, ed., *Jack Goldstein and the CalArts Mafia* (Ojai, California: Minneola Press, 2003).

Herzog, Jacques, and Pierre de Meuron, 'Just Waste', in *Herzog & de Meuron: Natural History*, ed. Philip Ursprung (Baden: Lars Müller, 2005).

Hickey, Dave, 'Naming the Colours', in *All Tomorrow's Parties: Billy Name's Photographs of Andy Warhol's Factory*, ed. Matthew Slotover (London: Frieze, 1997).

Jacob, Mary Jane, and Michelle Grabner, eds, *The Studio Reader: On the Space of Artists* (Chicago: School of the Art Institute of Chicago/University of Chicago Press, 2010).

Jones, Amelia, "'Presence' in Absentia: Experiencing Performance as Documentation', *Art Journal*, vol. 56, no. 4 (Winter 1997).

Jones, Caitlin, 'The Function of the Studio (When the Studio is a Laptop)', *Artlies*, no. 67 (Fall/Winter 2010) (www.artlies.org).

Jones, Caroline A., *Machine in the Studio: Constructing the Postwar American Artist* (Chicago: University of Chicago Press, 1996).

Kraynak, Janet, ed., *Please Pay Attention Please: Bruce Nauman's Words/Writings and Interviews*, (Cambridge, Massachusetts: The MIT Press, 2003).

Latour, Bruno, *Reassembling the Social: An Introduction to Actor-Network-Theory* (Oxford: Oxford University Press, 2005).

Lefebvre, Henri, *La Production de l'espace* (Paris: Éditions Anthropos, 1974); trans. Donald Nicholson-Smith, *The Production of Space* (Oxford: Blackwell, 1991).

Liberman, Alexander, *The Artist in His Studio* (New York: Viking Press, 1960).

Meyer, Laura, 'A Studio of Their Own: The Legacy of the Fresno Feminist Art Experiment' (September 2009) (www.astudiooftheirown.org)

Miller, Angela, 'Death and Resurrection in an Artist's Studio', *American Art*, vol. 20, no. 1 (Spring 2006).

Molderings, Herbert, 'It is Not the Objects That Count, but the Experiments: Marcel Duchamp's New York Studio as a Laboratory of Perception', *Re-Object* (Bregenz: Kunsthaus Bregenz, 2007).

Mytkowska, Joanna, and Andrzej Przywara, 'Edward Krasinski's Studio', trans. Marcin Wawrzynczak, in *Who if not we should at least try to imagine the future of all this?: 7 episodes on (ex)changing Europe*, ed. Maria Hlavajova, Jill Winder (Amsterdam: Artimo, 2004).

Nordgren, Sune, ed., *Artists at Work: Second BALTIC International Seminar* (Gateshead: BALTIC, 2001).

Obrist, Hans Ulrich, ed., *Do It* (Frankfurt am Main: Revolver, in association with e-flux, 2004).

Obrist, Hans Ulrich, and Barbara Vanderlinden, eds, *Laboratorium* (Antwerp: Roomade/Cologne: DuMont, 2001.

O'Connor, Francis V., 'Hans Namuth's Photographs of Jackson Pollock as Art-Historical Documentation', first published in French in Hans Namuth, *L'Atelier de Jackson Pollock* (Paris: Macula/Pierre Brochet, 1978); reprinted in *Art Journal*, vol. 39, no. 1 (Fall 1979).

O'Doherty, Brian, *Studio and Cube: On the Relationship between Where Art is Made and Where Art is Displayed* (New York: Columbia University Press, 2007).

Orozco, Gabriel, and Wesley Miller, 'Gabriel Orozco: Samurai Tree', *Art21 Blog* (6 November 2008).

Parker, Rozsika, 'Housework', *Spare Rib*, no. 26 (1975).

Peppiatt, Michael, and Alice Bellony-Rewald, *Imagination's Chambers: Artists and Their Studios* (Boston: Little Brown, 1982).

Richard, Frances, 'Seydou Keita: Sean Kelly Gallery', *Artforum* (April 2006).

Richards, Judith Olch, ed., *Inside The Studio: Two Decades of Talks with Artists in New York* (New York: Independent Curators International, 2004).

Roberts, John, *The Intangibilities of Form: Skill and Deskilling in Art after the Readymade* (London and New York: Verso, 2008).

Rodenbeck, Judith, 'Studio Visit', *Modern Painters* (March 2009).

Rubin, James Henry, 'The Studio of the Painter as History of the World', *Realism and Social Vision in Courbet and Proudhon* (Princeton, New Jersey: Princeton University Press, 1980).

Schmahmann, Brenda, 'Cast in a Different Light: Women and the "Artist's Studio" Theme in George Segal's Sculpture', *Woman's Art Journal*, vol. 20, no. 2 (Fall/Winter 1999–2000).

Schneemann, Carolee, *Imaging Her Erotics: Essays, Interviews, Projects* (Cambridge, Massachusetts: The MIT Press, 2002).

Schwabsky. Barry, 'The Symbolic Studio', in *The Studio Reader* (see Jacob, Mary Jane)

Sherlock, Maureen P., 'Piecework: Home, Factory, Studio, Exhibit', in *The Object of Labor*, ed. Joan Livingstone and John Ploof (Chicago: School of the Art Institute of Chicago Press/ Cambridge, Massachusetts: The MIT Press, 2007).

Simpson, Bennett, 'Can You Work as Fast as You Like to Think?', *Texte zur Kunst*, no. 49 (March 2003).

Smithson, Robert, *The Collected Writings*, ed. Jack Flam (Berkeley and Los Angeles: University of California Press, 1996).

Sobel, Dean, and Margaret Andera, eds, *Acconci Studio: Acts of Architecture* (Milwaukie: Milwaukie Art Museum, 2001).

Storr, Robert, 'A Room of One's Own, a Mind of One's Own', in *The Studio Reader* (see Jacob, Mary Jane).

Temkin, Ann, ed., *Martin Kippenberger: The Problem Perspective* (Los Angeles: The Museum of Contemporary Art/Cambridge, Massachusetts: The MIT Press, 2008).

Thornton, Sarah, *Seven Days in the Art World* (New York: W.W. Norton & Company, 2008).

van Bruggen, Coosje, *Bruce Nauman* (New York: Rizzoli, 1988).

Verwoert, Jan, 'Bernd Krauß', *frieze*, no. 97 (March 2006). www.frieze.com

Wallace, Ian, '*Corner of the Studio* and *El Taller*: A Reflection on Two Works from 1993', in *Ian Wallace: The Idea of the University* (Vancouver: Charles H. Scott Gallery, 2005).

Walter, Bernadette, 'Mats', trans. Catherine Schelbert, in *Roth Time: A Dieter Roth Retrospective*, ed. Theodora Vischer, Bernadette Walter (New York: The Museum of Modern Art/Baden: Lars Müller, 2003).

Watson, Steven, *Factory Made: Warhol and the Sixties* (New York: Pantheon Books, 2003).

Weiner, Lawrence, *HAVING BEEN SAID/WRITINGS & INTERVIEWS OF LAWRENCE WEINER 1968–2003*, ed. Gerti Fietzek and Gregor Stemmrich (Ostfildern-Ruit: Hatje Cantz, 2004).

Welish, Marjorie, 'The Studio Visit', *Art Criticism*, vol. 5, no. 1 (1988); reprinted in *The Studio Reader* (see Jacob, Mary Jane).

Welish, Marjorie, 'The Studio Revisited', *Arts Magazine*, no. 64 (September 1989); reprinted in *The Studio Reader* (see Jacob, Mary Jane).

Weschler, Lawrence, *Seeing is Forgetting the Name of the Thing One Sees: A Life of Contemporary Artist Robert Irwin* (Berkeley and Los Angeles: University of California Press, 1982).

Wood, Beatrice, 'Visit to Brancusi', *Archives of American Art Journal*, vol. 32, no. 4 (Washington, DC: Smithsonian Institution, 1992).

Wood, Jon, 'The Studio in the Gallery?', in *Reshaping Museum Space: Architecture, Design, Exhibitions*, ed. Suzanne MacLeod (London and New York: Routledge, 2005).

Yablonsky, Linda, 'The Studio System', *Art + Auction* (November 2007).

Zarrilli, Phillip B., 'The Metaphysical Studio', *The Drama Review*, vol. 46, no. 2 (Summer 2002).

Index

ACKNOWLEDGEMENTS

Editor's acknowledgements

I would like to thank Iwona Blazwick, Ian Farr, Hannah Holloway and Sarah Auld; and also Joanna Szupinska for her tireless support in researching the numerous texts from which this selection was made.

Publisher's acknowledgements

Whitechapel Gallery is grateful to all those who gave their generous permission to reproduce the listed material. Every effort has been made to secure all permissions and we apologize for any inadvertent errors or ommissions. If notified, we will endeavour to correct these at the earliest opportunity. We would like to express our thanks to all who contributed to the making of this volume, especially: Alexander Alberro, Jennifer Allen, Svetlana Alpers, Michael Auping, Albrecht Barthel, Mary Bergstein, Iwona Blazwick, Daniel Buren, Sarah Burns, Aimee Chang, Judy Chicago, Lynne Cooke, Crosby Coughlin, Barbara Dawson, Jeffrey Deitch, Manthia Diawara, Brian Dillon, Briony Fer, Elena Filipovic, Jori Finkel, Ulrike Groos, Carles Guerra, Elizabeth Harney, Carsten Höller, Amelia Jones, Caitlin Jones, Caroline A. Jones, Janet Kraynat, Sanford Kwinter, Paul McCarthy, Herzog & de Meuron, Laura Meyer, Wesley Miller, Herbert Molderings, Valérie Mréjen, Joanna Mytkowska, Bruce Nauman, Josephine New, Hans Ulrich Obrist, Francis V. O'Connor, Brian O'Doherty, Gabriel Orozco, Andrzej Przywara, Lane Relyea, Frances Richard, Carolee Schneemann, Ann Temkin, Sarah Thornton, Jan Verwoert, Ian Wallace, Bernadette Walter, Steven Watson, Lawrence Weiner, Lawrence Weschler, Jon Wood, Linda Yablonsky and Phillip B. Zarrilli. We also gratefully acknowledge the cooperation of: Afterall; ARS, New York; Artforum; Wiley-Blackwell; The Louise Bourgeois Trust; Oldenburg van Bruggen Studio; The Regents of the University of California; DACS, London; Duke University Press; The Estate of Jack Goldstein; Marian Goodman Gallery, New York; Hammer Museum, Los Angeles; Estate of Alexander Liberman; The MIT Press; The Museum of Contemporary Art, Los Angeles; Random House; Estate of Robert Smithson/VAGA; Hauser & Wirth; Yale University Press.

Whitechapel Gallery

whitechapelgallery.com

Whitechapel Gallery is supported by
Arts Council England